Carter County, Tennessee,

Marriages

1850 – 1876

Byron Sistler and Barbara Sistler

JANAWAY PUBLISHING, INC.
Santa Maria, California

Carter County, Tennessee, Marriages 1850-1876

Copyright © 1988 by Byron Sistler
All rights reserved.

Originally printed, Nashville, 1988
Byron Sistler and Associates, Inc.

Reprinted for Byron Sistler and Associates, Inc. by:

Janaway Publishing, Inc.
2412 Nicklaus Dr.
Santa Maria, California 93455
(805) 925-1038
www.JanawayPublishing.com

2007

ISBN 10: 1-59641-080-9
ISBN 13: 978-1-59641-080-0

Made in the United States of America

CARTER COUNTY, TN MARRIAGES

1850-1876

Where two dates appear on an entry, the first one is the date license was issued, the second (in parentheses) the date marriage was solemnized. If only one date, it usually means that the date of execution was the same as the date of license issuance.

Sometimes the execution of the marriage was not reported to the courthouse, and occasionally the clerk failed to note in the marriage book that the license was returned. We would usually make a notation in the entry to indicate the non-execution of a marriage if the book so stated.

The marriages are arranged alphabetically, the first half of the book by groom--the second by bride.

The records included in this book were transcribed by us directly from microfilm of the original marriage books. Error, where it occurs, may be attributed to us, or to the clerks of the period, many of whom did an appallingly sloppy job of entering the information.

If the bride and groom were black, a B is placed at the end of the entry.

It should be remembered that this and other marriage books we have prepared are indexes, and do not include all the information to be found in the original marriage book. Such data as names of bondsmen, ministers, justices of the peace, churches, etc., are omitted. Often such information is helpful to the researcher. Consequently the serious researcher, to obtain this additional information as well as to check on the accuracy of the transcriber, should examine the original marriage record if at all possible.

Byron Sistler
Barbara Sistler

Nashville, TN
January 1988

Adams, James W. to Saraphine Farr 11-14-1874 (11-15-1874)
Adams, John Q. to Nancy Myers 5-12-1866 (6-27-1866)
Adams, William to Sarah Emmert 12-31-1877 (1-31-1877?)
Akers, James to Emelin Smith 2-21-1869 (2-25-1869)
Akers, James to Emeline Smith 2-24-1869 (2-25-1869)
Akers, William to Matilda Perdue 12-21-1874
Akin, William to Malinda Perry? 12-21-1874
Aldrige, Wm. A. to Julia A. Tipton 10-30-1861 (10-31-1861)
Alen, Alexr? to Rebecca J. Crumly 12-14-1865
Alexander, B. F. to Mary Kibler 12-24-1861
Alford, James to Phebe Creed 7-12-1871 (2?-3-1871)
Alfred, James to Rebecca Creed 7-12-1870
Alison, Franklin to Elizabeth Daniel 9-9-1871 (9-10-1871)
Alison, L. C. to Marah E. Hampton 9-7-1876
Allen, Daniel S. to Mary Ann Campbell 11-15-1865 (11-18-1865)
Allen, Franklin to Elizabeth Daniel 9-9-1871 (9-10-1871)
Allen, John F. to Nancy A. E. Lacy 1-7-1873 (1-?-1873)
Allison, John to Martha Daniel 9-9-1871 (9-10-1871)
Almony, Nathan to Sarah Perry 2-10-1865
Anderson, Geo. Alex. to Mary E. Crockett 7-10-1876 (7-12-1876)
Anderson, Geo. T. to Rhoda Jane Williams 2-17-1855 (2-20-1855)
Anderson, James C. R. to Rebeca Jane Crumley 9-27-1865 (10-11-1865)
Anderson, James C. R. to Rebecca Jane Crumly 9-27-1865 (10-11-1865)
Anderson, James M. to Evaline Taylor 10-15-1872 (10-17-1872)
Anderson, P. C. to Roda C. Ellis 5-12-1873 (5-15-1873)
Anderson, P. C. to Roda Ellers 5-12-1873
Anderson, Wm. G. to Lucinda C. Bowman 7-5-1870
Angel, Geo. H. to Leelia? E. Custer 1-1-1872 (1-2-1872)
Angel, James R. to Elizabeth Montgomery 9-27-1856 (10-3-1856)
Angel, Samuel to Lorrina Smith 11-13-1865 (11-?-1865)
Angell, George H. to Lillia Roberts 1-1-1872 (1-2-1872)
Angell, George to Mary A. Butterworth 10-23-1858
Angell, Samuel to Lorena T. Smith 11-20-1865
Aram, William to Mary Taylor 4-24-1869 (4-25-1869)
Arance, William to Mary Arnell 1-1-1876
Archer, John to Sarah Pierce 10-14-1860
Archer, Smith? to Nancy Markland 8-14-1861
Archer, William Smith to Nancy A. Markland 8-14-1861 (8-16-1861)
Arnold, Geo. W. to Hannah Richardson 8-13-1876
Arnold, H. M. to Elizabeth A. Campbell 5-8-1874
Arnold, Harrison M. to Elizabeth Campbell 5-8-1874
Arnold, Powell to Rebecca Roberts 9-20-1855
Arnold, William to Ellen Dugger 8-3-1877 (8-4-1877)
Arrance?, William to Josephine White 1-22-1878 (1-25-1878)
Arrowood, John to Deby Houstin 3-2-1879
Ash, Grugham? to Susanna Smith 12-10-1853 (12-11-1853)
Austin, Henry C. to Molley J. Kidwell 12-3-1874 (12-10-1874)
Badgett, Thomas to Matilda E. Hampton 5-26-1855 (5-27-1855)
Badgett, Thomas to Matilda Hampton 12-14-1854 (no return)
Badgett, William P. to Tewanda Ballinger 12-31-1851
Badgley, A. S. to Jane E. Simerly 9-29-1865 (9-30-1865)
Badley, A. S. to Mary Jane E. Simerly 9-29-1869 (9-30-1869)
Bains, John M. to Mary M. Miller 11-7-1872
Baird, Benjamin to Cordelia Stout 12-19-1877 (12-20-1877)
Baker, Adam? to Martha Shell 3-19-1868
Baker, Charles to Sarah J. Garland 1-19-1861 (1-20-1861)
Baker, David A. to Joanah H. Furgason 12-22-1860 (12-23-1860)
Baker, Ezekiel to Martha L. Grindstaff 8-10-1866 (8-26-1866)
Baker, William to Jane Stephens 12-3-1857 (1-3-1858)
Baker, William to Jane Stephens 12-3-1857 (1-30-1858)
Baker, William to Martha Shell 3-18-1868 (3-19-1868)
Baker, William to Mary E. Lyle 12-23-1871 (12-24-1871)
Baker, William to Mary Leadford 3-2-1868 (3-5-1868)
Baker, Wilson to Margaret Keene 9-16-1875
Baker, Wilson to Margaret Kener 9-16-1875
Baker, Wm. to Mary E. Syler 12-23-1871 (12-24-1871)
Banks, John to Eliza Garland 4-17-1872 (12-18-1872)
Banner, F. V. to Martha C. Wilcox 12-11-1878 (12-15-1878)
Banner, J. T. to Cordelia Hyder 8-8-1878
Banner, Newton to Sefrony E. Mast 7-1-1867
Banner, Samuel to Jane A. Hydee 12-7-1868 (12-16-1868)
Bansy?, Isaac N. to Ann Hatcher 9-15-1872 (9-19-1872)
Barker, Joseph to Martha Jane Bishop 6-21-1858 (6-24-1858)

Barker?, Isaac M. to Malinda Campbell 4-?-1867 (4-12-1868?)
Barnes, Alen L. to Martha Sayler 3-7-1854
Barnes, James to Elizabeth Saylor 11-6-1861 (11-9-1861
Barnes, John to M. A. McLaughlin 7-24-1874 (7-27-1874)
Barnes, John to Martha A. McLouglin 7-24-1874 (7-26-1874)
Barnet, Nathan to Saraphina Troutman 12-22-1857 (12-23-1857)
Barnett, James to Bettie Vandeventer 11-13-1878 (11-14-1878)
Barns, Elbert A. to Mary A. Williams 12-19-1872 (12-24-1872) *
Barns, Elbert H. to Mary A. Williams 12-?-1871
Bashor, Joseph to Martha J. Bishop 6-21-1858 (6-24-1858)
Bates, Asa L. to Sarah Jane Moreland 8-2-1853
Bauk, Uriah to Margaret Morris 2-29-1828
Bayless, Andrew C. to Loucretia A. E. Hunt 7-20-1857 (no return)
Beam, William to Rebeca Moor 7-24-1866 (5?-26-1866)
Bearnia?, William to Rebecca Moore 7-24-1866 (7-26-1866)
Beasley, Henry c. to Susanna P. Crumley 3-6-1861
Beck, John to Mary Deloach 8-31-1870
Bell, H. E. to Harriet Miller 6-17-1875 (7-11-1875)
Bell, William V. to Mary A. Boyd 3-1-1860
Benet, Alfred to Jane Beener? 3-31-1864
Benfield, A. L. to Mary Brumit 6-26-1875 (7-18-1875)
Bennett, Nathan to Sophrona Troutmon 12-23-1857
Bentley, Martin to Lydia Smith 2-10-1874 (2-11-1874)
Beriens?, Wm. A. to Salley F. Williams 5-18-1875
Berry, Alfred J. to Sarah E. Carriger 1-29-1867 (1-31-1867)
Berry, David to Sarah Head 3-1-1875 (3-13-1875)
Berry, Elbert C. to Martha Crow 3-24-1875 (3-25-1875)
Berry, Henry T. to Martha A. Roddie 8-9-1854 (8-10-1854)
Berry, John W. to Emelin Burks 10-30-1874 (11-1-1874)
Berry, John W. to Evelin Banks 10-30-1874 (11-1-1874)
Berry, L. C. to Mary J. Folsom 6-3-1857
Berry, Leander to Elener Berry 8-12-1850 (8-15-1850)
Berry, Robert A. to Sarafinah Bishop 9-14-1877 (9-18-1877)
Berry, Samuel J. to Allice Yates 2-23-1872
Berry, Samuel M. to Mary C. Buckles 10-2-1878 (10-4-1878)
Berry, Thomas H. to Margaret Williams 3-9-1875 (3-11-1875)
Berry, Thomas H. to Margart Williams 3-9-1875 (4-11-1875)
Berry, William J. to Mary C. C. Pearce 2-15-1877
Bill, Lowis P. to Yanaby Whitehead 7-21-1847 (7-23-1847)
Birnham?, James C. to Adala Perry 1-18-1871
Bishop, Andrew E. to Martha Ann Barnett 3-12-1865
Bishop, Andrew E. to Martha E. Barrett 3-12-1865
Bishop, Henry to Elizabeth More 3-27-1855
Bishop, John to Margaret Jenkins 12-23-1861 (12-25-1861)
Bishop, Saml. to Alice O. Miller 12-30-1875
Bishop, William M. to Mary Newlin 9-11-1856
Bishop, William M. to Mary Newton 9-11-1856
Blackbourn, Larken to Malinda Campbell 10-6-1860
Blackburn, William to Emely Miller 10-31-1867 (11-2-1867)
Blankenship, W. H. to Martha Hopson 10-23-1872
Blevins, Alen to Lauza Cole 2-12-1853
Blevins, Allen to Amy Garland 12-1-1862 (12-6-1862)
Blevins, David P. to Sarah J. Pierce 8-7-1853 (8-8-1853)
Blevins, David to Hiley (Hilly) Whitehead 8-12-1870 (8-14-1870)
Blevins, Dillard to Malinda Garland 6-6-1861 (6-9-1861)
Blevins, Dillard to Matilda Garland 6-6-1861 (6-9-1861)
Blevins, Easterly to Rody Williams 3-29-1855
Blevins, George to Rebecca Rewir? 2-27-1862 (3-2-1862)
Blevins, James to Mary Richardson 6-27-1866 (7-1-1866)
Blevins, Jeremiah to Sarahfina Smith 8-2-1851 (8-3-1851)
Blevins, John to Adalin Nedeffer 4-22-1860 (4-24-1860)
Blevins, John to Adalin Nidefer 11-19-1866
Blevins, John to Adaline Nidiffer 11-29-1866
Blevins, John to Sarah Sewerly 8-25-1877 (no return)
Blevins, Swinfield to Nancy Carver 3-28-1864 (3-31-1864)
Blevins, Wesley to Mira Bowlen 4-8-1867 (4-11-1867)
Blevins, William to Delitha Lovless 11-20-1865 (11-?-1865)
Blevins, William to Serana Britt 3-4-1870 (3-24-1870)
Blevins, Willy to Eliza Johnson 9-30-1861 (10-5-1861)
Blevins, Willy to Eveline Carrier 2-15-1865
Blevins, Wm. to Elizabeth Eller 7-29-1878 (7-28?-1878)
Blevins?, William to Tobitha Lovless 11-20-1865 (11-21-1865)
Blum, William to Serana Brett 3-4-1870 (3-24-1870)
Bly, Abram to Dicy Taylor 4-21-1875
Bly, Alfred to Malinda Duffield 9-22-1874

Bolen, John to Jane Morgan 7-20-1866 (10-21-1866)
Bollen, S. P. to S. E. Perigory 6-19-1873
Bolling, Jacob B. to Elizabeth Jane Miller 1-13-1856 (1-14-1856)
Bolton, S. P. to S. E. Prigory 6-18-1873 (6-19-1873)
Boren, David C. to Nancy C. Hodges 12-23-1874 (12-24-1874)
Boren, David to Nancy Hodge 12-23-1874 (12-24-1874)
Boren, Joseph to Delial E. Range 8-17-1857 (8-20-1857)
Boren, Joseph to Delila E. Runge? 8-17-1857 (8-20-1857)
Boren, Willy W.(O?) to Arsilla Jane Williams 12-4-1859 (12-6-1859)
Bowe, Joseph C. to Mary Alice Ferguson 4-30-1878
Bowen, Benjamin W. to Nancy L. Louisa? 9-5-1852 (11-17-1851?)
Bowen, Christian B. to Susann Oliver 1-8-1875 (1-?-1875)
Bowen, David F. to Mary Ann Ruber 7-8-1857
Bowen, David T. to Marthey Crow 9-1-1860 (9-20-1860)
Bowen, John L. to Eliza J. Grindstaff 12-11-1866 (12-12-1866)
Bowen, John W. to Susan E. Smith 5-5-1868
Bowen, L. T. to Martha Collins 12-29-1874 (12-31-1874)
Bowen, Peter to Mary Anderson 8-6-1866
Bowen, William A. to Mary L. Bowen 6-16-1858 (6-17-1858)
Bowen, Wm. G. to Susanna Potter 9-5-1866
Bower, Andrew to Malinda Hodges 11-29-1870
Bower, David S. to Virginia J. Miller 9-14-1874 (9-15-1874)
Bower, Valentine to Babary Ellis 3-3-1871 (3-23-1871)
Bower, Volentin to Abigail Buck 9-30-1808 (10-1-1808)
Bowers, Abraham to Isey Alfred 6-22-1868
Bowers, Alfred R. to Rebecca S. Carriger 10-4-1876 (10-13-1876)
Bowers, Benjamin W. to Nancy Louisa Merly? 9-5-1852 (11-17-1851?)
Bowers, Benjamin to Louisa Morley 11-5-1852 (11-7-1852)
Bowers, C. B. to Susanna Oliver 1-8-1875 (1-9-1875)
Bowers, Christian N. to Martha Hollaway 11-15-1854 (11-17-1854)
Bowers, Daniel E. to Abigail Heaton 1-27-1873 (1-28-1873)
Bowers, Daniel S. to Eliza Berry 12-24-1867 (12-31-1867)
Bowers, Henry to Eliza Harkel 2-6-1871 (2-12-1871) B
Bowers, Henry to Rosanna Jane Dugger 6-8-1876
Bowers, Isaac M. to Matilda Campbell 4-12-1868
Bowers, Isaac N. to Emeline Bowers 3-8-1876
Bowers, Isaac S. to Margarett Tipton 8-20-1861
Bowers, Isaac to Racheal Carriger 4-14-1868 (9-15-1869)
Bowers, Isaac to Rachel J. Carriger 9-14-1867 (9-15-1867)
Bowers, James T. to Elizabeth Cannon 9-18-1852 (9-19-1852)
Bowers, John T. to Mary Pierce 4-19-1856 (4-20-1856)
Bowers, Joseph P. to Emeline Grace 10-15-1855
Bowers, L. T. to Martha Collier 12-29-1874 (12-31-1874)
Bowers, Landon C. to Loucreca Ensor 8-16-? (no return)
Bowers, Lenard A. to Ann Eliza Bishop 8-6-1856
Bowers, Leonard A. to Ann Eliza Bishop 8-6-1856
Bowers, M. S. to Eliza Pierce 11-27-1860
Bowers, Valentine to Barbra Eller 3-3-1871 (3-23-1871)
Bowers, William A. to Mary L. Bowers 6-16-1858 (6-17-1858)
Bowers, William A. to Sally F. Williams 5-18-1875
Bowers, William D. to Rody Stoner 5-16-1857 (5-17-1857)
Bowers, Wm. G. to Roda Stover 5-16-1857 (5-17-1857)
Bowers?, Telir? to Mary Anderson 8-6-1866
Bowman, Christopher C. to Mary E. Keen 6-8-1859 (6-9-1859)
Bowman, Daniel to Sarah Bunlain 10-10-1871
Bowman, Daniel to Sarah McIntyre 2-26-1850 (3-30-1850)
Bowman, David M. to Sarah I. Taylor 8-15-1876 (8-17-1876)
Bowman, David to Mary A. Bunton 10-10-1871
Bowman, E. K. to Caroline Julion 1-25-1852 (1-28-1852)
Bowman, Geo. W. to Martha E. McNatt 10-20-1857 (10-22-1857)
Bowman, George C.(W.?) to Martha E. McNabb 10-20-1857 (10-22-1857)
Bowman, George to Louvina Bowman 11-14-1870 (11-15-1870)
Bowman, Harison to Alvina Arwood 7-16-1868
Bowman, Harrison to Slavica? Arwood 7-16-1868
Bowman, Hyram to L. A. Johnson 3-25-1871 (3-28-1871)
Bowman, Jackson to Martha Jolly 7-22-1866 (7-23-1866)
Bowman, Jackson to Martha Tally 7-22-1866 (7-23-1866)
Bowman, Jacob to Abagail A. Gibs 1-24-1855 (1-25-1855)
Bowman, James to Sarah Ann Dunken 4-14-1853
Bowman, John H. to Jane R. Smith 1-1-1851
Bowman, John W. to Martha Peoples 11-17-1869
Bowman, Joseph to Eliza Jane Arwood 5-1-1865
Bowman, Lee to Nany Buck 12-20-1871
Bowman, Samuel to Nancy C. Price 1-13-1872 (1-14-1872)

Bowman, T. M. to Ann(a) I. (J?) McInturff 7-12-1873 (7-13-1873)
Bowman, Thomas to Mary Whittemore 10-2-1867 (10-7-1867)
Bowman, W. M. to Rebecca M. McInturff 5-7-1871
Bowman, William to Carolilne Carroll 9-11-1867
Bownell, Wm. M. to Rebecca McInturff 5-7-1871
Boyd, Andrew W. to Mary Ann Forbes 11-17-1864 (11-19-1865)
Boyd, J. J. R. to Martha Jane Tipton 10-2-1847 (10-7-1847)
Boyd, James I. (Jas. J.?) to Julia Miller 5-20-1852
Boyd, James I.(J?) R. to Rhoda Williams 2-7-1860 (2-28-1860)
Boyd, Marshall to Margaret P. McKinney 2-21-1871 (2-23-1871)
Boyd, Marshell to M. P. McKiny 2-20-1871 (2-23-1871)
Boyd, Samuel to Cathern Kughn 6-11-1851
Boyd, Samuel to Mary M. Lowe 11-30-1857 (no return)
Boyd, Samuell to Mary M. Rowe 11-30-1857
Boyd, William to Elizabeth Payne 2-24-1869 (2-25-1869)
Bradfute, Archabold to Louisa Moon 10-25-1834 (10-28-1834)
Bradley, Nathaniel T. to Sarah Carver 12-24-1872
Bradley, Robert B. to Hester Carter 8-24-1876
Bradley, William to Loucinda Buckles 4-12-1870 (4-17-1870)
Branch, Christopher C. to Amanda C. Waggoner 2-6-1877
Brent, John to Janie? Nave 5-1-1870 (5-8-1870)
Brett, Landon to Emeline Whitson 4-4-1871 (4-6-1871)
Brett, Thomas J. to Eva C. Miller 8-16-1878 (8-17-1878)
Brett, Worley to Mary Honeycut 3-21-1866 (3-22-1866)
Brevert?, John to Sarah A. McInturff 6-12-1872 (6-14-1872)
Brewer, Calvin to Mary A. Coffee 7-9-1878 (7-14-1878)
Briant, Elisha to Martha Overhulser 8-6-1858 (8-9-1858)
Briant, Jasper to Caroline Tucker 2-18-1879 (2-20-1879)
Bridget, Henderson to Susan Banner 8-4-1869
Bridgman, Mattison to Susana Richards 10-25-1868
Britt, David to Jane Britt 2-6-1855
Britt, John to Elizabeth Gilbert 9-8-1851
Britt, Martin to Lousinda McInturff 9-10-1862 (9-11-1862)
Britt, William to Matilda Linvill 10-17-1850
Britt, Wilson to Mirey Kenley 12-18-1850
Brooks, David to Angaline Grindstaff 3-23-1871 (3-26-1871)
Brooks, Jackson to Leodacia R. C. Pierce 4-22-1873 (4-23-1873)
Brooks, Jackson to Ludora E. L. Pain 5-22-18783 (4?-23-1873)
Brown, Alban M. to Hannah Jane Hendrix 5-10-1854 (5-11-1854)
Brown, Isaac H. to Margaret M. Williams 11-30-1855 (12-2-1855)
Brown, Isaac N. to Elizabeth Anders 8-21-1866
Brown, Isaac N. to Elizabeth Auder 8-21-1866
Brown, James to Rachael Tipton 11-4-1867 (11-6-1867)
Brown, John M. to Mary M. Coble 10-4-1876 (10-6-1876)
Brown, Nathanel to Phenith Dunken 2-7-1853
Browning, J. B. to Clamida J. Jenkins 7-22-1877
Broyles, Andrew C. to Loucretia A. E. Hunt 7-20-1857
Brumet, John A. to Lorina A. McInturff 6-12-1872 (6-14-1872)
Brumit, John to Mary Branch 4-18-1872 (4-19-1872)
Brumit, William to Susan Branch 8-26-1875
Brummet, William to Susan Branch 8-26-1875
Buck, George to Susanna Wilson 3-29-1863 (3-30-1863)
Buck, John to Mary Deloach 8-31-1870
Buck, Nat T. to Emelin Carrell 12-19-1868
Buck, Nathaniel T. to Etta Carrell 12-19-1868
Buck, Osborn D. to E. E. Taylor 12-4-1865 (12-7-1865)
Buck, Osburn D. to Eveline E. Taylor 12-4-1865 (12-7-1865)
Buck, Thomas to Mary McNabb 11-17-1866
Buck, William to Eliza E. Williams 3-5-1866 (3-8-1866)
Buckhannon, Thomas to Lew Miller 8-13-1876
Buckler, Andy to Catherine Nidefer 3-9-1876 (3-10-1876)
Buckles, Isaac B. to Ruthy Adaline Bowers 2-28-1866 (3-2-1866)
Buckles, Levie to Mary Jane Carriger 5-22-1860 (5-24-1860)
Buckles, Robert to Winey Berry 1-15-1851 (1-19-1851)
Buckles, Thomas J. to Selia Williams 4-14-1869 (4-22-1869)
Bukor?, Roner to Sally Cates Colend 6-27-1874 (no return)
Bunch, Robert to Rhoda Williams 7-6-1867 (7-7-1867)
Buntain, John F. to Mary E. Verick? 4-20-1874
Buntan, Jacob D. to Emily S. Cobb 1-12-1870 (1-17-1870)
Bunton, Jacob D. to Emily S. Cable 1-13-1870 (1-17-1870)
Burchfield, B. M. C. to Mary Burchfield 9-9-1871 (9-12-1871)
Burchfield, C. M. C. to Mary E. Burchfield 9-9-1871 (9-12-1871)
Burchfield, Ezekiel to Martha S. O'Brien 1-23-1853 (1-?-1853)
Burchfield, Ezekiel to Sarah Gauge 7-4-1859 (7-30-1859)
Burchfield, Ezekiel to Sarah Gouge 7-4-1859 (7-30-1859)

Burchfield, Robert to Mary Garland 12-23-1871 (12-28-1871)
Burchfield, William to Rebecca Carrell 5-2-1859
Burchfield, William to Rebecca Carroll 5-2-1859 (5-?-1859)
Burfield, A. L. to Mary Brummett 6-26-1875 (7-18-1875)
Burgon, Sandy to Ann Bruen 2-27-1872
Burk, John to Elizabeth Whalen 2-1-1865 (2-1-1866?)
Burlerson (Burlison), Greenberry to Jane Bell 11-27-1868 (11-29-1868)
Burrow?, Saml. to Jane A. Hyder 12-7-1868 (12-16-1868)
Bush, Solomon to Susan Hartly 7-8-1870
Bushong, William to Elizabeth C. Peoples 10-6-1862 (10-7-1862)
Butterworth, Charles E. to Julia A. Humphrey 11-23-1868 (11-25-1868)
Cable, Benjamin D. to Susanna Simerly 12-3-1855 (12-9-1855)
Cable, Noah to Eslie M. Collert 3-2-1874 (3-8-1874)
Cable, Richard to Malinda Whitehead 3-5-1875
Cagle, B. B. to Eliza McDalstrale 10-2-1877 (10-3-1877)
Cagle, Isaac to Sarah McQueen 7-26-1873 (7-27-1873)
Caldwell, Archabald to Edney Rusk 11-5-1868
Calis (Cates), W. F. to M. J. Cooper 7-26-1866
Caloway, T. C. to Mary L. Humphrey 12-19-1878
Camern, John W. to Mary E. Williams 12-31-1857
Camern, William M. to Mary J. Stover 2-22-1876
Cameron, Jas. M. to M. E. Tipton 2-6-1855
Campbell, Albert E. to Elizabeth Fry 11-6-1852 (11-9-1852)
Campbell, Alexander to Nancy Simmerly 3-9-1855 (3-11-1855)
Campbell, Alfred J. to Sarah Shea 3-25-1851 (3-27-1851)
Campbell, Calvin A. to Phebe Hart 9-1-1855 (no return)
Campbell, Calvin F. to Mary E. Campbell 2-2-1854
Campbell, Carter to Sarah A. E. Smith 3-23-1867 (3-24-1867)
Campbell, Charles N. to Bethana Yates 12-30-1869
Campbell, Charles N. to Elizabeth Jones 11-12-1840 (11-15-1840)
Campbell, Charles to Chany Pugh 1-1-1867
Campbell, Daniel to Elizabeth Anderson 4-28-1855 (4-29-1855)
Campbell, G. F. to Nancy Jane Goodwin 9-14-1874
Campbell, G. W. to Nancy J. Goodwin 9-14-1874
Campbell, Henderson to Tempy Jane Jenkins 5-14-1866
Campbell, Henry to Mary Grindstaff 1-2-1859 (1-8-1859)
Campbell, Hyder to Margaret Kincade 7-7-1869 (7-9-1869)
Campbell, Isaac to Adeline Cole 12-22-1876 (12-24-1876)
Campbell, J. R. to Sarah Hayes 5-17-1871 (5-21-1871)
Campbell, J. R. to Sarah Hays 5-17-1871 (5-21-1871)
Campbell, James D. to Dealy C. Hall 4-13-1876 (4-14-1876)
Campbell, James to Sarah Garland 3-17-1876 (3-20-1876)
Campbell, Jeremiah to Caroline Hamby 9-19-1874 (9-20-1874)
Campbell, John B. to Rebeca Hyder 11-9-1853 (11-10-1853)
Campbell, John F. to Loucinda(Loverda?) Goodwin 3-14-1870
Campbell, John H. to Mary A. Pean (Pruis?) 11-25-1857
Campbell, John H. to Mary A. Pierce 11-25-1857
Campbell, John R. to Melvina Lowe 2-5-1868 (2-6-1868)
Campbell, John T. to ___ Miller no date (with 1875)
Campbell, John to Jane Nave 12-6-1877
Campbell, John to Mary Smith 6-15-1867
Campbell, John to Rebecca Hyan? 11-9-1853 (11-10-1853)
Campbell, Joseph to Sarah Surena Stalcup 12-24-1865
Campbell, L. H. to Louisa Liply? 8-22-1857 (8-27-1857)
Campbell, Lawson H. to Louisa Lessley 8-22-1857 (8-27-1857)
Campbell, Lawson to Sarah Taylor 10-1-1870 (10-2-1870)
Campbell, Michael to Ann Blevins 5-29-1871
Campbell, N. T. to Fanny I. Campbell 11-8-1873 (11-9-1873)
Campbell, Nat T. to Margaret Jackson 3-1-1867 (3-3-1867)
Campbell, Samuel to Emiline Hardin 5-7-1864
Campbell, Thomas to Eliza Nedeffer 9-4-1874
Campbell, Thomas to Eliza Neffer 4-4-1874 (9-26-1874)
Campbell, Thomas to Eliza Nideffer 4-4-1874 (9-26-1874)
Campbell, Thomas to Elizabeth Glover 7-20-1877 (7-22-1877)
Campbell, W. H. to Delia C. Glover 12-21-1878 (12-29-1878)
Campbell, William C. to Mary A. Fry 10-31-1858
Campbell, William R. to Margaret Little 7-31-1854 (8-1-1854)
Campbell, William to Edney L. Lewis 12-18-1866 (12-23-1866)
Campbell, William to Elizabeth Carter 8-13-1870
Campbell, William to Elizabeth Cook 4-14-1866 (4-15-1866)
Campbell, William to Elva L. Rose 5-27-1873 (5-31-1873)
Campbell, Wm. G. to Nancy Glen 1-21-1865 (1-?-1865)
Campbell, Wm. to E. L. Nave 5-27-1873 (5-31-1873)

Campbell, Zachariah C. to Martha J. Fletcher 7-29-1867 (9-4-1867)
Cannon, Elbert F. to Isabela Hardin 5-3-1860 (5-6-1860)
Caps, William to Ruth E. Cox 4-30-1858 (5-1-1856?)
Caraway, James to Mary Ann Ferguson 10-26-1856
Caraway, James to Myria Maberry 5-10-1867 (5-11-1867)
Caraway, Larken to Ellen Shell 1-5-1878
Caraway, William H. to Martha Stout 11-1-1865 (11-3-1865)
Carden, Ansel C. to Sarah J. Oliver 6-18-1867
Carden, James W. to Ann Estep 3-6-1861 (2?-6-1861)
Carden, Kinchuls to Eliza Ann Anderson 11-6-1861 (11-7-1861)
Carden, Landon C. to Emily Goodwin 6-8-1867 (6-10-1867)
Carden, Landon to Emeline Goodwin 6-8-1867 (6-10-1867)
Carden, R. to Mary Nave 1-1-1875
Carden, Reuben to Mary K. Nave 1-1-1875
Carden, Vincent to Casander Lewis 4-16-1874
Carier, Robert to Ann Fitzsimmons 10-19-1867 (10-?-1867)
Carier?, Washington to Mary Lyons 11-23-1872 (11-24-1872)
Caron?, William to Raheal Swerin 10-9-1874
Carr, Alfred to Eliza Foster 7-29-1857 (8-1-1859)
Carr, Samuel to A. Peak 4-9-1870
Carr, William J. to Margaret Carter 3-4-1874 (3-5-1874)
Carray, William to Allan Wilson 9-9-1868 (9-12-1868) B
Carrel, John to Mary Buck 7-19-1872
Carrell, Alexander to Sarah Preen? 9-20-1860
Carrell, G. W. to Elizabeth Elliott 5-10-1858
Carrell, G. W. to Elizabeth Ellott 5-10-1858
Carrell, John C. to Caroline Britt 1-15-1856
Carrell, William S. to Mary Simerly 9-13-1866
Carrell, William to Ann Eliza Williams 10-8-1857
Carrell, William to Cleursy? Taylor 1-22-1878
Carrell, Wm. to Nancy Duncan 2-27-1855
Carrier, William to Rhoda A. Kelly 8-19-1873 (8-30-1873)
Carriger, Alen T. to Carline Pierce 9-21-1852 (9-22-1852)
Carriger, Christian to Rachael Buckles 9-1-1859
Carriger, Christian to Rachel Burkluts? 9-15-1859
Carriger, D. N. to Jane Treadway 5-23-1876 (5-25-1876)
Carriger, Godfrey to Jane Fen? Cannon 10-5-1857 (10-8-1857)
Carriger, Godfry to Jane T. Cannon 10-5-1857
Carriger, Isaac to Martha E. Hines? 2-26-1869 (7-28-1869)
Carriger, Isaac to Martha E. House 2-28-1869
Carriger, J. D. to Ediny Duggar 6-14-1866 (6-17-1866)
Carriger, J. D. to Edney Dugger 6-14-1866 (6-17-1866)
Carriger, Joel to Mary K. Ferguson 12-?-1861 (no return)
Carriger, John C. to Margaret J. Bowen 9-25-1876 (9-26-1876)
Carriger, Nicholas to Cashin (Cathan) Simerly 1-1-1873
Carriger, Wm. L. to Mary Morrell 4-10-1875 (4-11-1875)
Carriger, Wm. L. to Mollie Morrell 4-10-1875 (4-11-1875)
Carter, Archabald to Mary Emmert 1-21-1858
Carter, J. M. to S. C. Garrison 8-9-1850
Carter, James P. J.? to Margarette M. Dunn? 8-5-1851
Carter, James P. T. to Margaret M. Dunn 8-5-1851
Carter, John to Mary E. Morrell 12-30-1861 (2-10-1862)
Carter, Landon C. to Rebecca Garland 7-30-1877
Carter, Landon to Elizabeth A. Cameron 6-18-1866 (6-19-1866)
Carter, Landon to Elizabeth A. Camm? 6-19-1866
Carter, Robert to Sarah Moss 11-9-1871
Carter, William A. to Delia Bradley 6-15-1875
Carter, William to Malinda Wadkin 2-16-1869 (2-18-1869)
Carver, Adam to Tempy Hicks 2-25-1870 (3-1-1870)
Carver, George to Martha Davis 9-3-1866 (9-5-1866)
Carver, George to Martha Dover 9-5-1866
Carver, James T. to Nellie Escott 6-13-1873
Carver, John H. to Mary Smith 2-17-1870 (3-17-1870)
Carver, Risen to Sarah Swaner 1-28-1866 (4-28-1866)
Carver, William to Rachel Swan 10-9-1874 (10-11-1874?)
Carver, William to Rhoda Kelley 8-19-1873 (8-20-1873)
Carver, William to Viney Cates 10-21-1873 (10-27-1873)
Casa, William to Eveline Grindstaff 12-28-1870 (12-29-1870)
Cash, George W. to Maggie Droke? 7-28-1877 (7-29-1877)
Cash, William to Nancy J. Wagner 9-19-1851 (9-20-1851)
Cashaday, William to Margaret Bishop 7-13-1861 (7-15-1861)
Cassada, William to Margaret Bishop 7-13-1861 (7-15-1861)
Cassida, William to Mary Ann McAlister 11-24-1859
Cawer?, Washington to Mary Lyon 11-23-1872 (11-24-1872)
Chambers, David T. to Manervy Ellis 9-3-1866 (9-5-1866)

Chambers, David to Catharin Hamm? 3-23-1869
Chambers, David to Nancy C. Heltone 3-20-1869 (3-23-1869)
Chambers, James T. to Julia A. Dover 4-4-1878
Chambers, John to Emma Carter 3-6-1878 (3-7-1878)
Chambers, John to Mary Whitehead 10-15-1856 (10-16-1856)
Chambers, Turner? to Mary Ann Smith 10-1-1853 (10-18-1853)
Chambers, William to Catharine Simerly 10-12-1868 (12-29-1868)
Chanler, William to Clary Wellan 1-27-1875 B
Clark, D. T. W. to E. C. Shell 12-16-1870
Clark, D. T. W. to Emaline Catharine Shell 12-16-1870
Clark, Thos. to Louisa P. Williams 7-21-1860 (7-22-1860)
Clark, William to Elizabeth A. Krous 1-9-1854 (1-12-1854)
Clawson, Jas. L. to Sarah Ellen Potter 7-28-1854 (7-30-1854)
Claymon, John W. to Marget? E. Hayes 7-27-1863 (no return)
Clemens, William C. to Ema Hamley 5-5-1862 (5-8-1862)
Clemons, Benjamin to Sarah Lewis 2-27-1862 (3-2-1862)
Coble, Calvin F. to Susanna Buckles 3-6-1852 (3-18-1852)
Coble, Noah to E. M. Caldwell 3-2-1874 (3-8-1874)
Coble, Wallace D. to Nancy J. Williams 11-20-1868
Cochran, Markus G.(D?) to Mary Ann Simerly 7-8-1867 (7-14-1867)
Cochren, James W. to Darthula O'Brian 10-27-1865 (10-29-1865)
Cockren, Eldridge to Julian Carver 9-17-1874
Colbough, Teter to Lovinia I. Lewis 1-3-1868 (1-8-1868)
Colbough, William to Elizabeth Loe 12-23-1874 (12-24-1874)
Colbough, William to Elizabeth Smith 8-1-1850
Coldwell, Archabold to Edney Lusk 11-5-1868
Coldwell, Archabold to Racheal R. Newton 10-12-1865 (10-13-1865)
Cole, Anderson L. to Amanda Markland 2-22-1864 (2-24-1864)
Cole, Andrew to Amanda Markland 2-22-81864
Cole, James to Eliza Rasor 3-8-1875
Cole, James to Eliza Reason 3-18-1875
Cole, Jessee J. to Eliza Heatherly 5-4-1862
Cole, John H. to Martha E. Duisemer? 7-16-1875
Cole, John H. to Mmartha E. Dunsmore 7-16-1875
Cole, John to Sarah Carr 12-13-1860 (12-15-1860)
Cole, Joseph O. to Mahaley Hodge 6-14-1853 (6-19-1853)
Cole, Joseph R. to Docia D. Arnold 9-22-1864 (9-24-1864)
Cole, M. B. to Catherine Merideth 12-13-1877 (12-20-1877)
Cole, S. H. to Louisa Cole 3-20-1874
Cole, Solomon to Catharine Foust 1-6-1858 (1-7-1858)
Cole, Thompson to Martha Williams 4-15-1875
Cole, William to Clarecy Shuffield 8-10-1874 (8-13-1874)
Cole, William to Clary Shufferd 8-10-1874 (8-13-1874)
Coleman, Francis C. to Harriett Bowman 2-20-1877 (2-27-1877)
Colie, Andrew to Harrett Garland 11-15-1869 (11-17-1869)
Collett, Thomas to Mary Southerland 5-30-1874 (3?-31-1874)
Collett, Tolbert to Eliza Folsom 2-7-1872 (2-8-1872)
Collins, Elisha to S. E. Bowers 10-26-1854 (10-26-1854)
Collins, John N. to Permelia Nidiffer 9-2-1878 (9-5-1878)
Collins, Watson to Eveline Williams 8-6-1844
Combs, Johnathan to Aletha McKehn? 5-14-1851 (5-15-1851)
Conebson?, Eldridge to Julean Carver 9-17-1874 (9-20-1874)
Constable, John to Caroline McKehn 1-17-1867
Cook, Alexander to Sarah Davis 10-4-1873 (10-5-1873)
Cook, Andrew to Sarah Davis 10-4-1873 (10-5-1873)
Cook, John to Nancy Yarboro 11-16-1870 (11-17-1870)
Cook, John to Nancy Yearber 11-16-1870 (11-17-1870)
Cook, Ruben P. to Ruth Kite 7-16-1855
Cooper, James T. to Margaret C. McNabb 9-12-1857 (9-13-1857)
Cooper, James T. to Margarett McNabb 9-13-1857
Cooper, Montgomery C. to Rhoda Williamson? 1-24-1879
Cooper, Thomas to Elizabeth Maines 5-17-1834
Cooper, Thomas to Sarah Hatly 11-7-1877 (11-11-1877)
Cooper, William A. to Racheal C. Williams 5-7-1873 (5-8-1873)
Cooper, Wm. H. to Racheal Williams 5-7-1873 (5-8-1873)
Cooper, Wm. to Hannah Fair 9-26-1852
Cosbia, Joseph to Nancy A. Hampton 12-29-1869 (12-30-1869)
Cox, Thomas I. to Emily P. Fitzsimmons 12-9-1855
Crafford, Thomas to Phineda Hughes 4-30-1870 (5-1-1870)
Craig, Hiram to Harriet Cameron 6-9-1870
Crawford, David to Emeline Roberts 9-17-1864 (9-20-1864)
Creed, Geo. W. to Thereby A. Anderson 12-31-1861
Creed, George W. to Nancy Combs 5-1-1866 (5-3-1866)
Creed, Nepolion B. to Della Cathern Blevins 3-11-1876 (3-12-1876)
Crew, Levi N. to Margaret Duggan 10-2-1873 (10-9-1873)

Critcher, William C. to Martha C. Kinnick 7-11-1861 (7-23-1861)
Crocket, P. A. J. to Rhoda Ann Williams 9-27-1852 (9-30-1852)
Cromwell, W. H. to Mary Eliza Hamitte 11-5-1867 (11-7-1867)
Crouch, Geo. P. to Mary M. Brooks 2-13-1860
Crow, Daniel S. to Sarah Blevins 10-4-1871
Crow, David (Daniel) to Martha E. Wilcox 4-2-1873
Crow, G. W. to Nancy Combs 5-1-1866 (5-3-1866)
Crow, H. N. to Martha R. Pierce 1-11-1855
Crow, Isaac N. to Virginia A. Slagle 8-31-1878 (9-1-1878)
Crow, James C. to Theodosy Lacy 2-21-1878 (2-24-1878)
Crow, John to Eve Newsom Smith 10-16-1866 (10-18-1866)
Crow, John to Eveline Newton 10-16-1866 (10-18-1866)
Crow, John to Lavicy Carriger 2-18-1858
Crow, Levi N. to Margaret Dugger 10-2-1873 (10-9-1873)
Crow, Martin to Adalade Taylor 2-19-1873 (2-?-1873) B
Crow, R. G. to Emeline Carden 2-7-1864
Crow, Solomon to Lemier Folsom 2-12-1878 (2-14-1878)
Crow, Thomas to Elizabeth Nave 5-7-1859 (5-8-1859)
Crow, Thomas to Emma Daniels 8-29-1878
Crowe, William to Sarah Nave 4-29-1852 (5-2-1852)
Croy, Jerdon (Jorden) to Elizabeth Cooper 2-28-1861
Crucher, William J. to Matha? C. Kenik 7-11-1861 (7-23-1861)
Crumley, George W. to Emma Hickey 9-11-1860? (no return)
Crumley, James to Alice McKinney 2-27-1875 (2-28-1875)
Crumley, Thomas J. to Ann Hickey 12-25-1858 (12-24?-1858)
Crumly, Frederick F. to Anzella Pean 11-30-1865 (1-11-1866)
Crunly, Thomas J. to Ann Hicky 12-25-1858 (12-26-1858)
Crutcher, William C. to Martha C. Kennick 7-1-1861 (no return)
Culbert, Alexander to Emelin Lewis 7-5-1858 (12-6-1858)
Culbert, Alexander to Emeline Lewer? 2-5-1858 (1-3-1859)
Cunstabl, Jacob to Seally Stevens 8-17-1867 (8-18-1867)
Curren?, Wm. H. to Mary Smith 2-17-1870
Curten, John to Matilda Adkins 2-16-1869 (2-8?-1869)
Curtice, David to Sarah E. Lacy 7-26-1851 (7-27-1851)
Curtis, Andrew to Susan Morrell 12-29-1860 (12-22-1860)
Curtis, Archibald to Sarah Shell 5-25-1850 (5-27-1850)
Curtis?, John to Nancy Gill 5-26-1870 (5-27-1870) B
Custer, Calvin to Leticia E. Roberts 7-4-1861
Dane, Jacob to Margaret Tume 9-4-1865 (9-6-1865)
Daniel, B. F. to Sarah L. Lyles 2-6-1875
Daniel, James to Hariet Louisa Gourley 11-21-1850
Daniel, Ryby to Abegal J. Morrell 3-7-1857 (3-12-1857)
Davenport, Samuel S. to Elizabeth Gourley 12-24-1860
Davis, Alexander to Sarah Andrews 11-24-1862
Davis, Amos to Martha Gray 3-13-1854 (3-16-1854)
Davis, Brownlow to Louisa Morrell 4-28-1870
Davis, David to Matilda Chambers 7-29-1878 (7-28?-1878)
Davis, James to Sarah F. Smith 1-2-1871
Davis, Lank to Cheny R. Nave 11-26-1878 (11-27-1878)
Davis, Lankester to Margaret A. Segan 7-22-1871
Davis, Samuel to Nancy Brook 12-13-1874 (12-16-1874)
Davis, William P. to Margaret Lyon 1-14-1871
Davis, William P. to Margaret Lyons 1-14-1871 (1-15-1871)
Davis, William to Elizabeth Campbell 4-12-1866 (4-24-1866)
Deal, C. S. to Caroline Estep 3-3-1883 (3-4-1883)
Deals, Cosby S. P. to Mary P. Duglass 10-28-1859 (no return)
Deloach, J. M. to Elizabeth Beck 1-4-1879 (1-5-1879)
Deloach, James to Jane Williams 3-8-1869
Deloach, James to Matilda Bowers 4-17-1877
Deloach, John to Susan Oliver 1-20-1857
Deloach, John to Susanna Oliver 1-20-1857 (2-20-1857)
Deloach, Kineda to Margaret Mays 10-14-1874
Deloach, Kinedo to Margaret Macy 10-14-1874
Deloach, Samuel to Louisa Garrison 1-27-1865
Deloach, William to Elizabeth White 11-12-1869
Dempsey, William G. to Hannah Thompson 3-24-1854
Demsey, William to Susanna E. Shell 9-30-1865 (10-1-1865)
Dewit?, Riley to Abigail I. Morrell 3-7-1857 (3-12-1857)
Dice?, David to Mary A. Fulkerson 1-2-1871 (1-8-1871)
Dickson, Wm. H. to Nancy A. Smalling 9-10-1874
Dillard, Thos. to Sarah R. Welch 5-12-1865
Dougherty, John C. to Sarah Fulkerson 8-31-1866
Douglas, Thomas to Sarah Jane Osborn 11-13-1877 (12-18-1877)
Douthet, J. B. to Eliza I. Peirce 7-19-1861 (7-21-1861)
Dover, Samuel H. to Nancy Brooks 12-15-1876 (12-16-1874?)

Drake, Jacob I. to Sally Hulson 11-17-1871
Drake, Jacob J. to Sally Hutsen 11-17-1871
Due, David to Sarah Englishman 1-2-1871 (1-8-1871)
Duffield, Nelson to Mary Williams 4-25-1878 (4-26-1878)
Duffield, Samuel S. to Elza M. Furgason 11-20-1851
Duggar, David to Elizabeth Smith 3-31-1863 (4-1-1865)
Duggar, George M. to Susannah C. Campbell 2-14-1860 (3-8-1860)
Duggar, Joseph to Eliza C. Campbell 9-23-1861 (10-17-1861)
Duggar, Michael J. to Nancy C. Climon 6-2-1860 (6-5-1860)
Duggar, Thomas A. to Susanna C. Price? 5-9?-1859 (5-15-1859)
Dugger, Gasper to Jane Potter 10-20-1877 (10-21-1877)
Dugger, J. W. F. to Eliza A. Williams 9-30-1876 (10-1-1876)
Dugger, James A. to Margaret A.(S?) Stover 1-16-1866 (1-25-1866)
Dugger, James W. to Hannah R. Lunceford 11-8-1875 (11-13-1875)
Dugger, Michael I. to Nancy E. Cluner 6-2-1860 (6-5-1860)
Dugger, Tarlton to Elena W. Campbell 7-11-1856 (7-13-1856)
Dugger, Thomas A. to Sarah C. Pearce 5-7-1859 (5-15-1859)
Dugger, William H. to Mary J. Pierce 12-12-1868 (12-16-1866)
Dugless, William to Mary R. Campbell 10-12-1874
Dugless, William to Nancy Hyder 8-27-1861 (8-29-1861)
Dugless, William to Rebeca Campbell 10-10-1874 (10-12-1874)
Dugless, William to Rebecca Campbell 10-18-1874 (10-12?-1874)
Dunbar, Geo. W. to Mary J. Hart 1-21-1873
Duncan, Enoch to Catherin Arnold 6-22-1850
Duncy, William to Susan E. Shell 9-3-1865 (10-1-1865)
Dunken, Samuel H. to Marthy Crow 11-18-1859 (11-19-1859)
Dunkin, Saml. M. to Martha Crow 11-8-1859 (11-9-1859)
Dunney, W. F. to Eva M. Miller 7-19-1866
Dyke, William A. to Nancy J. Emmert 6-24-1857 (6-25-1857)
Dyke, Wm. A. to Nancy J. Lacy 6-24-1857 (6-25-1857)
Easley, Thomas to Allan Easley 3-24-1871 (3-26-1871) B
East, Lafayett D. to Mary E. White 12-2-1865
Eastep, Moses to Mary Grindstaff 4-11-1874
Edens, David I. to Mary Miller 10-22-1874
Edens, David to Mary Miller 10-22-1874
Edens, James to Elizabeth Berry 2-11-1850 (2-12-1850)
Edens, Millard to Mary Emmert 9-15-1877 (9-16-1877)
Edens, Nathanl. to Jane Lovy 5-6-1861 (5-12-1861)
Edins, John I. to Edna D. Taylor 1-1-1852
Edmundson, William to Sally Thompson 2-8-1877
Edwards, Abel to Catherin Nave 1-10-1874
Edwards, John W. to Catharin E. Woods 12-24-1858
Edwards, Wilson to Martha Ann Gouge 6-15-1867 (6-16-1867)
Egbert, Philander S. to Frances Pollums 9-27-1869 (10-11-1869)
Eliott, Joseph to Sarah Jane Gentry 9-11-1868 (9-13-1868)
Elis, Thomas A. to Margaret Forster 9-6-1856 (9-7-1856)
Ellers, John to Saraphine E. Seller 10-21-1869
Elliott, Daniel to Evaline Bartee 6-29-1878 (6-30-1878)
Elliott, David F. to Mary Fletcher 1-3-1867 (1-30-1867)
Elliott, Harrison H. to Margarett E. Lewis 12-17-1859 (12-18-1859)
Elliott, Harrison M. to Marga ___ 12-17-1859
Elliott, John to Carnelia Blevins 9-20-1876 (10-1-1876)
Elliott, M. B. to Ruth Estep 4-?-1878 (4-18-1878)
Elliott, Michael P. to Martha Anderson 10-6-1866 (10-18-1866)
Elliott, Peter B. to Susana Grindstaff 1-7-1835
Elliott, Thomas to Sarahfine Garland 3-7-1856 (3-10-1856)
Elliott, Thos. P. to Nancy Pierce 4-11-1868 (4-13-1868)
Elliott, William H. to Lourana Asher 7-15-1868 (7-21-1868)
Ellis, Daniel to Eliza C. Collins 9-2-1876 (9-3-1876)
Ellis, Guy H. to Matilda Ann Mothern 3-23-1876
Ellis, Jackson to Elizabeth Miller 2-7-1869
Ellis, James H. to Sarah A. Jones? 6-14-?
Ellis, James T. to Harriett Jobe 3-19-1868 (3-20-1868)
Ellis, John W. to Ann M. Angell 5-21-1857
Ellis, John W. to Ann M. Angle 5-21-1857
Ellis, John to Sarahfina J. Seller 10-18-1869 (10-21-1869)
Ellis, Joseph P. to Margaret Ritchie 10-7-1861 (10-10-1861)
Ellis, Landon C. to Mary Jane Lipps 4-19-1856 (4-20-1856)
Ellis, Levi N. to Jane Crowe 4-12-1856
Ellis, Solomon to Sarah Davis 1-15-1856 (1-20-1856)
Ellis?, Joseph P. to Margaret Raper? 10-7-1865 (10-10-1865)
Emit, Geo. W. to Kate E. Brook 4-27-1874 (4-29-1874)
Emmert, G. W. to Mary E. Scalp 2-3-1879
Emmert, John to Elizabeth Lacy 5-4-1857 (5-5-1857)
Emmert, Peter W. to Hester Ann Williams 2-3-1866 (2-4-1866)
Emmert, Peter W. to Loucinda C. Cotton 8-16-1860? (8-16-1860)
Emmit(Emmert), Caleb M. to Hester Ann Tipton 5-27-1873
Emmit, George D. to Catherine E. Brooks 5-27-1874 (4?-29-1874)
English, Isaac D. to Ann J. Row 10-19-1858 (4-7-1858)
Ensor, Aury P. T. to Margaret Taylor 11-30-1873 (12-4-1873)
Ensor, Avery C. P. to Margaret Taylor 11-30-1873 (12-4-1873)
Ensor, Preston to Martha A. Hyder 3-21-1870 (3-22-1870)
Ensor, William L. to Rachel E. Inmon 8-5-1853
Ensor, William to Blany Blue 3-9-1875 (no return)
Erwin, Adam to Caroline Hughes 7-16-1869 (7-17-1869)
Estep, Colonel A. to Evaline Hurley 10-2-1869
Estep, Harvey D. to Martha Carden 10-21-1875
Estep, Harvey D. to Martha M. Cardon 10-21-1875
Estep, Henry to Martha Garland 8-16-1866 (8-19-1866)
Estep, Isaac to Docia I. Robertson 7-31-1873 (8-1-1873)
Estep, Isaac to Elizabeth Oliver 9-17-1856 (9-18-1856)
Estep, Jno. to Julia Pearce 9-17-1886 (9-18-1886)
Estep, John to Julia Ann Hodges 1-12-1858 (no return)
Estep, John to Martha Taylor 7-6-1877 (7-10-1877)
Estep, Ransom to Nancy C. Garland 4-20-1866 (4-22-1866)
Estep, Samuel M. to Nancy Ann Campbell 10-31-1866 (11-11-1866)
Estep, William L. to Rebecca Arnold 2-23-1869 (2-26-1869)
Estip, John to Julia Ann Hodge 1-13-1858
Ewan, Preston to Martha A. Hyder 3-21-1870 (3-?-1870)
Fain, Millard F. to J. L. Hyder 1-24-1874 (1-26-1874)
Fainsworth, Wm. to Louretta A. Gourley 3-15-1858 (3-16-1858)
Fair (Farr), Samuel H. to Ann E. Turner 12-23-1869 (1-2-1870)
Fair, Geo. W. to Eliza J. Loveles? 10-5-1865 (10-7-1865)
Fair, J. N. to Alice Heltin 5-23-1877 (5-24-1877)
Fair, Shared to Martha Griffith 1-26-1870 (1-27-1870)
Fair, William to Emilin Floyd 10-10-1866
Farensworth, William B. to Loureth Gourly 3-15-1858 (3-16-1858)
Farr, Bethervill to Eliza E. White 5-2-1870 (5-3-1870)
Farr, George W. to Louesa Burrus 4-21-1870
Farr, Millard F. to J. L. Hyder 1-24-1874
Farr, Nathan to Mary A. Surland? 6-17-1874
Farr, Shared to Martha Grifeth 1-26-1870 (1-27-1870)
Farry?, Samuel W. to Roda E. Vanhuss 6-26-1867
Feaster, A. J. to C. A. Little 10-3-1874 (10-4-1874)
Feathers, John C. to Nancy A. Humphrey 12-23-1865 (12-24-1865)
Feathers, William A. to Hannah Pharr 3-2-1877 (5-10-1877)
February, Geo. G. to Elizabeth Wilson 11-2-1856
February, Mordica to Sarah Ann Baker 7-10-1857
Fellers, George to Ann Greenlee 3-2-1871
Fellig, B. F. to Susan Phinick 12-6-1856 (12-7-1856)
Felty, B. F. to Susan Phenix 12-6-1856 (12-8-1856)
Ferguson, A. J. to Sarah E. Ensor 9-25-1856 (9-26-1856)
Ferguson, Benjamin B. to Julia A. White 12-29-1868 (12-30-1868)
Fincanon, A. B. to Martha A. Arnold 3-4-1878 (3-7-1878)
Fletcher, A. J. to Luster Perry 9-9-1869
Fletcher, Andrew to Mary C. Blevins 6-21-1860
Fletcher, Andrew to Mary B. Blevins 6-21-1860
Fletcher, Andrew to Mary E. Blevins 6-?-1860 (6-21-1860)
Fletcher, James B. to Nancy M. Campbell 11-15-1871 (11-16-1871)
Fletcher, James D. to Nancy Campbell 11-15-1871 (11-16-1871)
Fletcher, James R. to Jenni G. Garrison 8-3-1869
Fletcher, Jno. L. to Nancy Nave 11-3-1875 (11-4-1875)
Fletcher, Lawson W. to Elizabeth Hathaway 2-29-1844 (3-30-1844)
Fletcher, William R. to Manervy Miller 8-1-1862 (8-3-1862)
Fletcher, Wm. R. to Manervy Miller 8-1-1862 (8-3-1862)
Floyd, Abraham to Elizabeth Williams 5-29-1851 (5-25?-1851)
Floyd, David to Sarafina Williams 7-5-1852
Floyd, James F. to Margaret C. Smith 3-12-1864 (3-17-1864)
Folsom, Benjamin F. to Sarah Ryon 7-24-1876
Folsom, Henderson M. to Sarah E. Berry 9-29-1855 (9-30-1855)
Folsom, William H. to Loyette S. Hilton 12-2-1865 (no return)
Folsom, William J. to Eliza E. O'Brian 12-8-1865 (12-10-1865)
Fondrin, Andrew C. to Hanna A. O'Brian 9-22-1865 (9-24-1865)
Forbes, Daniel R. to Mary J. Pleasant 12-29-1862 (1-6-1863)
Forbes, David to Jane Chambers 8-2-1877 (11-10-1877)
Forbes, Robert to Margaret Fletcher 12-26-1873
Forbus, Robert to Margaret Fluker? 12-28-1872 (12-26?-1872)
Ford, Benjamin to Vira Daniel 5-19-1866
Ford, George C. to Mary Jones 3-6-1871 (3-7-1871)
Forest, James to Elenor Arawood 3-9-1854

Forester, John H. to Louisa Grindstaff 12-9-1871
Foster, Asa H. to Manerva Lunier 4-3-1858
Foster, Asa to Manervy Lewis 4-3-1858
Foster, James H. to Frances Taylor 4-14-1871
Foust, Benjamin to Julia Ann Hays 10-8-1851 (10-9-1851)
Fox, Henry to Margaret Simmons 4-24-1874
Fox, Henry to Margret Ferris 4-24-1874
Franklin, Andrew to Jane Winters 3-4-1859 (3-13-1859)
Frasher, John W. to Ann Forbes 3-20-1858 (3-21-1858)
Frasher, William O. to Margaret Hinkle 10-2-1858 (10-4-1858)
Frasier, Alexander to Milly Ingle 11-9-1859 (11-22-1859)
Frasier, Jacob L. to Martha Fain 3-11-1876 (11-17-1876)
Frasier, William O. to Margaret Henkle 10-2-1858 (no return)
Frasure, John W. to Anna Forbus 3-20-1858 (3-21-1858)
Frazer, Thos. C. to Margarett E. McCalister 4-21-1859 (no return)
Freeman, Lewis to Ann B. Arnold 3-7-1853
Freeman, William T. to Mary J. Fleming 9-24-1866 (9-25-1866)
French, Brint P. to Elizabeth D. McKeehen 8-7-1860
French, Gorden to Causby Harmen 9-10-1851 (8?-11-1851)
French, James to Amanda Harmon 5-22-1851
French, Thomas to Elizabeth Harmon 8-2-1855
Frett, Geo. G. to Mary Jones 3-6-1871 (3-7-1871)
Fry, Eli to Mary Street 12-14-1856 (12-15-1856)
Fry, John to Elizabeth Campbell 12-15-1852 (12-20-1852)
Fuddle, Moses to Amanda McKee 12-5-1859 (12-9-1859)
Fulkerson, Abraham to Deborah Range 11-10-1856 (11-13-1856)
Fulkerson, Abraham to Eliza Range 11-17-1858 (11-18-1858)
Fulkerson, George to Nancy J. Kennick 12-12-1859 (12-15-1859)
Furguson, Andrew J. to Sarah E. Ensor 9-25-1856 (9-26-1856)
Gaddy, Charles to Nancy Duggar 11-26-1853
Gaddy, Clem to Mary Hamrick 12-6-1850
Gantt, Thomas to Miley Whitehead 7-8-1865 (7-12-1865)
Garitain?, Wm. to Viney Andrews 6-14-1873 (6-15-1873)
Garlan, William to Viney Andrews? 6-14-1873
Garland, Alexander to Eliza Engram 11-4-1870
Garland, Alexander to Eliza Ingram 11-4-1870
Garland, Benj. to Nancy Campbell 2-11-1865 (2-20-1865)
Garland, David to Nancy Garland 11-19-1859 (11-20-1859)
Garland, David to Nancy Garland 11-9-1859 (11-20-1859)
Garland, Elisha to Sarah Bell 2-26-1875 (3-4-1875)
Garland, Elisha to Sarah Campbell no date (1850-1876)
Garland, Elishey to Sarah Campbell (Bell) 2-26-1875 (3-4-1875)
Garland, Ezekiel L. to Nancy Standley 10-1-1853 (10-2-1853)
Garland, Henderson to Nancy S. Cole 12-29-1867
Garland, J. I. to Mary O'Brian 10-13-1874 (10-14-1874)
Garland, James D. to Saraphina Cole 10-31-1866 (10-10?-1866)
Garland, John M. to Mary Wilson 5-5-1875
Garland, John M. to Roda Estep 11-5-1872
Garland, John R. to Lettey Goarhand? 12-20-1868 (12-30-1868)
Garland, John R. to Lilly Garland 12-30-1868
Garland, John to Ann Hodges 1-15-1859 (1-19-1859)
Garland, John to Elzena Robertson 6-22-1875 (6-25-1875)
Garland, Jonathan B. to Susan Baker 2-1-1869
Garland, Joseph H. to Mary Lacy 12-5-1849
Garland, Kenedy to Eliza Wilson 11-4-1871 (11-8-1871)
Garland, Kenedy to Elizabeth Wilson 11-4-1871 (11-8-1871)
Garland, Nathan to Rhoda Jane Estep 3-21-1878
Garland, Pryor to Rhoda Ann Miller 2-14-1859 (3-7-1859)
Garland, Valentine to Dicey Anderson 10-21-1871 (10-22-1871)
Garland, Valentine to Mary Hurly 11-18-1863 (12-19-1863)
Garland, Valentine to Nancy Heatherly 5-6-1861 (5-8-1861)
Garland, William to Delila Hodges 9-24-1863 (9-29-1863)
Garland, William to Manervy Gouge 11-12-1867 (11-24-1867)
Garland, William to Viney Anderson 6-14-1873 (6-15-1873)
Garland, Wm. W. to Margaret A. Sellers 10-14-1871 (10-15-1871)
Garland, Wm. to Mary Blevins 1-22-1855 (1-27-1855)
Garvin?, David to Matilda Lenard 2-22-1854
Gates?, James W. to Mary E. Shell 12-21-1869
Geisler, William D. to Elizabeth Miller 8-16-1875 (8-26-1875)
Genetry, Ephraim to Sarah J. Olliver 12-27-1860 (1-5-1861)
Gentry, Ephrom C. to Sarah J. Oliver 12-27-1860 (1-5-1861)
Gentry, Furdinand to Carie Pearce 8-5-1877
Gentry, John to Susan Oliver 10-26-1871
Gentry, Joseph to Editha Hodge 2-6-1863 (2-8-1863)
Gentry, Joseph to Rebecca J. Maser? 12-26-1868

Gibbs, Frank to Sarah Harris 11-9-1873
Gibs, William to Mary Hickman 10-31-1860 (11-1-1860)
Gibson, Frederick to Sarah C. Martin 11-26-1875 (11-28-1875)
Gibson, John to Rosana Pharr 1-1-1866
Gibson, Pleasant to Adaline Hutsen 1-24-1852
Gibson, Pleasant to Malinda Fox 6-24-1865 (6-25-1865)
Gibson, Pleasant to Matilda Fox 6-24-1865 (6-25-1865)
Gibson, Pleasant to Nancy A. Gifferson 7-10-1866 (?-12-1866)
Gibson, Pleasant to Nancy A. Jefferson 7-12-1866
Gibson, Thomas to Catharine Trexwell? 8-9-1860? (8-10-1860)
Gibson, William A. to Sarah Jane Reno 1-18-1851 (1-19-1851)
Gibson, William to Nancy Hinkle 11-3-1866 (11-11-1866)
Gibson, Wm. to Hopper Curtis 2-19-1851 (2-20-1851)
Gilbert, Edmon to Malissa J. Smith 5-10-1877 (5-20-1877)
Glenn, Elcana to Harrett Guy 8-5-1871
Glenn, John A. to Martha A. L. Pearce 1-29-1873 (1-30-1873)
Glenn, William to Ellen Campbell 6-15-1877 (6-17-1877)
Gloone?, Thomas to Mary Lewis 1-14-1860 (1-15-1860)
Glover, Elbert to Emy C. Collins 9-27-1876
Glover, Elbert to Mary Loyd? 9-15-1872
Glover, Elbert to Mary Lyon 9-15-1872
Glover, Elcana to Hariet Guge 8-5-1871
Glover, Granville to Hariet Hutsen 3-5-1878
Glover, James to Mary Campbell 5-24-1876 (5-25-1876)
Glover, John A. to Martha A. L. Powers 1-29-1873 (1-30-1873)
Glover, Lervicy to Vina Robertson 1-12-1850
Glover, Marron to Mary A. Lilley 3-15-1870
Glover, Peter to Martha Ann Davenport 1-17-1879 (1-30-1879)
Glover, Richard to Charlotte Robertson 12-12-1863 (no return)
Glover, Samuel to Mary J. Robertson 1-3-1850 (no return)
Glover, Samuel to Mary Jane Robertson 1-3-1850
Glover, Thomas to Mary Louis 1-14-1860 (1-15-1860)
Glover, William to Elizabeth Perry 6-15-1859
Goan, David L. to Malinda Profett 6-12-1859
Golehor, James to Sarah Mathis 11-24-1868
Gomer, Thomas J. to Maggie E. Heatherly 1-23-1879 (1-26-1879)
Goodman, Thomas A. to Florance M. Perry 9-24-1871
Goodwin, James L. to J. M. Johnson 2-23-1874
Goodwin, James L. to Nancy J. A. Johnson 2-23-1874 (4-22-1874)
Goodwin, James M. to Nancy C. Lunsford 12-11-1866 (12-13-1866)
Goodwin, Thomas A. to Florance A. Perry 9-24-1871
Goodwind, Lawson L. to Mary E. Dugger 2-23-1861 (3-8-1861)
Gouge, Calvin to Catharin McKinny 12-28-1871 (12-29-1870?)
Gouge, Calvin to Catharn McKinney 12-28-1870 (12-29-1870)
Gouge, David to Mary J. Simerly 1-23-1873
Gouge, Nathan to Harriett Jenkins 12-7-1874 (12-13-1874)
Gouge, Nathan to Harriett Lenard 12-7-1874 (12-13-1874)
Gouge, Reuben to Hannah Simerly 1-29-1870 (1-30-1870)
Gourley, Adam to Mary Amanda Williams 8-14-1856
Gourley, C. M. D. to Martha Adalade Tipton 9-8-1856
Gourley, David N. to Sarah J. Simerly 11-9-1854
Gourley, Geo. W. to Caroline Shoemaker 5-18-1872
Gourley, Houston to Dicy? Stephens 12-26-1850
Gourley, Jno. C. to Lousinda McDoniel 2-25-1852 (2-26-1852)
Gourley, Lafayette to Julia A. Edens 1-20-1853
Gourley, N. T. to Evelin C. Taylor 8-13-1859 (8-14-1859)
Gourley, Thomas to Elizabeth Perry 1-25-1858 (1-28-1858)
Gourley, Thomas to Sarah Matherly 1-22-1879 (1-23-1879)
Gourley, Thos. H. to Delila Fair 1-2-1851
Gourley, W. M. to Viny Merritt 6-1-1877 (6-3-1877)
Gourley, William M. to Louisanda Edens 11-16-1851
Gourley, William to Jane Smalling 7-27-1878 (7-28-1878)
Gourley, William to Lucinda Jane Edens 11-16-1851
Gourley, William to Mahala Rockhold 8-15-1866
Gourly, David N. to Susannah Simerly 11-9-1854
Gourly, George F. to Mary Loveless 9-28-1876
Gourly, William M. to Lousarda Edens 11-16-1851
Govern, Shaderik W. to Eliza J. A. Carden 12-3-1850
Grag, William to Matilda Arnett 12-6-1872 (12-8-1872)
Grage?, Calvin to Mary Green 12-23-1877
Gragg, J. C. to Mary F. Greenwell 12-14-1877 (no return)
Gragg, Munroe to Rachel White 12-4-1868 (12-7-1868)
Gragg, Telanon to Jane Deddley 3-1-1873
Green, Daniel to E. J. Coble 2-22-1866 (2-24-1866)
Green, Jackson to Malinda Law 8-26-1872

Green, James to Catherine Coble 8-9-1863 (11-8-1863)
Green, Joseph W. to Rachel Whitehead 3-15-1866
Green, William S. to Martha A. Shuffield 8-22-1871 (8-24-1872)
Greene, David to Eliza Jane Coble 2-22-1866 (2-24-1866)
Greene, Timothy to Lena Love 3-1-1876 (3-3-1876)
Greenlee, William D. to Harne? H. Curtis 1-27-1869 (2-2-1869)
Greenlee, William D. to Harrieitt Carter 2-27-1869 (2-28-1869)
Greer, Aaron to Sarah Morgan 4-1-1873
Griffin, T. D. to M. E. Neely 3-3-1874 (3-4-1874)
Griffith, Francis M. to Louisa Gentry 10-2-1876 (10-4-1876)
Griffith, Thomas D. to Mary E. Neely 3-3-1874 (3-4-1874)
Grimes, Samuel to Sarah Ward 5-4-1878 (5-5-1878)
Grindstaff, A. J. to Nancy Moreland 7-9-1853 (7-10-1853)
Grindstaff, Alexander S. to Hannah J. Duggan 3-6-1868 (3-8-1868)
Grindstaff, Alexander to Dosha Campbell 3-7-1868 (3-8-1868)
Grindstaff, Alford L. to Eliza Britt 8-15-1874 (8-24-1874)
Grindstaff, Alfred L. to Eliza Brutt 8-15-1874
Grindstaff, Amos to Ellen Hyder 8-13-1872 (8-15-1872)
Grindstaff, Arwine? to Ellen Hyder 8-13-1872 (8-15-1872)
Grindstaff, Charles to Judy Baker 11-20-1860 (11-24-1860)
Grindstaff, D. K. to Selia J. Shuffield 12-4-1872 (12-5-1872)
Grindstaff, David H. to C. J. Shuffield 12-4-1872 (12-25-1872)
Grindstaff, David to Eliza Garrison 10-26-1876 (10-26-1879?)
Grindstaff, David to Eliza Slimp 8-9-1856? (8-10-1856)
Grindstaff, David to Louisa Slimp 8-9-1856 (8-10-1856)
Grindstaff, Elijah to Emelin Overhulser 9-16-18871
Grindstaff, Isaac to Emily Boyd 8-5-1834
Grindstaff, Jackson to Nancy L. Bowen 5-8-1866 (5-14-1866)
Grindstaff, Jackson to Nancy L. Bowers 5-8-1866 (5-14-1866)
Grindstaff, John to Claricy Morland 8-12-1854 (8-31-1854)
Grindstaff, Michael to Mabla? Stout 7-26-1862 (7-27-1862)
Grindstaff, Thomas to Hilley Whitehead 7-8-1865 (7-12-1865)
Grindstaff, William to Mahala Roberts 10-30-1869 (10-31-1869)
Grindstaff, Wilson to Mary Ann Berry 10-14-1860
Grindstaff, Wm. to Mary Campbell 5-26-1854 (no return)
Grogen, Isaac to Sarah Jane Stout 11-9-1865 (11-13-1865)
Guardner, J. B. to Mildred Baker 10-21-1845 (11-20-1845)
Guin, Amos to Sarah Morgan 4-1-1873
Guinn, Amos to Carolin Robert 9-9-1873
Guinn, H. D. to Martha Whitehead 11-3-1874 (11-5-1874)
Guy, Samuel to Delila McKinney 11-9-1854
Haardin, Alvlin P. to Eveline Peters 7?-25-1857 (7?-28-1867)
Hail, James L. to N. A. Williams 10-21-1875
Hail, William to Sarah Ann Grindstaff 6-20-1861
Hall, Hyram to Nancy Ballard 9-26-1850
Hall, Oliver to Elizabeth Grindstaff 11-27-1855 (11-29-1855)
Hamby (Harnby), Thomas to Elizabeth White 8-9-1856 (8-10-1856)
Hamby, Allen to Eliza Radin 2-8-1871 (2-9-1871)
Hamby, Allen to Eliza Readie 2-8-1871 (2-9-1871)
Hamby, Allen to Mary Sims 11-12-1877 (11-24-1877)
Hamby, Leander to Georgie A. Nave 4-2-1876
Hamet, John to Margret Robison 10-19-1869
Hamit, Ezekiel to Lydia Trusler 6-21-1866 (6-22-1866)
Hamm, G. A. to Mary E. Taylor 11-12-1868
Hammer, Henry H. to Louisa E. Cooper 8-7-1855 (8-9-1855)
Hammer, Isaac C. to Rebecca Carrell 12-24-1858
Hampton, A. C. to Loucretia M. Williams 12-22-1870
Hampton, E. W. to Annie J. Miller 4-25-1879 (5-7-1879)
Hampton, Jacob S. to Emeline Snider 2-12-1853
Hampton, John B. to Catharin Hoss 8-11-1860 (8-18-1860)
Hampton, John B. to Catharn Hose 8-11-1860 (8-18-1860)
Hampton, S. E. to Martha A. Rasor 12-26-1878
Hampton, Thomas to Sarah Williams 12-30-1876 (12-31-1876)
Harden, Andrew J. to Fereby Roberts 8-15-1868 (8-16-1868)
Harden, Daniel to Jane Collins 1-1-1869 (1-2-1869)
Harden, Elija D. to Caroline Potter 10-9-1858
Harden, J. N. to Sally Hinkle 11-29-1878 (11-30-1878)
Harden, James C. to Caroline Whitacre 2-24-1874 (2-25-1874)
Harden, John H. to Mary E. Grindstaff 10-10-1870 (10-13-1870)
Harden, William to Anne J. Nave 9-14-1853 (9-15-1853)
Hardin, Daniel to Mary J. Richie 1-4-1862
Hardin, Eli to Elizabeth Forbess 10-6-1866 (10-19-1866)
Hardin, Eli to Elizabeth Peters 10-6-1866 (10-14-1866)
Hardin, Eli to Josephine Poor 4-2-1859 (4-3-1859)
Hardin, Elija D. to Lydia Forbes 1-2-1852 (1-22-1852)
Hardin, Elija D.(C?) to Antonette Stover 2-11-1857
Hardin, Elijah D. to Clarisy Hinton 2-21-1869
Hardin, James U. to Martha Whitacer 2-24-1874
Hardin, John to Ellen Bowers 10-8-1866 (10-10-1866)
Hardin, Jorden C. to Julia C. Williams 11-24-1861 (12-4-1861)
Harkland, Charles D. to Amanda E. Campbell 11-26-1870 (11-7?-1870)
Harly, Wright to Sarah Richardson 10-23-1876
Harmon, Adam to Martha C. Hyder 12-29-1852 (12-30-1852)
Harris, John to Nancy Baker 5-8-1872
Harris, Lewis to Julia Love 7-9-1866 (7-15-1866) B
Harris, Lewis to Margaret Ollee? 1-4-1875 (no return)
Harris, William to Delia Taylor 12-24-1875 (12-29-1875)
Harris, William to Lylie Taylor no date (with 1875)
Hart, Campbell to Sarah Ann Newton 1-10-1856
Hart, George to Margaret Taylor 9-2-1875
Hart, Isaac to Julia A. February 7-10-1852 (7-11-1852)
Hart, James L. to Nancy J. Williams 12-21-1875
Hart, Leonard to Eliza Jenkins 4-19-1856 (4-24-1856)
Hart, Peter E. to Martha Stoner 8-20-1867 (8-22-1867)
Hart, Peter E. to Martha Stover 8-20-1867 (8-22-1867)
Hart, Thomas to Eliza Newton 11-20-1860 (1-20-1860?)
Hart, William to Emey Cobler 9-23-1868 (9-24-1868)
Hart, William to Emey Kibler 9-22-1868 (9-24-1868)
Hatcher, Jas. to Martha Beats? 12-25-1874
Hatcher, Jas. to Martha Blevins 12-25-1874
Hatcher, William Y.? to Mary Garrison 1-2-1879
Hately, John F. to Mary White 5-5-1866 (5-13-1866)
Hately, Reby B. (Riley B.) to Rachel Green 8-13-1866 (8-18-1866)
Hately, Willey S. to Emily O. Green 1-14-1866
Hathaway, Abraham to Martha J. Lester 2-18-1855
Hathaway, Elija C. to Lavicy Campbell 11-14-1853 (11-15-1863?)
Hathaway, Elija C. to Mary Leslie 3-21-1852 (no return)
Hathaway, John W. to Mary E. Smith 6-28-1872
Hatley, Willy S. to Emily C. Green 1-12-1866 (1-14-1866)
Hauger, Cornelius to Sealy Foster 9-27-1873 (9-28-1873)
Hauger, J. R. A. to Sarah Foster 3-29-1875 (3-30-1875)
Haun, George A. to Harriet J. N. Tipton 1-8-1856
Haynes, Nathanel T. to Elizabeth L. Bowman 7-12-1865 (7-13-1864?)
Haynes, W. D. to M. P. Haynes 8-25-1859 (9-1-1859)
Haynes, William D. to Margaret P. Haynes 8-25-1859 (9-1-1859)
Haynes?, Nathanl. to Levina E. Bowman 7-12-1864 (7-13-1864)
Hays, Elcana to Ann Peep 4-27-1874
Hays, James L. to Rebecca F. Lyon 3-17-1855 (3-18-1855)
Hays, Jehue to Elizabeth Glover? 12-15-1856
Hays, John to Elizabeth Glover 12-15-1857 (12-15-1856?)
Hays, John to Elizabeth Stover 12-15-1857
Hays, Ranson M. to Lyda A. Winters 3-19-1878 (3-28-1878)
Hazelwood, Pleasant to Jane Smith 10-14-1871 (10-16-1871)
Hazelwood, R. F. to Carolin Pean 7-22-187? (with 1871)
Hazlewood, John to Rarey Morton 5-18-1870 (6-19-1870)
Hazlewood, Richard to Elizabeth A. Campbell 12-24-1870 (12-25-1870)
Head, Andrew to Mary A. Mathis 2-20-1872 (2-22-1872)
Head, Andrew to Mary Masters 2-20-1872
Head, David A. S. to Eveline Stover 8-9-1866
Head, John to Sarah David 3-15-1873 (3-16-1873)
Head, John to Sarah Dover 3-15-1873 (3-16-1873)
Head, Jonathan to Martha Wallace 8-26-1873 (8-29-1873)
Head, Jonathan to Martha Walters 8-26-1873 (8-29-1873)
Headerick, Robert M. to Matilda E. Helton 1-11-1872
Headrick, John W. to Cardelia Fletcher 3-23-1866 (3-24-1866)
Headrick, Robert M. to Mahelda E. Hellin 1-11-1872
Heard, Clingman to Sarah McKinney 4-14-1864 (4-15-1864)
Heatherly, Landon to Nancy Blevins 2-28-1855 (2-29-1855)
Heatherly, R. C. to Sarah Campbell 3-11-1875
Heaton, Edward T. to Mollie T. Bowers 5-18-1874 (5-24-1874)
Heaton, Edward T. to Molly T. Bowen 5-18-1874 (5-26-1874)
Heaton, Elcana D. to _____ Simerly ?-?-1871 (with spring)
Heaton, Isaac M. to Catherine E. Treadway 3-28-1877 (3-29-1877)
Heaton, Isaac M. to Cathern Treadway 7-31-1875
Heaton, Johnson to Mary Ann Snider 8-11-1855 (8-13-1855)
Helton, A. T. to Nancy C. Grindstaff 12-18-1860 (12-20-1860)
Helton, David S. to Jenney Perry 4-13-1869
Hendrix, Harrison to Nancy Campbell 3-4-1851

Hendrix, Philip to Sarah B. McIntire 6-23-1854 (6-25-1854)
Hendrix, William N. to Sarah E. Hart 9-13-1870 (9-16-1870)
Hendrix, Wm. H. to Mary Taylor 1-23-1853 (1-24-1853)
Henry, John L. to Julia Sims 2-4-1877
Henry, William B. W. to Mary P. Hyder 2-19-1850
Hester, William to Martha Caroway 12-25-1873
Heuston?, Thomas E. R. to Jane Brooks 9-15-1857
Hick, Jacob to Emy J. Carriger 12-15-1874
Hickey, George to Elizabeth O'Brien 7-4-1852 (7-25-1852)
Hickey, James M. to Sarafina Bishop 10-21-1850 (10-24-1850)
Hickey, Timothy to Sina Motham 5-11-1850 (5-12-1850)
Hicks, Daniel to Nancy Campbell 11-27-1869 (11-28-1869)
Hicks, Eli H. to Martha C. Edens 1-3-1868
Hicks, G. W. to Martha J. Loudermilk 11-28-1858 (12-2-1858)
Hicks, G. W. to Martha Jane Lowdermilk 11-28-1858 (12-2-1858)
Hicks, Henry to Fanney Bank 4-2-1869
Hicks, Henry to Fanny Banks 4-1-1869 (4-2-1869)
Hicks, Henry to Sarah Carver 2-23-1878 (2-24-1878)
Hicks, Jacob H. to Emi J. Carriger 12-15-1874 (12-16-1874)
Hicks, Jacob to Susannah M. Carriger 8-30-1858 (9-1-1858)
Hicks, Merit L. to Amassa A. R. Closson 4-29-1878 (4-30-1878)
Hicks, Wilborn to Martha A. Whitehead 1-25-1878
Hicks, William to Elizabeth Simons 2-19-1867
Hicks, Willis to Hannah A. Reeser 10-1-1872 (10-3-1872)
Hicky, William to Safrona Montgomery 7-10-1852 (7-18-1852)
Hill, Albert to Malinda Ingram 1-30-1861 (2-10-1866?)
Hill, Albert to Matilda Ingrum 1-30-1866 (2-10-1866)
Hill, Ezekiel to Biddy Whitehead 5-8-1857
Hill, James M. to Amah Morrison 10-15-1857
Hill, Samuel to Ellen E. Townsend 11-23-1865
Hill, Wilson to Eliza Smith 1-6-1858 (1-8-1858)
Hill, Wilson to Louisa Eliza Smith 1-6-1858 (1-8-1858)
Hillard, Harrison to Sarah McFally 1-4-1865 (1-6-1865)
Hilliard, John to Louisa Masten 5-16-1877
Hilton, Robert to Sarah Ann Haynes 11-25-1858 (11-30-1858)
Hilton, Samuel to Priscilla Hughs 11-18-1858 (11-20-1858)
Hilton, Samuel to Prulla Hughes 11-18-1858 (11-20-1858)
Hilton, William to Sarah Williams 1-?-1875
Hinkle, David to Maryann Henley 1-26-1876
Hinkle, David to May A. Hurly 1-26-1876
Hinkle, Frank to Mary Jane Blevins 11-7-1877 (11-9-1877)
Hinkle, George to Amanda Taylor 3-19-1876
Hinkle, James to Eliza Stover 11-22-1862 (11-23-1862)
Hinkle, James to Margaret Shell 8-18-18871 (8-20-1871)
Hinkle, James to Rebecca Scalf 9-2-1856 (no return)
Hinkle, John to Nancy Miller 6-5-1850 (6-6-1850)
Hinkle, William to Dilley C. Robertson 8-8-1874 (8-9-1874)
Hochs, Willis to Hanah A. Reece 10-1-1872 (10-3-1872)
Hodge, Doc to Eliza J. Wilson 5-2-1875
Hodge, Francis to Nancy Phillips 8-15-1875 (8-17-1875)
Hodge, Isaac to Elizabeth Campbell 12-23-1872
Hodge, John M. to Nancy Ann Roberts 8-2-1877 (8-5-1877)
Hodge, Josiah to Cathane Little 2-27-1871 (3-2-1871)
Hodge, Levi to Angaline Garland 8-22-1865 (8-24-1865)
Hodge, Samuel W. to Martha Hartly? 12-25-1867 (12-29-1867)
Hodge, Simon to Caroline Church 2-23-1858
Hodge, Solomon to Catharin Church 2-23-1858
Hodge, Wellington to Pricilla Wilson 10-10-1865 (10-15-1865)
Hodges, Josiah to Cathan L. H. Law? 2-27-1871 (3-2-1871)
Hodges, Waitsel A. to Loucretia Hodge 1-5-1870 (1-6-1870)
Hodges, Wartsel A. to Loucretia Wyatt 1-5-1870 (1-6-1870)
Hodges, William R. to Emiline Hyder 3-25-1852
Hollen, John to Ellian? Coble 12-18-1868 (12-19-1868)
Hollen?, John to Ellen Cable 12-18-1868 (12-19-1868)
Holley, Robert to Hannah C. Hyder 2-20-1871 (2-22-1871)
Holloway, John to Mary A. Truman 1-7-1871 (1-10-1871)
Hollowman, John to Nancy West 1-2-1867 (1-3-1867)
Holly, David to Mary Ann Ellis 11-27-1856
Holly, M. L. to M. L. Potter 9-26-1875
Hollyfield, A. S. to Sarah Caraway 7-23-1873 (7-27-1873)
Hollyway, John to Mary A. Frasure 1-7-1871
Holtsclaw, Burton to Angaline Hoss 1-18-1878 (1-20-1878)
Honeycut, Robert to Nancy Miller 11-26-1872
Honycut, Nathan to Mary Bowman 3-23-1873
Hopson, Isaac to Susanah Whitehead 2-23-1871 (2-26-1871)

Hopson, Isaac to Susanah Whitehead 2-23-1871 (7-26-1871)
Hoss, James H. to Nancy Perry 1-30-1866 (1-31-1866)
Hotticlaw, John to Mary A. Moreland 3-7-1860 (3-12-1860?)
Houston, H. B. to Clemy J. (Clericy?) Smalling 10-14-1875 (10-17-1875)
Houston, James M. M. to Rebecca Maring? 3-29-1866
Houston, James to Lou Williams 12-25-1875 (12-30-1875)
Houston, James to Lue Williams 12-25-1875 (12-30-1875)
Howard, Alphaus to Pernina Lucas 10-12-1850 (10-13-1850)
Howard, Benjamin to Emilin M. Folsom 7-28-1865
Howard, Samuel to Hannah Simerly 8-12-1867 (8-13-1867)
Howard, Wm. G. to Lidia Cole 12-16-1854 (12-21-1854)
Howell, John to Margaret Roberson 10-19-1869
Huck?, Daniel to Nanevy Campbell 11-27-1869 (11-28-1869)
Huckler, William to Delley C. Robertson 8-8-1874 (8-9-1874)
Huff, William to Martha E. Johnson 5-7-1856
Hugh, Albert to Martha E. Hodge 2-4-1869
Hughes, James W. to Margaret A. Perringer 12-8-1856 (12-11-1856)
Hughes, James W. to Margaret Ann Persinger 12-8-1856 (12-11-1856)
Hughes, James to Rosanna J. Linville 11-17-1853 (11-20-1853)
Hughes, Joseph to L. M. McCorkle 5-23-1868 (5-24-1868)
Hughes, Joseph to S. McKorkle 5-23-1868 (5-24-1868)
Humphrey, A. C. to Loucretia M. Williams 12-22-1870
Humphrey, Andrew M. to Martha A. Shell 4-30-1877 (5-6-1872?)
Humphrey, Francis M. to Reda (Roda) J. Campbell 11-25-1874 (11-26-1874)
Humphrey, Geo. to Deleny Taylor 8-3-1878 (8-4-1878)
Humphrey, J. D. to —— Bolin 9-28-1870
Humphrey, Pleasant G. to Eliza T. Curtice 4-16-1861 (4-18-1861)
Humphrey, W. J. to Fanney J. Gourley 4-13-1875
Humphrey, William H. C. to Martha Alice Garrison 4-17-1878
Humphrey, William J. to Fanny J. Gourly 4-13-1875
Humphrey, Wm. to Elizabeth Grindstaff 2-14-1877
Humphrey, Young to Eliza Chambers 8-15-1855 (8-16-1855)
Humphreys, James D. to Myrey Ann Bolen 9-28-1870 (9-29-1870)
Humphreys, William G. to Elizabeth Little 5-2-1866 (5-3-1866)
Hunley?, Thomas to Elizabeth Jenkins 6-9-1877 (6-10-1877)
Hunt, Thomas H. to Margaret A. Mast 8-19-1856
Hunt, W. C. to Amanda V. Paulett 4-10-1860
Hunt, W. C. to Lousea J. Berry 6-26-1855 (6-28-1855)
Hunter, E. E. to Mary Jane Jobe 9-19-1871
Hunter, Henderson to Mahala Deloach 4-25-1852 (4-26-1852) B
Hunton, Thomas E. R. to Janie Brooks 9-15-1857
Hurley, Hamilton to Selia Smith 8-25-1877 (8-26-1877)
Hurley?, Allen to Matilda Blevins 10-23-1867 (10-25-1867)
Hurly, M. E. to M. E. Humphrey 5-21-1873
Huston, J. M. M. to Rebecca Manning 3-29-1866
Hyder, A. J. F. to Magie A. Hyder 6-18-1872 (6-19-1872)
Hyder, Benjamin G. to Tobitha Taylor 2-21-1852 (2-22-1852)
Hyder, Benjamin to Charlotte Catton 3-19-1855
Hyder, Daniel C. to Martha Hyder 2-25-1877
Hyder, David H. to M. E. Williams 2-21-1872 (2-22-1872)
Hyder, David H. to Mary E. Williams 1-21-1872 (1-22-1872)
Hyder, David H. to Mary E. Williams 2-21-1872
Hyder, F. M. to Martha Gourley 7-6-1866 (8-22-1866)
Hyder, Henry H. to Rhoda J. Williams 12-19-1866 (1-9-1869)
Hyder, Henry to Mary S. Gourley 9-26-1877 (9-30-1877)
Hyder, J. O. L. to Martha A. Carriger 5-21-1857 (5-29-1857)
Hyder, Jacob K. to Rebecca Merrett 10-24-1871 (10-26-1871)
Hyder, Jacob to Rebeca Merit 10-24-1871 (10-26-1871)
Hyder, James E. to Eliza Jane Carriger 11-2-1859 (11-3-1859)
Hyder, James E. to Margaret J. O'Brian 3-4-1858 (2?-4-1858)
Hyder, John L. to Catharn Simerly 9-12-1859
Hyder, John to Carlin Simerly 9-1-1859
Hyder, John to Susanna Range 8-29-1865 (9-7-1865)
Hyder, Jos. to Sally L. Hyder 1-23-1878 (3-28-1878)
Hyder, Joseph O. L. to Martha A. Carriger 5-31-1857 (5-29?-1857)
Hyder, Lawson F. to Margaret R. Brooks 3-29-1871 (3-30-1871)
Hyder, Michael B. to Elizabeth (Hannah)C. Lany 9-7-1857 (9-10-1857)
Hyder, Michael B. to Hanah C. Lacy 9-7-1857 (9-10-1857)
Hyder, Michal E. to Julia Williams 11-21-1877 (11-22-1877)
Hyder, N. E. to Amanda J. Hyder 4-18-1871 (4-20-1871)
Hyder, N. H. to M. T. Williams 6-6-1870 (6-9-1870)
Hyder, Nelson to Hannah Haynes 8-27-1867 (9-3-1867)

Hyder, S. W. to Sarah E. Fair 7-1-1872 (7-2-1872)
Hyder, Samuel W. to Sarah E. Farr 7-1-1872 (7-16-1872)
Hyder, William P. to Jane Duglass 3-5-1873 (3-13-1873)
Hyder, Wm. P. to J. Duglus 3-5-1873 (3-13-1873)
Ingram, David to Mariah J. Cates 12-3-1872
Ingram, John to Nancy Jane Tipton 12-23-1854
Ingrum, Nathaniel to Eliza Parker 10-14-1875
Jackson, Andrew to Nancy C. Donathan 11-24-1850
Jackson, James to Florence? Angell ?-?-1875 (with spring)
Jackson, James to Mary Campbell 10-11-1868
Jackson, James to Mary Camphen? 10-11-1868
Jacobs, William C. to Pantitha Heatherly 9-21-1864
James, Thos. to Nancy Campbell 1-25-1855 (1-27-1855)
Jane, Robert to Ann E. Nave 8-23-1871 (8-24-1871)
Jenkins, Abraham to Rebecca Nave 12-14-1874 (12-15-1874)
Jenkins, David B. to Eveline Stover 10-13-1869 (10-14-1869)
Jenkins, Elijah to Angaline Crow 5-31-1856 (6-1-1856)
Jenkins, Levi to Ann E. Nidiffer 2-17-1875
Jenkins, Robert to Mary Cariger 7-19-1877 (9-20-1877)
Jenkins, Saml. to Eliza Williams 10-28-1875
Jenkins, Samuel to Eliza M. Campbell 2-20-1873
Jenkins, Samuel to Elizabeth Campbell 2-20-1873
Jenkins, Thomas to Emily Salls 4-27-1870
Jenkins, W. H. to Josephine Arwood 2-20-1879 (2-25-1879)
Jenkins, William D. to Elizabeth J. Snider 3-11-1853 (3-15-1853)
Jenkins, William to Eliza C. Peters 12-22-1875
Jensbuck?, Henry to Lillie Wilson 10-2-1872
Jentry, Andrew to Nancy Ann Wilson 6-9-1867
Jobe, E. D. to Mary E. Taylor 2-8-1877
Johnson, Albert M. to Ann Smith 3-6-1866 (3-15-1866)
Johnson, Alexander to Maria Bolem? 12-21-1875 (12-22-1875)
Johnson, Alexander to Marier Bolen 12-21-1875 (12-22-1875)
Johnson, Alexander to Mary Miller 10-26-1859 (10-29-1859)
Johnson, Andrew H. to Susaner Smith 2-22-1873 (2-23-1873)
Johnson, Andrew J. to Alis Harmon 4-5-1878
Johnson, Andrew J. to Amanda Harmon 4-5-1878
Johnson, Andrew to Ellen Grindstaff 9-25-1876 (10-1-1876)
Johnson, Andrew to Susana Smith 2-23-1873
Johnson, Carter to Martha Keen 11-2-1861 (11-5-1861)
Johnson, D. O. to Nancy E. Campbell 8-1-1886 (8-8-1886)
Johnson, Francis M. to Nancy Ann Keen 5-8-1861 (5-9-1861)
Johnson, Henry to Lover? Carter 3-26-1874
Johnson, James to Jane A. Tripp 8-27-1872 (8-28-1872)
Johnson, James to Jane A. Zapp 8-27-1872
Johnson, James? H. to Nancy Ann Kean 5-8-1861 (5-9-1861)
Johnson, John H. to Lovena Morris 10-23-1876
Johnson, Moses to Margaret Morsley 10-5-1850 (10-6-1850)
Johnson, Moses to Rachel McIntush 10-3-1855
Johnson, N. H. to Margaret Carver 2-16-1856 (2-17-1856)
Johnson, N. M. to Mary Ann Jenkins 4-1-1855
Johnson, Patrick H. to Susan Combs 10-4-1860 (10-5-1860)
Johnson, Samuel to Olive Daniel 3-7-1853 (3-10-1853)
Johnson, Wesley to Elizabeth McNabb 7-12-1873 (7-13-1873)
Johnson, Westly to Rebecca J. Young 10-1-1870
Johnson, William to Beddy Gouge 12-23-1867 (12-26-1867)
Johnson, William to Jane Campbell 12-20-1856
Johnson, William to Jane Campbell 12-23-1856 (12-27-1856)
Johnson, William to Mary Simerly 3-22-1851 (3-27-1851)
Joins, Peter to Lorena Meredith 11-3-1874 (11-7-184)
Jolley, Miles to Jane Morton 8-10-1855 (8-30-1855)
Jones, Amber C. to Elizabeth Edens 11-30-1871
Jones, Ambrose to Selia Shuffield 4-19-1862 (4-20-1862)
Jones, Ambrous to Elizabeth Edin 11-30-1871
Jones, Henry to Eliza Williams 10-1-1853 (10-2-1853)
Jones, Isaac to Jane McKeene 5-18-1872 (5-19-1872)
Jones, Isaac to Jane McKissic? 5-18-1872 (5-19-1872)
Jones, Jeremiah R. to Mary E. McKehen 10-2-1865 (10-5-1865)
Jones, John M.(W?) to Martha J. Tipton 7-16-1867
Jones, John W. to Rebecah J. Bowers 12-17-1859
Jones, John to Hanah Potter 11-12-1877 (11-19-1877)
Jones, Nathaniel to Matilda A. R. Keener 9-6-1871 (9-7-1871)
Jones, Robert to Mary Prichard 3-8-1855 (no return)
Jones, Samuel to Lavicy Hensley 5-25-1869 (5-27-1869)
Jones, Samuel to _____ 3-25-1869
Jones, Stephen to Elizabeth Vandeventer 12-31-1850 (1-9-1851)

Jones, Thomas J. to Mary A. Garland 6-17-1874 (6-25-1874)
Jones, Wesley to Mary A. Eden 10-12-1869
Jones, Wesley to Nancy Meredas? 8-24-1867 (8-20?-1867)
Jones, Wesly to Mary A. Edens 10-12-1869
Jones, Willy W. to Tempey Stone 4-19-1866
Jorden, William to Eliza Good 1-5-1872 (1-7-1872)
Jordon, Mat to Delila Stoner 11-5-1865
Jordon, William to Martha J. Angel 8-31-1854
Julian, James N. to Eliza Heaton 10-16-1858 (10-21-1858)
Julian, Jas. N. to Eliza Heaton 3-8-1850 (3-10-1850)
Justice, James H. to Martha Navey? 12-24-1869 (12-26-1869)
Justis, Elcana to Sarah J. Jackson 4-15-1862 (4-6?-1862)
Kaner (Keener), David to Caroline Baker 12-21-1875 (12-23-1875)
Kates, David A. to Martha Whitehead 12-29-1877 (12-30-1877)
Keane, William to Ann Bowman 8-1-1860 (8-2-1860)
Kearne, David M. to Mary A. Cole 6-4-1873 (6-5-1873)
Kee, Henry to Jamima Lains 6-29-1865 (7-2-1865)
Kee, Henry to Jemima Laws 6-29-1865 (7-2-1865)
Keen, Francis K. to Susan J. Garland 5-5-1872 (5-3?-1872)
Keen, John V. to Hannah Daniel 12-27-1871
Keen, Jonas M. to Mary Slagle 1-24-1875 (1-25-1875)
Kees, William to Eliza Carden 7-10-1872 (7-11-1872)
Kehn?, Daniel C. to Nancy E. Carrell 4-3-1866 (4-29-1866)
Kelly, James A. to Emma Jobe 3-14-1878
Kelly, James T. to Mary F. Range 4-20-1867 (5-19-1867)
Kelly, John to Nancy Williams 11-3-1847
Ker, William to Eliza Cardin 7-10-1872
Kethporal, W. to Emma R. Rusell 3-24-1875 (4-1-1875)
Keton, Peter D. to Barbra Holafield 5-18-1878 (5-19-1878)
Kichen, Millard to Margaret Davis 12-5-1872 (12-6-1872)
King, Albert to Amanda Horton 12-28-1865
King, Albert to Amanda Houston 12-28-1865
King, Albert to Leah Lacy 6-7-1856 (6-8-1856)
King, John T. to Saraphina L. Johnson 9-11-1866
Kinley, John to Elizabeth Church 1-10-1863 (1-11-1863)
Kinnick, Jacob C. to Louretta Culbert 4-7-1877 (4-8-1877)
Kite, Daniel C. to Nancy E. Carroll 4-27-1866 (4-29-1866)
Kite, Malden to Tempy Potter 9-28-1859 (10-13-1859)
Kite, Russell to Sarah Doby 5-1-1866 (5-2-1866)
Kite, Samuel W. to Catharn Davenport 4-9-1866 (4-10-1866)
Kitzmiller, A. N. to Mary J. Taylor 1-30-1855
Kolluff?, Ira J. to Jane Lipps 1-16-1869 (1-17-1869)
Krouse, James E. to Mary J. Rowen 10-17-1870 (10-18-1870)
Krouse, James M. to Mary J. Rourk? 10-17-1870 (10-18-1870)
Kughn, Joseph to Margarett Ellis 7-1-1851
Kughn, Joseph to Viney Perry 8-23-1854 (8-24-1854)
Kuhn, Millard F. to Margaret Davis 12-5-1872 (12-6-1872)
Lacy, Albert to Mary A. Seller 4-16-1873
Lacy, Alexander to Mary E. Bowers 1-10-1870 (1-16-1870)
Lacy, B. M. to Mary Mattern 11-28-1878
Lacy, Isaac to Clarkey Hutsen 9-6-1851
Lacy, James to Martha Duncan 1-24-1870 (1-23?-1870)
Lacy, Jeremiah to Martha Smith 10-23-1855 (10-28-1855)
Lacy, John C. to Elizabeth Robertson 3-19-1868
Lacy, John W. to Martha N. Nave 1-3-1867 (2-23-1867)
Lacy, Joseph to Elizabeth McAlister 3-22-1875 (3-23-1875)
Lacy, Samuel to Mary D. Spring 3-25-1871
Lacy, William S. to Mary Jane Lyon 3-13-1855 (3-15-1855)
Lacy, William to Evelin Taylor 11-26-1860 (11-27-1860)
Landingham, Julias T. to H. Martin 8-11-1873 (8-12-1873)
Landingham, Julius to Harriet Mathis 8-11-1873 (8-12-1873)
Landreth, Wm. to Lydia B. McNabb 7-16-1870
Lane, James to Susanna McClain 12-24-1853 (12-25-1854)
Laner?, John to Amanda Fox 8-19-1872
Lany, Reuben to Salley Hutsen 10-4-1827 (10-7-1827)
Laudermilk, Noe D. to Elizabeth L. Davis 2-29-1876
Laws, Healy to Sefrona Agner 9-5-1877
Laws, Isaac C. to Mancy Richey 9-10-1858
Laws, Isaac L. to Jamima Ruber 9-10-1858 (2-18-1871)
Laws, John to Manda Fox 8-20-1872
Laws, William to Martha C. Eggers 6-23-1877 (6-24-1877)
League, Simon to Ellen Beekin 5-28-1867 (5-29-1867)
Lee, James to Catharin Simerly 6-5-1865 (6-8-1865)
Lee, Tandy to Mahala Robertson 2-2-1875
Lenard, Geo. W. to Elizabeth O'Brian 12-26-1865 (12-28-1865)

Lenard, Jacob to Lydia A.? Range 11-15-1871 (11-16-1871)
Lenard, James O. to Martha Jane Whitehead 12-29-1858 (1-12-1859)
Lenard, James to Martha Easir? 1-28-1878 (1-29-1878)
Leslie, Paxton to Melvina C. Rowe 1-1-1857 (1-2-1857)
Leu?, James to Catharn Simerly 6-5-1865 (6-8-1866?)
Lewceford, S. A. to Mary E. Dugger 10-2-1875 (10-8-1875)
Lewis, Alfred to Delia Humphrey 4-7-1877 (4-8-1877)
Lewis, Carlos W. to Rachel N. Welcus? 9-23-1867 (9-24-1867)
Lewis, Corlos W. to Rachel Allenella Wilcox 9-23-1867 (9-24-1867)
Lewis, D. B. to Sarah M. Nidiffer 10-21-1869 (10-24-1869)
Lewis, Gideon to Evellin Oliver 12-4-1866 (12-9-1866)
Lewis, Gideon to Martha E. Goodwin 8-21-1860
Lewis, J. F. M. to Mary A. Jenkins 8-5-1878 (8-8-1878)
Lewis, James C. to Elizzie J. Berry 6-9-1875 (6-10-1875)
Lewis, James C. to R. E. Peters 1-22-1878 (1-23-1878)
Lewis, James D. to Elizabeth Jane Berry 6-9-18785 (6-10-1875)
Lewis, James G. to Nancy J. Duggar 12-30-1865 (1-4-1866)
Lewis, James G. to Nancy J. Dugger 12-3-1865 (1-4-1865)
Lewis, James L. to Elizabeth Mararity 2-6-1873
Lewis, James L. to Elizabeth Murray 2-6-1873
Lewis, James L. to ___ Vance 6-17-1875
Lewis, James M. to Emeline Heatherly 2-19-1876 (2-28-1876)
Lewis, Jessee to Elizabeth McQueen 12-1-1855 (12-2-1855)
Lewis, John F. to Mary A. M. Lyon 11-27-1869 (11-29-1869) *
Lewis, John F. to Nancy Loveless 7-15-1870
Lewis, John F. to Nancy Lovless 7-15-1870
Lewis, John to Elizabeth Oliver 12-23-1871 (12-25-1871)
Lewis, Jos. L. to E. E. Frasier 4-3-1878 (4-4-1878)
Lewis, Lawson L. to Sarah J. Campbell 8-27-1858 (8-29-1858)
Lewis, Nicholas R. to Angeline Housley 10-12-1868
Lewis, Samuel B. to Sarah M. Nidiffer 10-21-1869 (10-24-1869)
Lewis, Stephen to Manerva Fletcher 6-14-1876 (6-20-1876)
Lewis, Tobias to Edy Livingston 1-2-1856 (1-4-1856)
Lewis, William A. to Celia J. Campbell 12-29-1856 (1-4-1857)
Lewis, William A. to Selia Jane Campbell 12-29-1856 (12-30-1856)
Lewis, William M. to Nancy Garland 4-15-1871 (4-16-1871)
Lewis, Wm. L. to N. C. Goodwin 11-4-1861 (11-10-1861)
Lilley, John to Lue (Luisa) Barnes 1-16-1876
Linby, Paxton to Melviny C. Roe 1-1-1857
Lincoln, George to Ellen Gordon 11-5-1867 (11-11-1867)
Lindaman, Jas. M. to Mary M. Carr 6-25-1875
Lineback, Henry to Charlotty Willson 10-2-1872 (10-4-1872)
Linus?, David J. to Emilin E. Pearce 2-4-1848 (2-24-1848)
Linville, Worley to Margaret Swanger 1-24-1857 (1-25-1857)
Lipford, William A. to Elizabeth C. Rainbolt 8-14-1866 (8-16-1866)
Liphford, L. D. to Malinda Powell 12-7-1864 (12-20-1864)
Lipps, Daniel W. to Mahala Estep 12-29-1871 (12-30-1871)
Lipps, Daniel W. to Mahala Estepp 12-29-1871 (12-30-1871)
Lipps, Nelson to Elizabeth Pierce 8-21-1886 (8-23-1846?)
Little, George W. to Charlotte Ann Raly 3-23-1866 (3-25-1866)
Little, George W. to Charlottie A. Lany? 3-23-1866 (3-25-1866)
Little, James F. to Pheby E. Claimore 10-23-1876 (10-24-1876)
Little, James K. to Sarah Jane Cox 12-3-1857
Little, James R. to Sarah J. Cox 12-3-1857
Little, John to Mary Ann Range 8-11-1854 (8-13-1854)
Livingston, George W. to Carolin Richardson 12-28-1872 (12-29-1872)
Livingston, George W. to Susanna White 12-29-1868 (12-19?-1868)
Livingston, George W. to Susannah White 12-29-1868 (1-30-1869)
Livingston, John W. to Drusilla Hyder 12-19-1853 (12-30-1853)
Livingston, John to Martha Grace 10-1-1870
Livingston, Mary to Martha Kites 1-26-1874
Livingston, Murray to Martha C. Kite 1-26-1874
Livingston, Saml. to Mary Grindstaff 8-24-1873
Livingston, Samuel to Sarah Grindstaff 8-24-1873
Logan, Joseph to Bettie Carson 4-16-1872
Long, Alexander to Mary E. Bowers 1-10-1870 (1-16-1870)
Long, James to Martha Dunkin 1-23-1870
Loudermilk, Geo. to Sarah Kettle 11-4-1867 (11-14-1867)
Loudermilk, John to Rody E. Bowman 9-30-1858
Loudermilk, Thadeous(Theopholus) to Mary E. Taylor 3-10-1872
Loudymilk, John to Roda E. Bowman 9-30-1858
Love, Alexander to Eliza Taylor 4-28-1873 (no return)
Lovelass, E. D. to Mary Ann Wilson 11-19-1876
Loveless, A. M. to Delitha Smith 3-16-1860 (3-18-1860)
Loveless, John to Eveline Smith 2-13-1869 (2-14-1869)

Loveless, Joseph B. to Sarah Ann Ambrose 6-4-1855 (6-7-1855)
Lovett, Michael G. to Mary E. Holden 2-14-1853 (2-15-1853)
Lovless, Elijah G. to Elizabeth Williams 12-19-1870 (12-22-1870)
Lovless, John to Emelin Smith 2-13-1869
Lovless, John to Mary J. Crow 1-8-1867 (1-13-1867)
Lovless, Joseph to Sarah J. Ambrous 6-4-1855 (6-5-1855)
Lovless, Joseph to Sarah Jane Ambrouse 6-7-1855
Low, Geo. J. to Jemima J. Colbaugh 12-29-1865 (12-31-1865)
Low, George J. to Jemima C. Collough 12-29-1865 (12-31-1865)
Low, Stephen to Elve M. Colbough 6-13-1872 (6-15-1872)
Lowe, David R. to Mary C. Elliott 12-26-1878
Lowe, John A. to Martha W. Lips 3-13-1861 (3-14-1861)
Lowe, John to Ann Cole 6-20-1856 (6-23-1856)
Lunaford?, Marion V. to Mary E. Goodwin 5-27-1872 (6-9-1872)
Lunceford, Jos. to Mary Clementine 12-30-1865 (1-7-1866)
Luner?, F. J. to Nancy Ann Hinkle 3-14-1863 (3-15-1863)
Lunis?, Hasten J. to Mary Culbert 4-19-1860
Lunis?, John to Elizabeth Obrien 12-23-1871 (12-25-1871)
Lunsford, John F. to Caroline Goodwin 11-12-1866 (11-18-1866)
Lunsford, Marion to Mary E. Goodrum 5-27-1872 (6-9-1872)
Lusk, F.(Q?) H. H. to Mary F.(S?) Snodgrass 1-30-1872 (2-1-1872)
Lusk, J. A. C. to Mary J. McKehen 1-27-1866 (1-28-1866)
Lusk, John A. C. to Mary Jane McKeehen 1-27-1866 (1-28-1866)
Lusk, Richard J. to Elizabeth Hart 7-25-1872
Lusk, Robert J. to Elizabeth S. Hart 7-25-1872
Lusk, Samuel N. K. T. to Saraphina Gourley 5-3-1860
Luvies?, H. H. to Lorena Hyder 2-12-1862 (2-27-1862)
Lyle, Willy B. to Nancy Ann Wilson 4-15-1862 (9-24-1862)
Lyles, Geo. W. to Jane Lyles 1-2-1867 (1-3-1867)
Lyles, Willey B. to Nancy Ann Wilson 9-22-1862 (9-24-1862)
Lynch, John A. to Elizabeth Hyatt 10-2-1857 (no return)
Lynch, John A. to Elizabeth Hyett 10-2-1857
Lynvill, G. W. to Mary A. Bowman 9-24-1870
Lynvill, John to Emely Hyder 7-8-1865 (7-9-1865)
Lyon, A. J. to Mary Ann Hays 12-8-1860 (12-9-1860)
Lyon, Ezekiel to Adaline Carr 12-24-1877
Lyon, George to Mary A. M. Lyon 11-27-1869 (11-29-1869)
Lyon, George to Masora Duncan 7-17-1875
Lyon, Henry to Elizabeth Russell 10-17-1868 (10-18-1868)
Lyon, Jeremiah to Martha Moresby? 9-27-1873 (9-28-1873)
Lyon, Jeremiah to Selia C. Smith 8-20-1856
Lyon, John L. to Margaret Elis 1-5-1854
Lyon, John N. to Mary E. Sayler? 5-30-1874 (5-31-1874)
Lyon, John N. to Mary Lee 5-30-1874 (5-31-1874)
Lyon, Joseph P. to Eveline Smith 7-27-1859
Lyon, Landon C. to Catharn Carr 8-21-1872 (8-25-1872)
Lyon, Landon C. to Cathrin Carr 8-21-1872
Lyons, Jeremiah to Martha Moses 9-27-1873 (9-24?-1873)
Lyons, Jeremiah to Selia C. Smith 8-2-1856 (no return)
Lyons, Samuel B. to Louisa A. B. Ellis 10-13-1855 (10-14-1855)
Maberry, Grover B. to Myrey R. Bailey 2-19-1855
Mackland, James to Della Hodge 6-9-1855
Magee, Daniel to Rosetta Magee 1-3-1866 (no return)
Magee, Drewry S. to Margaret S. Carlton 10-30-1850
Magee, G. T. to Mary N. Cameron 3-13-1850
Magee, Mompy to Amanda Worley 12-24-1869
Mallance?, William G. to Emmy B. Hendrix 9-1-1875 (9-2-1875)
Malloner, William G. to Emily B. Hendrix 9-1-1875 (9-2-1875)
Malone, Geo. to Mary Ann Humphrey 1-8-1879 (1-9-1879)
Maloney, Thomas to Eliza M. Stover 10-14-1875
Manis, Jno. to Evaline Smith 7-22-1878 (8-2-1878)
Manning, H. H. to S. L. McKinney 6-8-1878 (6-13-1878)
Manning, Jackson to Elizabeth Campbell 8-16-1853 (8-18-1853)
Manning, Jas. M. to Elizabeth Fletcher 4-17-1876 (4-20-1876)
Maple, Henry to Rebeca Barne 4-25-1865 (4-29-1865)
Maples, A. D. to Margret Nidiver 3-12-1870 (3-24-1870)
Maples, A. Demsey to Margaret Neddon? 3-12-1870 (3-24-1870)
Markland, Charles D. to Amanda E. Campbell 11-26-1870 (11-7?-1870)
Markland, Henry to Mary J. Campbell 6-27-1868
Markland, Nelson J. to Nancy Pierce 2--19-1851 (3-16-1851)
Markland, Nelson to Martha L. Wilson 8-2-1853 (8-7-1853)
Markland, Philip to Eviline Pearce 3-7-1878
Markland, Philip to Jane Lipps 4-3-1864 (4-10-1864)
Marlen (Martin?), David to Hannah Jones 12-31-1870 (1-1-1871) B

Marshall, Landon to Allice Borders? 3-1-1875
Martin, Geo. W. to Saraphina Kite 10-17-1850
Martin, Jacob to Delia McKiney 10-1-1877 (11-18-1877)
Martin, James M. to Elizabeth Lane 12-24-1851 (12-25-1851)
Martin, M. M. to Sanora F. Paregoy 3-17-1873 (3-19-1873)
Martin, M. M. to Sanora Perrigory 3-17-1873 (3-19-1873)
Martin, M. Y. to Carolin McKiny 7-27-1871
Martin, Meridith Y. to Carolin McKinny 7-27-1871
Master, Geo. W. to Mary Gourley 6-14-1850
Maston, Jas. to Ann Forslit 9-13-1877
Mather, John to Emily Crow 8-7-1869 (no return)
Matherly, Alexander to Jane Sims 6-24-1857 (6-29-1857)
Matherly, Alexander to Jane Sims 6-28-1857 (6-29-1857)
Matherly, William to Sarah Fritts 1-30-1854 (2-2-1854)
Mathis, Jesse to Elizabeth Helton 5-15-1855
Mathis, John to Emelin Crow 8-5-1869
Matison, James F. to Mary J. Overholser 10-8-1868 (10-11-1868)
May, Andrew to Sarah Peeps 2-19-1867
May, Elcana to Ann Peek 4-27-1874
Mayton, Andrew W. to Elizabeth Duglass 3-27-1852 (3-28-1852)
McBee, R. L. to E. A. S. Lane 5-19-1852 (5-20-1852)
McCathern, Jas. to Elizabeth Headrick 9-4-1878 (9-8-1878)
McClocklin, John to Rebecca Lessly 6-13-1867 (6-14-1867)
McClure, John F. to Sarah C. Cried? 9-17-1864 (9-18-1864)
McCorkle, John J. to Rutha E. Hendrix 9-18-1866 (9-20-1866)
McFall, John to Alla (Alta) Caraway 12-8-1858 (12-16-1858)
McFall, John to Nancy A. Caraway 12-8-1858 (12-16-1858)
McFall, John to Nancy Allos Carraway 12-8-1858 (12-16-1858?)
McFarland, N. G. to Mary Sayler 5-25-1870 (5-26-1870)
McFarland?, Joseph to Charlotte Smith 6-19-1868
McGinis, T. N. to Marah Ann Potter 8-25-1874 (8-24?-1874)
McIntosh, David M. to Harriet Turner 12-26-1853 (1-1-1854)
McIntosh, Fielding to Edalin Walker 8-21-1861 (8-23-1861)
McIntosh, James to Elizabeth McIntosh 8-1-1852 (8-4-1852)
McInturf, Wilson to Sarah Burchfield 2-1-1851 (2-2-1851)
McInturff, C. C. to Mahala Toney(Tomy) 1-9-1851 (1-30-1851)
McInturff, Ebanna W. to Mary E. Anderson 12-28-1871 (12-29-1871)
McInturff, Elcana W. to Mary E. Anderson 12-28-1871 (12-29-1871)
McInturff, Elcana W. to Mary E. Anderson 12-28-1871 (12-31-1871)
McInturff, Emanul to Sarahfina Bowman 9-30-1873
McInturff, Israel to Darkus Bailley 3-6-1850 (3-7-1850)
McInturff, John S. to Mary E. Noris 11-2-1853 (11-3-1853)
McInturff, John W. to Julia A. Rowe 12-29-1868 (1-3-1869)
McInturff, John to ___ Miller 1-25-1872
McInturff, William to Mary Hyder 4-26-1877
McInturff, Wm. A. to Sarah J. O'Brian 4-13-1874 (4-16-1874)
McIntush, Fielding to Adelin Walker 8-21-1861 (8-22-1861)
McKassay, Charles to Eliza Dunbar 8-31-1864 (10?-30-1864)
McKee, Smith to Lerunsa? Pearce 12-9-1871 (12-10-1871)
McKeehan, Landon to Martha Overholser 10-20-1855
McKeehen, George to Synthey Owens 6-23-1865 (6-25-1865)
McKeehen, William M. to Perlina J. Simerly 5-31-1862 (6-1-1862)
McKehen, Geo. W. P. to Arzella Jane Hyder 7-4-1855 (7-12-1855)
McKehen, Saml. to Hannah McKeehen 5-10-1860
McKehen, Wm. W. to Julia F. Fair 1-6-1868 (1-9-1868)
McKehin, George W. P. to Arzella J. Hyder 7-11-1855 (7-12-1855)
McKehn, Geo. to Mary French 6-14-1855
McKiney, Wilson to Ann Merrett 4-6-1861 (4-7-1861)
McKinney, John to Emily Grindstaff 3-27-1857 (3-29-1857)
McKinney, John to Viney Merrit 7-2-1860 (7-15-1860)
McKinney, Saml. to Sarahfinna Kent 11-1-1876 (11-2-1876)
McKinney, Samuel to Biddy Stephens 11-3-1860 (11-4-1860)
McKinney, Thomas to Martha Hyder 3-21-1874 (3-22-1874)
McKinney, William to Rebecca Treadway 10-30-1852 (11-2-1852)
McKinney, William to Selia Simerly 2-8-1868 (2-9-1868)
McKinney, Wm. to Sudia Scott 9-22-1886
McKinny, Joseph to Catharin Carriger 9-19-1865 (9-24-1865)
McLain, J. B. to Marah Hoss 7-3?-1873
McLaughlin, John to Rebecca Leslie 6-13-1867 (6-14-1867)
McLaukin?, Nelson to Lousinda L. Norris 12-27-1873
McLean, James to Martha Hope 7-5-1873
McNabb, Isaac to Elizabeth Watson 10-9-1856 (10-16-1856)
McNabb, James K. P. to Hanna Philips 8-21-1861 (8-22-1861)
McNabb, Saml. B. to Lydia E. Topp 1-11-1858 (1-17-1858)
McNabb, Samuel B. to Lydia E. Tapp 1-11-1858 (1-17-1858)

McNealey, Reuben to Mary Duncan ?-?-1875
McQueen, W. L. to Elizabeth White 5-11-1870 (5-15-1870)
Meredith, John to Phebe Jones 11-25-1862 (12-2-1862)
Meridith, Andrew J. to Louisa Glover 7-27-1865
Meridith, James to Susanna Moreland 3-23-1850 (3-25-1850)
Meridith, John to Elizabeth Estep 1-7-1855
Meridith, John to Phebee Janes 11-25-1862 (12-2-1862)
Meridith, Samuel H. to Malinda Smith 2-17-1868
Meridith, Samuel H. to Malinda Smith 7-17-1868
Meridith, William G. to Elizabeth February 8-30-1856 (8-31-1856)
Meridith, William G. to Marah Morgan 10-12-1874 (no return)
Meridith, Wm. G. to Sarah Morgan 10-12-1874
Merit, James to Mary Ann Garrison 10-27-1854 (11-26-1854)
Merrit, John to Harriet Garrison 1-4-1851 (1-5-1851)
Merritt, John to Susan Hays 9-3-1855 (9-6-1855)
Merritt, Lenard to Martha Hayes 2-20-1858
Merritt, Lenard to Martha Hays 2-20-1858
Milem, Calvin to Mary Pruett 7-6-1876 (7-10-1876)
Milhorn, George to Nancy C. Lilley 12-9-1868
Millard, S. H. to M. J. Kitzmiller 10-25-1873 (10-26-1873)
Miller (Mills?), James M. to Rebecca A. Hyder 2-4-1875 (2-2?-1875)
Miller, Alben to Elizabeth Dover 3-27-1858
Miller, Allen to Elizabeth David 3-27-1858
Miller, Allen to Elizabeth Dover 3-27-1858 (no return)
Miller, D. L. to Sarah Badgett 4-20-1856
Miller, David H. to Louisa Meridith 9-10-1870 (9-16-1870)
Miller, David T. to Ednay Poyner? 12-25-1867
Miller, David T. to Edney Payne 12-25-1867 (12-26-1867)
Miller, David to Margaret Miller 12-16-1850 (12-19-1850)
Miller, Francis to Hannah Heaton 1-6-1868 (1-10-1868)
Miller, G. W. to Sarah Shell 9-24-1870
Miller, Georg to Martha Bollin 5-31-1865 (6-3-1865)
Miller, George W. to Tempy Potter 2-16-1849 (2-18-1849)
Miller, George to Martha O'Brian 5-31-1865 (6-3-1865)
Miller, Henry to Mary Krouse 3-3-1857 (3-5-1857)
Miller, Jacob A. to Mahilda Moreland 10-31-1867 (11-5-1867)
Miller, Jacob B. to Julia A. Leonard 6-7-1856 (6-10-1856)
Miller, Jacob to Luona Shell 6-10-1876 (6-?-1876)
Miller, Jacob to Sarah M. Gragg 4-12-1877 (4-15-1877)
Miller, James H. to Caroline Whitehead 2-5-1869
Miller, James to Eliza Jane Whitehead 11-7-1865 (1-25-1866)
Miller, James to Malinda Wilcox 1-16-1855 (1-17-1855)
Miller, Jeremiah B. to Emeline Jobe 3-23-1867 (3-24-1867)
Miller, Jeremiah to Matilda Hickeny 12-9-1842 (12-13-1842)
Miller, John K. to Mary R. Minea? 7-20-1852 (7-22-1852)
Miller, John K.(R?) to Fanny C. Tipton 1-22-1866 (1-23-1866)
Miller, Johnson to Manervy Gouge 2-9-1869 (2-21-1869)
Miller, Johnson to Monisany? Gouge 2-9-1869 (2-21-1869)
Miller, Kinchen to Jane McNabb 9-7-1855 (9-9-1855)
Miller, Lawson to Susan Miller 9-28-1877
Miller, Loranze to Marilda Heaton 3-12-1866 (3-15-1866)
Miller, Moses A. to Mary A. Patton 8-19-1858
Miller, Rewfus to Helen Ingram 8-29-1860 (8-30-1860)
Miller, Rufus to Helia McGraw 8-29-1860 (8-30-1860)
Miller, S. H. K. to M. S. Lelsmiller 11-17-1873
Miller, Samuel to Clarisa Fair 12-18-1857
Miller, Samuel to Saraphina Jane Taylor 3-20-1858 (3-21-1858)
Miller, Samuel to Surrena Hodge 6-16-1869
Miller, Sanford to Elizabeth Simerly 9-18-1854 (no return)
Miller, Solomon to L. J. Crow 1-15-1853 (1-16-1853)
Miller, William R. to Deborah Williams 8-27-1866 (9-2-1866)
Miller, William R. to Deborah Williams 8-29-1866 (9-12-1866)
Miller, William to Sarah Ingram 7-21-1859 (7-22-1859)
Miller, Wm. K. to Caroline White 2-4-1869 (3-1-1869)
Miller, Wm. to Mary Blevins 12-16-1855
Mills, David H. to Louisa Merdith 9-10-1870 (9-16-1870)
Mims?, John C. to Lydia J. Moss 8-16-1855
Minton, Rufus G. to Phebe Peters 10-16-1858 (10-17-1858)
Minton, Rufus to Jane Carriger 9-15-1858 (not executed?)
Minton, Ruphus G. to Phoeba Peaters 10-16-1858 (10-17-1858)
Minton, Ruphus to Jane Carriger 9-15-1858 (no return)
Mires, A. T. to Rebeca J. Crumley 12-14-1865
Mollen, John H. to Emilie Slagle 1-13-1873 (1-14-1873)
Montgomery, Samuel to Mary Potter 2-17-1859
Montgomery, William E. to Elizabeth Merritt 1-7-1850 (1-10-1850)

Moody, Geo. W. to Jane Fair 5-7-1858
Moody, George W. to Jane Pharr 5-7-1858
Moon, John to Mary Britt 9-2-1858
Moore, John to Mary Butt 9-2-1858
Moore, Samuel to Margaret Chapman 3-22-1858 (3-23-1858)
More, Robert to Louisa Blevins 2-15-1853 (2-16-1853)
More, Wm. to Mary Carver 12-8-1854 (12-16-1854)
Moreland, Charles to Elizabeth Main 7-14-1854 (7-15-1854)
Moreland, James L. to Hanah A. Overhulser 2-13-1875 (4-5-1875)
Moreland, Materson L. to Lousinda J. Hyder 10-24-1871 (10-26-1871)
Mores, Abraham to Sarah Rusell 10-17-1868 (10-18-1868)
Morgan, James to Caroline Roberts 9-9-1873 (9-12-1873)
Morgan, James to Rossella? Stout 9-24-1873 (9-26-1873)
Morgan, James to Rosseller Stout 9-24-1873 (10-26-1873)
Morgan, John W. to Eliza Richardson 3-18-1874 (5-22-1874)
Morgan, John W. to Mary A. Potter 9-14-1873
Morgon, Thomas to Evaline Glover 12-29-1877 (12-30-1877)
Moris, Jefferson to Hannah Lacy 3-9-1851
Morland, M. L. to Louisa J. Hyder 10-24-1871
Morliver?, D. N. to Lidda M. Robert 10-8-1871
Morrell (Murrell?), Joseph to Rhoda A. E. Anderson 9-14-1856 (9-24-1856)
Morrell, C. C. to Alvena Cariger 1-18-1862 (1-19-1862)
Morrell, Christian C. to Alizina Carriger 1-18-1862 (1-19-1862)
Morrell, Isaac O. to Mary Ann Peters 4-2-1856 (4-26-1856)
Morrell, Isaac to Mimi Vanhuss 2-23-1877
Morrell, John S. to Emily Floyd 3-12-1866
Morrell, Thomas H. to Ester P. Lacy 3-2-1872 (2?-5-1872)
Morrell, Thos. to Hester P. Lacy 3-1-1872
Morrell, William E. to Susan Hendrix 10-1-1873 (10-2-1873)
Morrell, William R. to Sarah E. Mothern 2-12-1868 (2-13-1868)
Morrell, Wm. R. to Eliza J. Peters 1-16-1851
Morris, Franklin to Eliza A. Lenderwood 1-20-1866 (1-21-1866)
Morris, Franklin to Eliza Ann Lindermood 1-20-1866 (1-?-1866)
Morris, Henry to Lucilla Jane Carr 6-12-1875 (6-13-1875)
Morris, Jefferson to Catharin Smith 2-9-1866 (2-10-1865?)
Morton, Alexander to Mary Stout 6-22-1875 (7-4-1875)
Morton, D. N. to Lidda M. Roberts 10-8-1871
Morton, M. Y. to Barbery Thompson(Jenkins) 12-12-1861 (12-21-1861)
Morton, Meredith Y. to Caroline McKinney 7-27-1871
Morton, William to Phebe Richardson 12-30-1856 (12-31-1856)
Morton, Zacariah to Susan Grindstaff 2-2-1875
Morton, Zacariah to Susanna Grindstaff 2-2-1875 (2-7-1875)
Moser, Abraham to Sarah Russell 10-17-1868 (10-18-1868)
Mosley, John to Hanah Ann Carrell 8-15-1857 (8-16-1857)
Mosley, John to Hannah Ann Carroll 8-15-18857 (8-16-1857)
Mosley, Reuben to Sarah Simerly 10-2-1853 (10-4-1853)
Mosley, Reuben to Sarah Simmerly 10-3-1853 (10-4-1853)
Mothern, Geo. to Harriett Shell 4-30-1877 (5-6-1877)
Mothern, Henry to Ruth Ann Lacy 7-17-1878 (7-18-1878)
Mothern, Isaac H. to Eveline G. Lacy 1-11-1862 (1-12-1862)
Mothern, John S. to Margaret Holly 11-21-1877 (11-22-1877)
Mothern, William H. to Mary Eliza Range 2-20-1867 (2-28-1867)
Mothern, Wm. E. to Elizabeth Lewis 1-11-1854 (1-12-1854)
Mothison, John C. to Rhody A. E. Lewis 12-8?-1866 (12-11-1866)
Mothorn, Geo. to Catharin E. Smallen 8-24-1850 (no return)
Mottern, John H. to Emilin Slagle 1-13-1873 (1-14-1873)
Mottern, William to Elizabeth J. Lyons 11-8-1876 (11-9-1876)
Murdox, Howard to Saraphina Drake 9-23-1865 (9-27-1865)
Murphy, Preston W. to Nancy Ann Badget 5-20-1852
Murry, Andrew to Elizabeth Hicks 11-17-1873 (12-17-1873)
Murry, John L. to Rebecca Martin 11-26-1851 (11-27-1851)
Murry, Thomas O. to Delila A. Dover 2-27-1877
Myer, Christian C. to Phebe S. Hardin 12-1-1851? (12-15-1857)
Myers, E. D. to Mary E. Grindstaff 12-30-1876 (12-31-1876)
Myers, Harmon to Mary Taylor 5-4-1875 (5-9-1875)
Myers, Harrison to Mary Taylor? 5-4-1875 (5-9-1875)
Myers, James to Ann Livly 4-16-1861 (4-17-1861)
Myers, James to Ann Loveless 4-16-1861 (4-17-1861)
Myers, Saml. M. S. to Lovina V. Pierce 2-26-1876 (2-3?-1876)
Nance, James to Sarah Phuen? 3-8-18783
Nave, Abraham to A. B. D. Vanhouse 11-8-1861 (11-9-1861)
Nave, Abraham to Nancy A. Crumbley 6-18-1852 (6-20-1852)
Nave, Daniel S. to Elizabeth Bowers 3-15-1860 (3-18-1860)

Nave, David F. to Amanda M. Matherson 7-30-1873 (7-31-1873)
Nave, David F. to Amanda Mathison 7-30-1873 (7-31-1873)
Nave, David N. to Ruth E. Lyon 10-13-1855 (10-18-1855)
Nave, Henry J. to Sabina J. Hyder 3-23-1876
Nave, Henry J.? to Phebe Crow 12-9-1865 (12-10-1865)
Nave, Isaac to Elizabeth Fair 12-26-1866 (12-27-1866)
Nave, James A. to Mary Fair 3-8-1873
Nave, Pleasant G. to Delila Hardin 2-1-1868 (2-2-1868)
Nave, Samuel N. to Sarah Berry 1-20-1869 (1-21-1869)
Nave, William T. to Mary E. Matherly 4-16-1874 (4-17-1874)
Nave, Wm. P. to Mary E. Motherly 4-16-1874
Neal, James H. to Evaline M. Brewer 9-23-1852
Nediffer, Calvin to Mary A. Miller 7-31-1873 (8-3-1873)
Nediffer, G. W. to Elizabeth A. Taylor 9-9-1872
Nelson, Thomas A. R. to Ellenor Boyd 3-21-1858 (3-22-1858)
Nelson, Thos. A. R. to Ellen Boyd 3-20-1857
Nideffer, James C. to Martha A. Colbaugh 6-28-1871 (6-29-1871)
Nideffer, Robert to Frankey Morgan 1-6-1875 (12?-6-1875)
Nideffer, Thomas to —— Robertson 1-23-1875
Nidifer, Isaac to Levicy Abner 4-24-1868 (5-3-1868)
Nidifer, James to Catharin Lewis 11-20-1855 (11-14?-1855)
Nidifer, Samuel to Amanda Loveless 11-15-1851 (11-16-1851)
Nidiffer, Isaac to Lavica Blevins 4-14-1868 (5-3-1868)
Nidiffer, James C. to Marthy A. Calboch 6-28-1871 (6-29-1871)
Nidiffer, Levi to Margaret Estep 4-30-1877 (5-6-1877)
Nidiffer, Robt. to Emiline Estep 5-20-1856 (5-21-1856)
Nidiffer, Samuel to Francy Morgan 12-6-1875
Nidiffer, Thomas to Mary Robertson 1-23-1874 (1-24-1875?)
Nidiffer, William to Mary Calbaugh 5-7-1877 (6-3-1877)
Nidiffer, Wm. E. to Elizabeth Peters 3-14-1872
Night, Mathew to Sarah Campbell 7-8-1865 (no return)
Noris, James P. to Lovenia Baker 9-18-1857 (9-27-1857)
Norris, Christopher to Racheal McInterff 2-13-1855 (2-14-1855)
Norris, W. F. to Caroline McInturff 11-28-1867
O'Brien, J. S. to Ann E. Burchfield 10-16-1852 (10-21-1852)
O'Brien, B. M. G. to Elizabeth J. Singletary 9-16-1869
O'Brien, David P. to Sarah Mottern 2-19-1850 (2-21-1850)
O'Brien, George to Sarah Jane Gentry 2-27-1867
O'Lenard, James to Martha J. Whitehead 12-29-1858 (1-12-1859)
Odaner, Waits to Rhoda Whitehead 10-3-1878 (10-8-1878)
Odell, Joseph to Eliza J. Foster 2-2-1850 (2-3-1850)
Odell, Thomas to Eveline Nave 10-14-1852
Olive, John to Martha Tronell 7-14-1873
Oliver, Chrisley to Nancey C. Oliver 12-23-1871 (12-25-1857?)
Oliver, Christian to Lavicy Nave 9-14-1865 (9-24-1865)
Oliver, Christian to Margaret Pharr 11-20-1858 (11-21-1858)
Oliver, Christley to Winny L. Oliver 12-23-1871 (12-25-1871)
Oliver, Elijah D. to Malinda Collins 8-6-1866
Oliver, Geo. to June Johnson 11-13-1868 (11-15-1868)
Oliver, George to Jane Talley 11-13-1868 (11-15-1868)
Oliver, George to Mary Bunton 9-10-1858 (9-11-1859?)
Oliver, Jackson to Elizabeth Myers 8-23-1863 (no return)
Oliver, James to Jane Jenkins 12-24-1866 (12-26-1866)
Oliver, Nicholas to Elizabeth Fair 9-29-1862 (10-1-1862)
Oliver, Nicholas to Elizabeth Farr 9-29-1862 (10-1-1862)
Oliver, William D. to Abigail J. Nave 9-20-1871
Oliver, Wm. J. to Nancy A. Jolly 11-9-1874 (11-15-1874)
Oller, Isaac to Amanda Isham? 1-22-1875 (1-29-1875)
Olliver, George to Mary Buntain 9-10-1858 (9-11-1858)
Olliver, Isaac to Amanda J. Fair 1-25-1875 (1-29-1875)
Overbee?, Lawson to Eury Overbee 1-13-1871?
Overby, Lawson to Every Pearce 1-13-1871
Overholser, William J. to Martha E. Cooper 11-7-1865 (11-23-1865)
Owen, A. H. to Matilda Benfield 3-9-1871
Owens, A. H. to Mahala Burfield? 3-7-1871 (3-9-1871)
Owens, Alexander H. to Emeline Robinson 5-2-1857 (5-3-1857)
Owens, David to Elizabeth Robertson 8-25-1861 (8-26-1861)
Owens, James A. to Sarah J. Stout 1-6-1852 (1-22-1852)
Parker, Franklin to Ann Carter 7-12-1861
Parker, Jos. W. to Emaline Hilton 7-30-1855 (7-31-1855)
Parker, Mathew E.(F?) to Malinda Taylor 9-9-1856
Parker, Pleasant to Matilda Buntern 3-4-1871 (3-12-1871)
Parker, Pleasant to Matildad Burton 3-11-1871 (3-12-1871)
Parks, Franklin to Ann Carter 7-12-1866
Patrick, Thomas J. to Eliza Jane Buckles 9-1-1870 (9-4-1870)

Patterick, Thomas J. to Eliza Jane Buckles 9-1-1870 (9-4-1870)
Patterson, Ninevy to Rachael E. Hartly 7-17-1867 (8-18-1867)
Patton, D. M. to Joanah L. Hyder 6-16-1860 (6-17-1860)
Patton, Joshua M. to Julia Phillips 6-1-1859 (6-2-1859)
Patton, Thomas Y. to Mary Jane Phillips 10-17-1861 (10-24-1861)
Payne, James J. to Mary Nave 12-5-1868 (12-10-1868)
Payte, Nathaniel to Vina Garland 10-27-1871 (10-29-1871)
Peace, Lafayett to E. E. Campbell 5-13-1871
Peace?, Christian H. to Martha J. B. Crow 12-23-1869
Pean (Pierce?), William C. to Sarah J. Duggar 7-6-1857 (8-30-1857)
Pean, Nathanl. J. to Rebecca Stover 12-24-1857
Pearc?, Elbert S. to Rosey J. Duggar 12-20-1852 (12-21-1852)
Pearce, A. B. to Salina J. Lewis 1-12-1852 (1-15-1852)
Pearce, Alfred to Mary White 8-2-1873 (8-3-1873)
Pearce, Camern to Amanda Oliver 9-21-1875 (9-23-1875)
Pearce, Christian A. A. to Martha J. B. Crow 12-23-1869
Pearce, Elbert S. to Rosy Jane Dugger 12-20-1852 (12-21-1852)
Pearce, Henry to Phebe J. Crow 5-11-1854 (5-13-1854)
Pearce, Jackson to Virginia Bowers 1-19-1878 (1-20-1878)
Pearce, James to Mary O. Carter 1-26-1852 (7-27-1852)
Pearce, John to Sabra Taylor 3-25-1870 (3-27-1870)
Pearce, Layfaette to Ellen E. Campbell 5-13-1871
Pearce, Lewis to Darthula Elliott 12-25-1868 (12-29-1868)
Pearce, Richard to Margaret Hampton 9-12-1857 (no return)
Pearce, Robert to Elizabeth Rasor 4-8-1875 (4-9-1875)
Pearce, W. A. D. to Selia A. Lewis 12-29-1856 (1-4-1857)
Pearce, William A. D. to Celia Ann Lewis 12-29-1856 (12-30-1856)
Pearce, William A. to Mary C. Nave 10-9-1860
Peare, Elber S. to Rosy Jane Duggar 12-20-1852 (12-21-1853?)
Pearson, Alexander to Elender Anderson 10-26-1867
Peaters, Geo. F. to Sealy Grindstaff 1-21-1876 (1-27-1876)
Peck, Alfred to Selia Lyons 2-3-1866 (2-4-1866)
Peler?, Alfred to Nancy Nideffer 7-18-1874
Penland, Milton to Louisa Williams 12-23-1877 (12-27-1878?)
Penland, Milton to Rachel Williams 7-21-1867
Peoples, David H. to Tabitha J. Hyder 7-5-1866
Peoples, David H. to Tobitha E. Hyder 7-5-1866
Peoples, James H. to Julia C. Parker 11-19-1870
Peoples, James M. to Delia C. Parker 11-29-1870
Peoples, John W. to Cornelia J. Houn 10-17-1877 (10-18-1877)
Peoples, Kenedy to Mary Williams 6-6-1859 (6-12-1859)
Peoples, Nathaniel T. to Harriet E. Britt 1-18-1879 (1-19-1879)
Pepper, Jesse to Mary C. Taylor 12-9-1867
Perdue, Silas to Melvena Shuffield 7-12-1871 (7-14-1871)
Perkins, Isaac to Jane Burchfield 5-14-1860 (5-15-1860)
Perkins, J. F. to Sary J. L. Menen? 12-13-1851 (12-14-1851)
Perkins, James to Martha Potter 11-8-1872 (11-9-1872)
Perkins, Joseph to Nancy E. Thomas 10-8-1860 (10-14-1860)
Perkins, W. A. to Nancy Shuffield 8-28-1851 (8-31-1851)
Perkins, William R. to Nancy A. McFall 6-21-1865 (6-29-1865)
Perrigan, John H. to Sinah Mothin? 4-19-1869
Perry, Andrew to Margaret Royston 2-17-1871 (2-18-1871)
Perry, David to Elizabeth Collins 6-25-1867 (6-26-1867)
Perry, G. W. to Martha Sams 6-28-1873
Perry, Geo. M. to Cathern Hilton 3-28-1875
Perry, Geo. W. to Mary Helton 7-10-1869 (7-11-1869)
Perry, Henderson F. to Eva C. Custer 11-28-1878
Perry, Isaac to Eliza Richardson 3-6-1875 (3-7-1875)
Perry, James to Sarah J. Collins 2-1-1868 (2-4-1868)
Perry, Landon C. to Elizabeth A. Buchanon 3-15-1858 (3-16-1858)
Perry, Landon C. to Elizabeth A. Buckhannon 3-15-1858 (3-16-1858)
Perry, William to Emilin Collins 4-14-1866
Perry, Wm. R. to Sarah T. Taylor 8-18-1868
Peters, A. J. to Evelin Crumley 7-23-1861 (8-1-1861)
Peters, A. Jackson to Eveline Crumley 7-23-1861 (8-1-1861)
Peters, Alfred C. to Elizabeth Bishop 7-12-1863 (7-13-1863)
Peters, Alfred C. to Louisa Nidiffer 10-2-1869 (10-5-1869)
Peters, Alfred to Nancy Nidiffer 7-18-1874
Peters, B. H. to Aneliza Bowers 3-14-1866
Peters, B. H. to Levisa Oliver 3-2-1861 (3-3-1861)
Peters, Benj. H. to Phebe Peters 5-26-1858
Peters, Cherstly to Eliz. J. Lewis 2-5-1866 (2-22-1866)
Peters, David to Sarah Frazier 7-2-1866 (7-8-1866)
Peters, Jackson to Eveline Crumly 7-23-1861 (8-1-1861)
Peters, James H. to Elizabeth Forbes 3-6-1861 (3-8-1861)

Peters, James H. to Elizabeth Forbus 3-6-1861 (3-8-1861)
Peters, Jas. T. to Elizabeth Miller 1-13-1860 (1-15-1860)
Peters, Reuben to Elizabeth Fletcher 11-30-1867 (12-1-1867)
Peters, Reuben to Nancy Oliver 9-1-1865 (9-2-1865)
Peters, Rheuben to Evelina Berry 11-29-1853
Peters, Thomas to Nancy Morton 10-5-1856
Peters, William to Charlotte Heatherly 11-25-1858
Petty, William to Tiney J. Britt 8-24-1853
Phair?, David to Nancy J. Estep 3-13-1868 (3-15-1868)
Pharr, Geo. W. to Louisa Burrow 4-21-1870
Pharr, George W. to Eliza J. Lovless 10-5-1865 (10-7-1865)
Pharr, J. H. to Elizabeth Fletcher 7-3-1866 (8-5-1866)
Pharr, Jackson C. to Ellen Fletcher 5-3-1868
Pharr, Rethual to Eliza E. White 5-2-1870 (5-5-1870)
Philips, Powell to Edana Britt 5-17-1862 (5-22-1862)
Phillip, Wm. O. to Laura Pearce 10-8-1875 (10-14-1875)
Phillips, Barnett to Catharn Hampton 2-2-1858 (no return)
Phillips, Edmond to Susanna Smith 2-2-1866 (no return)
Phillips, W. M. to E. A. Hyder 12-21-1872 (12-23-1877)
Phipps, Peter to Elizabeth Blevins 11-7-1865 (11-8-1865)
Phipps, Taylor to Monas Phipps 12-13-186
Pierce, George L. C. to Mary C. White 11-6-1869 (11-7-1869)
Pierce, Jacob C. to Vicey J. Carriage 2-28-1856
Pierce, Nathaniel J. to Rebeca Stover 12-24-1857
Pilkington, Enoch to Hannah C. Noras 3-25-1878 (3-27-1878)
Pippen, J. W. to Mary J. Crow 11-10-1875 (11-11-1875)
Pippin, J. H. to Mary E. Taylor 12-9-1867 (12-?-1867)
Pippin, John W. to Mary C. Crow 11-10-1875 (11-11-1875)
Plep, R. P. to Amanda Hamby 11-11-1873 (11-21-1873)
Plessee?, P. P. to Amanda Hunby 11-11-1873 (11-10?-1873)
Plurty, Paddy O. to Mary J. Genely? 6-22-1874
Poland, Jonathan to Emeline Akins 3-14-1874 (3-15-1874)
Poland, Jonathan to Nancy Kelley 8-12-1862
Poland, Jonathan to Nancy Kelly 8-12-1862
Pollero?, Jonathan to Cambe? Akner 3-14-1874 (3-15-1874)
Pool, Robert to Gillen (Gillie) M. White 9-3-1874 (9-6-1874)
Potter, James B. to Sarah Bunton 10-31-1851 (11-1-1851)
Potter, James B. to Sarah Bunton 11-7-1854 (11-11-1854)
Potter, Johnson to Martha Gillen 3-5-1874 (7-11-1874)
Potter, Johnson to Martha Giller 3-3-1874 (7-11?-1874)
Potter, Peter H. to Mary E. Cable 1-9-1859 (2-10-1859)
Potter, Peter H. to Mary E. Coble 1-9-1859 (2-10-1859)
Potter, Peter to Lousana Shell 10-10-1870 (10-23-1870)
Potter, William H. to Sarah M. Nave 3-1-1862 (3-9-1862)
Potts, Johnson to Martha Gillen 3-5-1874 (7-11-1874)
Powell, William L. to Rachel L. Powell 3-18-1866 (3-19-1866)
Prestly, Henry B. to Martha J. Clemens 2-26-1868 (3-1-1868)
Price, Christopher F. to Carolin Grimsley 10-13-1861 (10-15-1861)
Price, Christopher to Sarah Kenley 12-15-1850 (12-22-1850)
Price, F. M. to Sary Ann Dugger 10-15-1857 (10-16-1857)
Price, Geo. to Adaline Kinley 3-7-1864
Price, James P. to Manery J. Pugh 1-9-1861 (1-10-1861)
Price, John E. to Sabra E. Taylor 3-25-1870 (3-27-1870)
Price, John to Mary McInturff 2-24-1872 (2-25-1872)
Price, John to Mary McInturff 2-24-1873 (2-25-1873)
Price, Joseph D. to Emeline E. Hyder 9-5-1855 (9-6-1855)
Price, Joseph W. to Emma E. Wyatt 8-22-1873 (8-24-1873)
Price, William H. to Elizabeth Pickerieng 10-18-1859
Pricharad, W. D. to Leriza Perry 11-29-1877
Prichard, John to Hester Ann Shell 4-4-1866 (4-5-1866)
Prichard, Thomas S. to Alis E. Twigs 4-5-1877 (4-8-1877)
Prichard, William to Rebecca Hopkins 7-26-1862 (7-27-1862)
Prichard, William to Rebecca Hopson 7-26-1862 (7-27-1862)
Pters, Chrisley to Eliza L. Lewis 2-5-1866 (2-22-1866)
Pugh, David to Nancy Johnson 3-30-1871 (4-2-1871)
Pugh, William to Hester Combs 3-2-1868 (3-3-1868)
Puket?, John F. to Lorana Wilson 12-17-1868
Rain (Ryan), George to Elizabeth C. Singletary 4-30-1856 (5-4-1856)
Rainbolt, John H. to Matilda Venable 9-3-1848
Raines, William J. to Louisa J. Grindstaff 7-21-1864 (7-24-1864)
Rains, Jacob K. to Sarah A. Hopkins 4-7-1856 (1-21-1856?)
Ramsom, George to Emile Walker 7-26-1873 (7-27-1873)
Ramsour?, John to Rebecca J. Gouge 10-22-1870
Range, Alfred to Lydia Claymore 1-2-1873
Range, Elbert? H. to Mary C. Beagles 9-27-1852 (9-30-1852)

Range, Elcana D. to Barshaby Range 8-3-1866 (8-5-1866)
Range, Harrison H. to Harriet C. Mothern 7-24-1865 (8-1-1865)
Range, Harrison H. to Harritt Mathorn 7-24-1865 (8-1-1865)
Range, Jacob to Mary Jane Range 9-10-1866 (9-13-1866)
Range, Jeremiah B. to Sarah E. McKeehen 10-2-1865 (10-5-1865)
Range, Jonathan M. to Nancy J. McKeehen 6-11-1866 (6-14-1866)
Range, K. K. to Sarafina Lusk 6-11-1860 (6-21-1860)
Range, Landon P. to Okaperdelia Humphrey 2-19-1866 (1-1-1867)
Range, William to Sarah Morrell 11-14-1877
Range, Wm. T. to Julia Williams 8-30-1865 (8-31-1865)
Rasmor, Robert to Margaret Grisham 10-2-1868
Ratliff, Ira to Mary Jane Lipps 1-16-1869 (1-17-1869)
Ray, Samuel to Alice Tate 2-23-1872
Ready, John A. to Rebecca A. Loudermilk 9-18-1878 (9-26-1878)
Reason, Wilferman to Margaret Buckles 12-30-1873
Reasor, Vaught to Mary Arnold 1-9-1854 (1-28-1854)
Reed, Clemmons to Sarah Anderson 4-25-1854
Reed, James to Rebecca Leonard 12-3-1877
Reeser, R. B. to Amanda Shuffield 2-16-1875
Reeves, John D. to Rhoda E. Taylor 4-17-1876 (4-18-1876)
Reges?, James to ____ Taylor 8-21-1874
Remine, John to Jane O'Brian 1-11-1863
Renfro, Henry M. to Martha J. Duffield 11-25-1867 (11-26-1867)
Renfro, Jos. to Parmellia C. Brooks 12-26-1876
Renfro, Joseph C. to Mary A. O'Brian 5-1-1856
Renolds, Andrew L. to Elizabeth Lucas 11-1-1867 (11-8-1867)
Renolds, Andrew R. to Elizabeth Lucus 11-1-1867 (11-8-1867)
Rhodes, Abraham to Martha Brewer 2-22-1860
Richards, Benja. to Jane Morris 7-22-1865
Richards, G. W. to Mary Ann McKinny 8-16-1862 (8-17-1862)
Richards, Geo. W. to Mary Ann McKimay 8-16-1862 (8-17-1862)
Richards, Jas. to Louisa Woods 9-30-1863
Richards, John S. to Nancy M. Hyder 10-23-1859 (10-25-1859)
Richardson, Alexander to Martha Perry 12-16-1856
Richardson, Andrew to Carrie Smith 3-11-1875
Richardson, Elcana to Mary Ann Smith 11-9-1853 (11-11-1853)
Richardson, Elijah to Fanny Blevins 4-10-1861 (4-11-1861)
Richardson, H. P. to Frelove? Oliver 11-26-1871 (11-28-1871)
Richardson, H. P. to Susan Oliver 11-26-1871 (11-28-1871)
Richardson, Harvey to Elizabeth A. Crow 8-5-1852
Richardson, Henry to Matilda Wilson 7-6-1878
Richardson, Hillsberry? to Malinda Shell 12-24-1844 (1-8-1845)
Richardson, James M. to Nancy C. Pleasant 8-5-1875 (8-8-1875)
Richardson, James to Margaret Arnold 9-12-1866 (9-17-1866)
Richardson, John to Matilda Estep 11-22-1855 (11-23-1855)
Richardson, John to Nancy C. Estep 12-19-1868
Richardson, Joseph P. to Charlotte Smith 6-18-1868 (6-19-1868)
Richardson, Sampson to Nancy E. Campbell 9-24-1874 (9-29-1874)
Richardson, Samuel to Delana E. Crow 2-16-1875 (2-18-1875)
Richardson, Samuel to Delcena E. Crow 1-30-1869 (1-31-1869)
Richardson, Wm. F. to Martha E. Garland 6-7-1861 (6-8-1861)
Richardson, Wm. M. to Nancy Oaks 3-29-1877 (4-1-1877)
Riche?, Silas M. to Mary D. Bishop 12-31-1867 (1-2-1868)
Richer?, Elbert to Josephin Green 1-23-1872 (1-25-1872)
Richie, David to Jane Creed 5-10-1862 (5-25-1862)
Riles?, Samul W. to Cathan Debenport 4-9-1866 (4-10-1866)
Rine, Thomas to Elizabeth Sumers 9-12-1871 (9-14-1871)
Ritchie, Alvin P. to Martha L. Cass 12-8-1869
Ritchie, Carac N. to Martha L. Blevins 12-9-1876 (12-10-1876)
Ritchie, Elbert to Josephine Green 1-20-1872 (1-25-1872)
Ritchie, J. R. to Margaret A. Dover 4-18-1871 (4-20-1871)
Ritchie, James P. to Mary Ann Bucklen 11-17-1865 (11-23-1865)
River, Andrew to Manerva Lewis 6-2-1862 (6-3-1862)
Roberson, Moses P. to Margaret E. Bowers 12-?-1865 (12-14-1865)
Roberson, Thomas to Phenith Watson 6-11-1855 (6-16-1855)
Roberts, A. H. to Mary (Nancy?) Morgan 4-13-1874 (4-14-1874)
Roberts, Alfred to Elizabeth Heatherly 8-21-1867 (8-25-1867)
Roberts, Geo. D. to Emy Burrow 10-29-1866 (10-30-1866)
Roberts, George D. to Emily D. Burrow 10-29-1866 (10-30-1866)
Roberts, John to Emmy T. Lacy 8-22-1870 (8-23-1870)
Roberts, John to Sarah Fletcher 6-16-1876 (6-18-1876)
Roberts, Michael to Eliza Jane Nidifer 5-20-1865 (5-22-1865)
Roberts, Wm. C. to Rebecca McNeese 2-13-1879 (2-16-1879)
Robertson, Daniel to Catharin Elliott 6-16-1866 (6-18-1866)
Robertson, Daniel to Jane Lowe 2-25-1873 (2-26-1873)

Robertson, David to Jane Lawe 2-25-1873 (2-26-1873)
Robertson, Moses P. to Margaret E. Bowers 12-12-1865 (12-14-1865)
Robertson, Sampson to Louisa Rains ?-?-1875 (with spring)
Robison, David L. to Eliza C. Buckles 8-24-1878 (8-25-1878)
Rockhold, Dimmond to Martha Foust 10-14-1865
Rowe, Daniel to Martha Scott 12-21-1865 B
Rowe, J. E. to Emiline E. Boren 12-31-1859 (1-1-1860)
Rowe, J. E. to M. E. Boren 12-31-1859 (1-1-1860?)
Rowe, L. L. to Allen Jones 6-14-1867 (6-15-1867)
Rowe, Loranzo D. to Allom Jones 6-14-1867 (6-15-1867)
Rowe, Robert L. to Margaret Stafford 1-15-1857
Rowe, Thomas to Elizabeth Simons 9-12-1871 (9-14-1871)
Rowe, William H. to Lydia McNabb 11-13-1866 (maybe Dec.)
Rucker, Silas M. to Mary D. Bishop 12-27-1867 (1-2-1868)
Rucker, W. T. to Mary C. Johnson 12-17-1867
Ruhn, J. R. to M. A. Dorun? 4-18-1871 (4-20-1871)
Rusell, John S. to Urry? Melvina Low 8-21-1865
Rusell, Thepholus to Rhoda A. Dugless 10-2-1874 (11-5-1874)
Russell, Theaplus to Rhoda A. Duglass 11-20-1874 (11-5?-1874)
Rutledge, William to Eveline Odell 12-31-1875 (1-1-1860)
Ryefield, William to Selia Laws 5-30-1874 (5-31-1874)
Ryon, Thomas S. to L. J. Pearce 12-26-1854 (12-28-1854)
Sams, Owen to Eliza J. Glover 3-24-1859
Sams, Owen to Eliza Perry 8-19-1872
Sams, Owen to Elzina Perry 8-19-1872 (8-25-1872)
Sayler, David to Hannah Prock 11-8-1865 (11-10-1865)
Saylor, David to Hannah Porch 11-8-1865 (11-10-1865)
Saylor, Joseph to Amanda Oliver 3-7-1862 (4-15-1862)
Saylor, Noah to Susanna Loudermilk 1-1-1856 (1-3-1856)
Saylor, Noh? D. to Rachael Carrell 5-14-1877 (5-15-1877)
Scalf, Benjamin to Rarsanna Hilton 1-14-1860 (3-27-1860)
Scalf, Benjamin to Rosanna Helton 3-22-1860
Scalf, William J. to Mary E. Foust 9-20-1865
Scott, G. H. to Ellen V. O'Brian 7-12-1875 (8-5-1875)
Scott, Geo. H. to Ellen V. O'Brien 7-12-1875 (8-5-1875)
Scott, Jackson to Elizabeth Little 7-19-1866
Scott, John to Elizabeth Dun 11-15-1871 (1?-29-1871)
Scott, John to Elizabeth Dunn 11-15-1871 (11-16-1871)
Scott, S. to Hannah Hendrix 3-2-1869
Scott, Samuel J. to Josephine Hickey 1-12-1871 (2-19-1871)
Scott, Samuel J. to Saraphin Hickey 1-12-1871 (2-19-1871)
Scott, W. T. L. to Racheal A. C. Williams 4-8-1869
Scott, William H. to Racheal A. Williams 4-8-1869
Scott, William to Hannah E. Handrix 3-1-1869 (3-2-1869)
Seal, Cornelius to Jane Stover 6-11-1870 (6-12-1870)
Seal?, Cornelus to Juie? Stern 6-12-1870
Seals, Corneleas to Ann Ward 3-13-1868 (3-14-1868)
Sellers, John H. to Ann Hatcher 1-17-1867
Sharp, James K. to Adelia J. Nance 4-7-1870
Shell, A. J. to L. F. Hammer 5-7-1878 (5-26-1878)
Shell, Aaron to Abby Shell 12-24-1853 (12-25-1853)
Shell, Aaron to Joanah Freese? 10-3-1874
Shell, Aaron to Joanah Miller 10-3-1874 (10-4-1874)
Shell, Alfred M. to Elizabeth Johnson 6-18-1866 (6-19-1866)
Shell, Alfred to Lucinda Deel 1-10-1854
Shell, Alvin P. to Barsha A. Range 1-24-1862 (1-30-1862)
Shell, Cane to Hannah Thompson 4-18-1859 (4-19-1859)
Shell, Elkanah to Catharine Toppins 10-4-1854
Shell, Findly to Jane Wilson 5-9-1852
Shell, H. F. to Rebecah Hopson 12-2-1877
Shell, Henderson J. to Sarah (Susah?) Wright 5-18-1871 (5-21-1871)
Shell, James E. to Cordelia Loudermilk 7-11-1874 (7-12-1874)
Shell, James to Martha Casper 10-3-1863 (10-4-1863)
Shell, James to Matilda Hampton 8-24-1874 (9-1-1874)
Shell, John A. to ____ McNabb ?-?-1871 (with spring)
Shell, John G. to Susan M. Angel 10-12-1865 (9?-19-1865)
Shell, John G. to Susanna E. Angell 10-12-1865 (10-19-1865)
Shell, Leonard to Jane Grindstaff 10-13-1871 (10-15-1871)
Shell, R. P. to Mary J. Luncey? 9-30-1865 (10-1-1865)
Shell, Robert P. to Mary J. Duncey 9-30-1865 (10-1-1865)
Shell, Samuel P. to Jane E. Taylor 6-12-1867 (6-13-1867)
Sherass?, W. B. to Hannah E. Harnett 2-28-1872
Shipley, William to Sarah E. McKinney 10-28-1871 (11-2-1871)
Shipley, William to Sarah E. McKiny 10-28-1871 (11-2-1871)
Shipley, William to Sarah E. McKiny? 3-28-1870

Shoun, John to Eliza J. Goodwin 5-23-1858
Shown, Frederik to Margaret Hardin 3-2-1872
Shown, John to Highly (Hilley) Campbell 3-13-1858 (3-14-1858)
Shown, William to Catharin Goodwin 2-25-1858 (3-4-1858)
Shuffield, Alfred to Mary A. Shuffield 7-14-1870 (7-15-1870)
Shuffield, Alfred to Mary L. Shuffield 7-4-1870 (7-16-1870)
Shuffield, Landon to Rebecca Heatherly 3-9-1878
Shuffield, W. S. to C. J. Gilber 12-26-1874 (12-27-1874)
Shuffield, Willey S. to C. J. Gillen 12-26-1874 (12-27-1874)
Shull, David H. to Martha Lewis 9-19-1865 (10-31-1865)
Shull, David H. to Martha Luner? 9-19-1865 (10-31-1865)
Silvers, Edmond to Edney Payne 5-25-1859
Silvers, Edmond to Emiline Payne 5-25-1859
Silvers, William J. to Sarah A. Patton 9-7-1859 (9-8-1859)
Simbs, Charley to Mary J. Mongumery 11-1-1878 (11-3-1878)
Simerely, Henry to Ellen Carlton 12-8-1860 (12-9-1860)
Simerliln, John to Mary A. Rulen 12-27-1857
Simerlin, John to Mary Ann Richie 12-27-1857 (12-17?-1857)
Simerly, Christly to Jane Matherly 9-11-1862
Simerly, David M. to Judah C. McKinney 12-30-1865 (1-1-1866)
Simerly, David to Judah McKinny 12-30-1865 (1-1-1866)
Simerly, George to Nancy Guinn 11-30-1868
Simerly, J. H. to Laura C. Campbell 11-2-1878 (11-3-1878)
Simerly, James to Nancy Blevins 12-4-1872 (12-5-1872)
Simerly, James to Nany? Blevins 12-4-1872 (12-9-1872)
Simerly, John M. to Allace T. Williams 10-6-1870
Simerly, John to Eliza C. Lipps 1-5-1865 (6-22-1865)
Simerly, John to Susan Oliver 5-2-1871
Simerly, N. G. T. to Molly C. Folsom 8-20-1876 (8-24-1876)
Simerly, N. T. to Janie Hodge 2-22-1873 (2-23-1873)
Simerly, N. T. to Mary J. Hodge 2-22-1873 (2-23-1873)
Simerly, William B. to Malinda Prichard 7-14-1862 (7-16-1862)
Simerly, William H. to Emaline Oak 2-15-1873 (2-16-1873)
Simerly, William to Margaret E. Hopson 5-18-1876 (7-8-1876)
Simmerly, John to Susanna Chambers 3-22-1850 (3-24-1850)
Simmerly, William B. to Matilda Prichard 7-14-1862 (7-16-1862)
Simmons, James M. to Jane Sharp 9-26-1866 (9-27-1866)
Simons, Lewis to Allace Cates 11-14-1871 (11-19-1871)
Sims, Henery to Sarah (Susannah) Gourley 8-1-1867 (8-4-1867)
Sims, Henry to Eliza J. Merrett 9-4-1878
Sims, Henry to Susanna J. Gourly 8-1-1867 (8-4-1867)
Sims, Jackson to Rachel Glover 6-24-1856
Sims, Jackson to Rachel Sims 6-24-1856
Sims, Jackson to Rachel Stover 6-2-1856
Sims, Thomas to Mary J. Crose? 3-13-1867 (3-14-1867)
Sizemore, Nathaniel to Emeline Merritt 7-25-1878 (7-28-1878)
Slage, Henry to Cynthia E. C. Sagle 8-26-1845
Slagle, Abner to L. J. Smith 1-8-1857
Slagle, Abner to Lucinda Ann Smith 1-8-1857 (1-15-1857)
Slagle, John W. to Nancy A. Holly 9-2-1865 (9-3-1865)
Slagle, Peter to Sarah J. Claymore 2-9-1856 (2-10-1856)
Slagler, John W. to Nancy A. Walling? 9-2-1865
Slimp, Thos. M. to Priscilla Turner 9-30-1865 (10-2-1865)
Smallin, A. B. to Lou V. Boy 9-13-1873
Smalling, Martin to Evelin Payne 1-30-1878
Smith, A. B. to Mary A. Bowman 4-23-1878 (4-22?-1878)
Smith, Alpheus? to Sarah A. Smith 11-9-1875
Smith, David H. M. to Sarah E. Smith 2-16-1878 (2-24-1878)
Smith, Elijah to Mary J. Stephens 10-4-1864 (10-15-1864)
Smith, Findley M. to Lorina T. Smith 12-7-1847 (11?-18-1847)
Smith, Geo. F. L. to Betty E. Vernon 6-10-1869
Smith, Geo. H. M. to Nancy? Hathaway 1-24-1877 (1-25-1877)
Smith, George to Jane Johnson 11-27-1859 (11-29-1859)
Smith, Guy to Jane Johnson 11-27-1859 (11-29-1859)
Smith, H. C. to Sarah G.? McIntosh 3-8-1876 (3-9-1876)
Smith, Hardin to Sarah A. Pharr 10-1-1859 (10-6-1859)
Smith, Henderson to Martha J. Mast 3-27-1866 (4-10-1866)
Smith, J. A. to C. A. Crockett 12-31-1877 (1-1-1878)
Smith, J. L. to Eva Campbell 11-20-1878
Smith, James L. to Eliza A. Lewis 4-5-1871 (4-9-1871)
Smith, James L. to Eliza Livers 4-5-1871 (4-9-1871)
Smith, James M. to Eliza J. Odell 7-12-1855 (7-15-1855)
Smith, James S. to Sarah Blevins 5-21-1859 (5-29-1859)
Smith, James to Ann J. Miller 9-17-1871 (9-19-1871)
Smith, John B. to Mary E. Steve 5-12-1875 (5-13-1875)
Smith, John B. to Mary E. Stover 5-12-1875 (5-13-1875)
Smith, John C. to Eve V. Tipton 12-22-1868
Smith, John H. to Eliza Jane Hamby 6-5-1865 (6-11-1865)
Smith, John W. to Delila Lows 1-5-1857 (1-8-1857)
Smith, John W. to Delilah Laws 1-5-1857 (1-8-1857)
Smith, John to Ann Bradley 10-25-1853
Smith, John to Matilda Johnson 2-13-1875
Smith, John to Molita Johnson 2-9-1875 (2-13-1875)
Smith, John to Nancy Glover 1-29-1851
Smith, John to Nancy Jobe 2-16-1865
Smith, John to Nancy Miller 1-24-1864
Smith, Joseph R. to Nancy J. Hacher 1-2-1873
Smith, Joseph R. to Nancy J. Hatcher 1-2-1873
Smith, Joseph to Sarah Baker 10-25-1860 (10-26-1860)
Smith, Nathanel T. to Mary A. Smith 11-12-1866 (11-22-1866)
Smith, Nathaniel T. to Mary Richardson 11-13-1867 (11-16-1867)
Smith, Robert A. to Elmira E. Roberts 7-22-1873 (9-22-1873)
Smith, Robert L. to Mary C. White 4-8-1866 (4-19-1866)
Smith, Samuel E. (T.?) to Phebe E. Crow 11-30-1858
Smith, Samuel to Phebe E. Crew 11-30-1858
Smith, W. H. M. to Nanie E. Range 3-10-1877 (3-22-1877)
Smith, William to Malinda Miller 5-28-1854 (5-29-1854)
Smith, Wm. B. C. to Lydia E. Barker 10-12-1865 (10-17-1865)
Smithpeter, Alphna to Mary C. Dugger 7-7-1857 (7-11-1857)
Snapp, Alfred to Polly Klux 4-6-1874 (4-9-1874)
Sneyd, Sith? to Martha Woodby 10-15-1853
Snider, Jacob to Nancy Hughes 1-7-1853 (1-13-1853)
Snider, Solomon B. to E. J. E. Buck 12-12-1869 (12-16-1869)
Snodgrass, C. G. to S. C.(E) McKehen 2-26-1875 (2-28-1875)
Snodgrass, Emery to Drusilla J. Brewer 2-6-1872 (7-7-1872)
Snodgrass, Emery to Loucille J. Brown 2-6-1872 (2-7-1872)
Snodgrass, John S. to Matilda Shell 8-21-1871
Snodgrass, T. Y. to Mattie E. Smith 3-6-1872
Snodgrass, Thomas Y. to Mollie C. Smith 3-6-1872
Soner?, Jackson to Eliza Lyon 3-20-1857 (3-21-1857)
Spears, John to Amy Fletcher 4-10-1852 (4-11-1852)
Spergin, Henry to Susan Waller 11-19-1878 (11-24-1878)
Stafford, Clayton R. to Mary Carrell 12-4-1856
Stafford, Clayton to Mary Camu? 12-11-1856 (12-24-1856?)
Stafford, Clayton to Mary Carrell 12-11-1856 (12-24-1856)
Stafford, Clayton to Mary Cassell 12-4-1856
Steffey, John W. to Margaret Fondern 6-24-1871 (6-25-1871)
Step, George O. to Martha Slagle 12-2-1873
Stephen, Michael to Fanny J. Morton 8-15-1866
Stephens, Charles to Susanna Gouge 8-11-1855 (8-12-1855)
Stephens, John to Elizabeth Stout 10-12-1865
Stephens, John to Elizabeth Street 10-10-1865 (10-12-1865)
Stephens, Michael to Fanny Jane Martin 8-5-1866 (8-15-1866)
Stephens, Welcom to Emily Dyar 8-30-1856
Stephens, William to Mary McKinney 3-24-1859 (3-?-1859)
Stepp, Geo. O. to Mollie E. Slagle 12-12-1873 (12-18-1873)
Stepp, James S. to Susan Fair 10-24-1877
Stepp, John W. to Eliza Barnes 6-18-1872 (6-26-1872)
Stern (Stover?), Isaac N. to Martha J. Hart 7-25-1869? (no return)
Stewaert, John to Elizabeth Church 11-14-1861 (11-15-1861)
Stout, Anderson R. to Julia A. Cassina 11-2-1877 (11-7-1877)
Stout, David to Lorena Hodges 3-30-1851 (3-23?-1851)
Stout, David to Lurana Hodge 3-3-1851 (3-23-1851)
Stout, Granvill W. to Martha C. Coble 10-19-1857
Stout, Granville W. to Martha C. Cable 10-19-1857
Stout, James to Sarah Cable 8-2-1867 (8-15-1867)
Stout, John to Edilin Perry 4-6-1866
Stout, Joseph R. to Sarah A. Heatherly 11-8-1876 (11-9-1876)
Stout, Kennedy to Cealy Ann Cole 1-9-1852 (6-13-1852)
Stout, Matison to Hannah Younce 7-25-1868 (7-26-1868)
Stout, Saml. to Adaw? Meridith 7-30-1875 (8-1-1875)
Stout, Vol to Margaret Morrell 2-6-1870
Stout, Volentin B. to Martha Morrell 2-6-1870
Stover, Alexander to Levicy Nave 7-21-1877 (7-22-1877)
Stover, Robert to Littitia Carter 5-28-1870 (6-1-1870)
Stover, Samuel to Mary C. McKiny 1-19-1871
Stover, Samuel to Mary J. McKinney 1-19-1871
Stover, William to Nancy N. Carriger 1-21-1856
Street, Jonathan to Eviline Stephens 11-8-1875 (11-11-1875)
Street, Samuel to Emily McKinney 12-16-1865

Street, Samul to Emily McKiney 12-16-1865
Struls?, James to Emeline Carr 1-12-1854 (6-15-1854)
Sullivan, George to Kenah Carriger 9-16-1871 (9-18-1871)
Swamer, Geo. W. to Amanda J. Keen 2-4-1856 (2-10-1856)
Swiney, Wesley to Lusinda Lacy 3-13-1861 (3-17-1861)
Swingle, Geo. W. to Elizabeth C. Hunt 9-12-1876
Tapp, William to Elizabeth Mayton 10-19-1850 (10-20-1850)
Tate, Andy to Nancy Gorman 10-7-1878 (10-27-1878)
Taylor, A. D. to Sally Cooper 6-8-1878 (8-15-1878)
Taylor, Alfred M. C. to Cornelia E. Tipton 7-22-1856 (7-24-1856)
Taylor, Allen to Cordelia Lewis 11-29-1878 (11-30-1878)
Taylor, Alvin to Sarah Markland 4-12-1862 (4-13-1862)
Taylor, Andrew to Hannah Shoemaker 11-30-1865
Taylor, Caswell C. to Frances T. Williams 11-21-1867
Taylor, David M. to Nancy J. Loudermilk 12-29-1866 (1-10-1867)
Taylor, David W. to Joanna Gourley 3-17-1862 (3-23-1862)
Taylor, David to Elizabeth J. Smith 3-1-1851 (4-3-1851)
Taylor, Edmond (Edward) to Harrett Baker 9-12-1866
Taylor, Edmond W. to Christena Foust 6-28-1856 (6-29-1856)
Taylor, Eli C. to Amanda C. Peters 12-19-1865
Taylor, Eli C. to Mandy Puden 12-19-1865
Taylor, G. W. to Levicy Elliott 7-6-1868 (7-13-1868)
Taylor, General Jackson to Hariet J. Combs 10-28-1856 (10-29-1856)
Taylor, General to Amanda Combs 1-2-1855
Taylor, Isaac N. to Catharin Berry 5-28-1859 (5-29-1859)
Taylor, Isaac N. to Catharine C. Berry 5-28-1859 (4?-29-1859)
Taylor, Isaac to Ellen Lawson 8-1-1863 (8-3-1863)
Taylor, Jacob P. to Malinda S. A. Cooper 7-16-1862 (7-27-1862)
Taylor, Jacob to Beloadory? White 10-3-1878 (10-4-1878)
Taylor, Jacob to Sarah Heatherly 6-17-1868 (6-20-1868)
Taylor, James L. to Saraphina Campbell 2-26-1875
Taylor?, James P. to Mary S. George 12-24-1865 (12-28-1865)
Taylor, James P. to Mary S. George 12-24-1865 (12-28-1865)
Taylor, James to Eveline Campbell 3-8-1867
Taylor, Jas. M. to Mary Peoples 11-3-1859
Taylor, John to Ellen Anderson 4-21-1877
Taylor, John to Loritia Pearce 11-13-1872 (11-15-1872)
Taylor, John to Lousa Taylor 3-29-1873 (3-30-1873)
Taylor, John to Permelia Hathaway 3-13-1872 (no return)
Taylor, Jon to Milli Pendeana? 11-1-1875
Taylor, Jonathan to Nancy A. Taylor 12-25-1869
Taylor, Landon C. to Fanny Love 10-8-1870
Taylor, Landon C. to Fanny Lowe 10-8-1870
Taylor, Levi to Emelin Peters 7-10-1875 (7-11-1875)
Taylor, Lewis D. to Elizabeth Reckey 3-2-1872 (3-3-1872)
Taylor, Lewis D. to Elizabeth Richie 3-2-1872 (3-3-1872)
Taylor, Luny B. to Eliza J. Wilson 8-30-1878 (9-4-1878)
Taylor, M. N. to Molley C. Stepp 8-3-1873 (9-2-1873)
Taylor, Mailer N. to Molley C. Stepp 8-30-1873 (9-2-1873)
Taylor?, Nathaniel W. to Harritt G. Jobe 9-13-1875
Taylor, Noah D. to Sarah J. Taylor 1-1-1856
Taylor, Robert C. to Margaret A. McLoud 4-15-1873 (4-16-1873)
Taylor, Robert R. to Margaret McLeod 4-15-1873 (4-16-1873)
Taylor, Rufus to Amanda Duffield 12-15-1876 (12-16-1876)
Taylor, S. M. to Celia A. Cole 10-28-1878 (10-30-1878)
Taylor, Samuel to Sarah Robertson 12-18-1871 (12-19-1871)
Taylor, Sion to Amanda J. Johnson 7-9-1850
Taylor, Thomas to Angeline Treasure 8-22-1856 (8-23-1856)
Taylor, Thomas to Angeline Frasure 8-22-1856
Taylor, Thomas to Lucinda Lowe 12-29-1877 (12-30-1877)
Taylor, W. A. to Ditha? Range 12-20-1875
Taylor, William to Elizabeth Culbert 12-28-1867 (12-29-1867)
Taylor, William to Mary Caman 10-2-1873 (no return) B
Taylor, Wm. H. to Sarah J. Williams 4-4-1860 (4-5-1860)
Teague, W. A. to Nancy Bowlin 1-26-1879
Tener, Alexander to Caroline Hampton 1-1-1870 (1-16-1870)
Terrin, Henry T. to Julia Mastin 7-24-1869 (7-25-1869)
Thomas, Samuel to Elizabeth Young 12-28-1866
Thomas, Strawberry to Modena Whitehead 10-19-1865 (12-26-1865)
Thomas, Treg to Jane Brown 11-13-1867 B
Thomas, William S. to Jane Farr 11-12-1870
Thomas, Wm. S. to Jane Fair 11-12-1870
Thompson, Samuel to Sarah Jane Emmert 3-13-1866 (3-18-1866)
Tilson, Nathanel F.? Y. to Rhoda A. Vanhulser 11-18-1869 (11-20-1869)

Tinen, William J. to Sarah C. Williams 10-15-1868
Tinnen?, John to _____ 12-31-1872
Tipton, George to Elizabeth Campbell 12-27-1870 B
Tipton, Joseph P. to Susan E. Carden 6-22-1852 (6-24-1852)
Tipton, Saml. A. to N. J. Crumley 8-5-1853 (8-7-1853)
Tipton, Samuel to Nancy Long 7-25-1824 (7-27-1824)
Tipton, Thomas J. to Allice P. Coffman 5-10-1875 (5-11-1875)
Tipton, W. S. to Sarah Stover 11-15-1870
Tolly, Daniel to Rebecca Whitehead 4-28-1864 (5-7-1864)
Tolly, Francis to Sarah Griffin 8-1-1872
Tolsom, William H. to Loyett S. Helton 12-2-1865 (12-12-1865)
Tolson?, N. T. Y. to Rhoda A. Overhulser 11-18-1869 (11-20-1870)
Toncray, A. R. to Sarah Smith 12-30-1872
Toncray, Charles P. to Margaret L. Williams 3-9-1859
Toncray, William J. to Sarah C. Williams 10-15-1868
Toney, Jesse to Sabina McNabb 1-10-1857 (1-15-1857)
Toney, Wm. to Evelina Price 1-25-1855
Toppens, George to Eliza J. Williams 9-20-1864
Townsend, John G. to Jane Hill 4-17-1866 (4-19-1866)
Townson, James D. to Marah Townson 4-13-1878
Treadway, Jacob F. to Cathan Collins 2-10-1866 (2-11-1866)
Treadway, John B. to Mary Smith 11-22-1877 (11-24-1877)
Treadway, John H. to Mary M. Pugh 9-23-1868
Treadway, Jonathan H. to Mary Ann Gourley 3-28-1878 (4-21-1878)
Treadway, Lilbern to Mary L. Bowers 11-17-1850
Treadway, Morgan to Jane Pagin (Pugh) 2-19-1867
Treadway, Robert to Eva Chrisly 9-3-1872 (9-4-1872)
Treadway, Robert to Evelin Crumley 9-3-1872 (9-4-1872)
Treadway, William H. to Sarah E. Pugh 6-20-1866 (6-24-1866)
Treadway, William to Delila Potter 3-3-1867 (3-30-1867)
Trivet, James W. to Luisey Church 4-13-1878 (4-18-1878)
Troanner, Amon to Catharine Banks 2-19-1853 (2-?-1853)
Troxell, William to Emalin Floyd 8-19-1865
Troxwell, Jas. to Sarah Spears 12-25-1876 (12-27-1876)
Truman, John to Susana Armey 12-31-1872 (1-5-1873)
Trusler, James to Caraline Arwood 10-10-1858
Trusler, James to Patsy Arawood 4-5-1864 (4-7-1864)
Trusler, Joseph to Mary Arwood 9-5-1860 (9-14-1860)
Trusler, Lewis to Martha Arwood 2-16-1867
Turin?, John A. to Mary Angell 11-29-1865
Turner, Henry T. to Julia Mastin 7-24-1869 (7-25-1869)
Turner, John A. to Mary Angel 11-29-1865 (11-28?-1865)
Turner, Solomon to Mary Darnel 6-24-1860
Umphrey, Young to Eliza Chamber 8-15-1855 (9-16-1855)
Usry, jr., Thomas to Sarah Walker 6-6-1856
Vance, Abner to Mary Whitehead 4-17-1853 (4-24-1853)
Vance, John H. to Mary Ann Willcox 8-2-1859 (8-10-1859)
Vance, John to Rinda Mosley 4-19-1850 (4-24-1850)
Vanconer?, Jno. L. to Cathern A. Kennick 11-22-1875 (11-25-1875)
Vandeventer, J. P. to Nancy J. Buckle 5-30-1870 (6-2-1870)
Vandeventer, Joseph P. to Nancy J. Buckles 5-30-1870 (6-2-1870)
Vanhuss, Thomas D. to Elvinah Campbell 8-7-1851
Vaughn, Benjamin to Fany Garland 11-4-1871 (11-6-1871)
Vaughn, William to Charlott Stewart 8-21-1875 (8-26-1875)
Vaughn, Wm. A. to Clementine Carr 9-29-1873
Vaught, Jonah to Julia Barber 3-23-1873 B
Vest, Archibald A. to Nancy A. Jackson 7-10-1867 (7-11-1867)
Vest, William to Cathrine Emmit 3-27-1871 (3-24?-1871)
Waggoner, Joseph L. to Louisa C. Smith 9-17-1866 (9-20-1866)
Wagoner, David to Catharine Wagoner 6-12-1879
Wagoner, Jas. to Martilia Voncanon 9-5-1877 (9-10-1877)
Walery, P. L. to Hannah Irick 9-7-1869
Walin, Wm. H. to Nancy Blevins 10-1-1870 (10-2-1870)
Walker, John P. to Mary C. Simery? 10-23-1867 (10-31-1867)
Walker, John P. to Mary C. Swiney (Swinney) 10-23-1867 (10-31-1867)
Walker, John S. to Martha J. Sanders 10-19-1868
Walker, Joseph to Mary Jane Lyon 12-4-1877 (12-5-1877)
Ward, Andrew J. to Nancy Yarbrough 12-13-1851 (1-11-1852)
Ward, John to Rachel Ervin 9-16-1871 B
Ward, William C. to Nancy L. Greenvill 10-15-1864 (10-16-1864)
Ward, Wm. C. to Nancy R. Grenwell 10-15-1864 (10-16-1864)
Warren, John N. to Mary Arwood 10-27-1868 (11-1-1868)
Warren, John to Joanna Morton 10-23-1866 (11-1-1866)
Washam, William J. to Mary P. Buckles 8-30-1876 (9-10-1877)

Water, P. L. to Hannah Irick 9-7-1869
Waters, William H. to Nancy Blevins 10-1-1870 (10-2-1870)
Watson, John to Rachel Robertson 11-29-1850 (12-1-1850)
Weaver, David to Hester A. Carr 12-26-1877 (12-18?-1877)
Weaver, Russell to Susan E. Lewis 4-18-1878
Webb, A. H. to Mary F. McCulloch 5-28-1877
Webb, Patrick H. to Phebe Roberts 5-12-1858 (5-13-1858)
Webb, Rodney A. to Mary McKorkle 12-21-1857 (12-24-1857)
Werley, Joseph to Margaret P. Brown 3-13-1871 (3-21-1871)
West, Hampton to Rachel A. Overhulser 9-5-1866 (9-9-1866)
West, Jackson to Susan Jones 6-6-1870
West, Jackson to Susanna _____ 6-6-1870
West, James to Sarah Arwood 7-22-1858 (7-25-1858)
West, John to Jane Nave 5-8-1870
West, William to Martha J. Overhulser 10-1-1866 (10-2-1866)
West, William to Rebecca Day 12-23-1870 (12-25-1870)
Whaley, A. H. to Marret Clemons 6-3-1862 (6-8-1862)
Whisenhunt, Adam to Lousanda Watson 12-30-1852
Whisenhunt, Noah to Loucinda Roberts 5-5-1873 (5-6-1873)
White, A. C. to Laura Perkins 12-14-1877 (12-20-1877)
White, David W. to Malicia C. Smith 9-21-1866 (9-23-1866)
White, Geo. to Mary Buckles 9-22-1866 (9-28-1866)
White, Isaac to Easther Pearce 5-12-1866 (5-13-1866)
White, Isaac to Esther Reese 5-12-1866 (5-13-1866) B
White, James L. to Julia Lewis 4-27-1859
White, James L. to Julian S. Lewis? 4-27-1859
White, James L. to Rhoda E. Stout 11-27-1864 (12-7-1864)
White, James to Mary Shuffield 11-26-1862 (12-8-1862)
White, John V. to Jane Lewis 7-26-1872 (8-4-1872)
White, R. C. to Elizabeth Kendall 3-21-1861 (3-24-1861)
White, Richard L. to Belvedora White 1-3-1867
White, Richard to M. J. Shuffield 5-25-1877 (5-27-1877)
White, Robert to Julia Blevins 8-23-1877
White, Thos. C. to Mary A. Smith 8-9-1862 (8-14-1862)
Whitehead, Andrew to Mary Lunsford 4-7-1871 (4-23-1871)
Whitehead, Andrew to Susanna Meridith 3-25-1858 (4-1-1858)
Whitehead, Caleb to Cordelia Howell 3-13-1871
Whitehead, David A. to Margaret Whitehead 11-19-1869
Whitehead, Jas. H. to Julia Cates 2-2-1874 (2-8-1874)
Whitehead, Jas. M. to Sarah Carver 2-12-1868 (2-16-1868)
Whitehead, Jas. to Sarah Chambers 2-2-1852 (1?-4-1852)
Whitehead, John to Nancy A.(E?) Snider 12-4-1857 (10?-4-1857)
Whitehead, John to Nancy Allen 7-13-1866
Whitehead, Landon to Elizabeth Hicks 5-27-1858 (1-28-1859)
Whitehead, Thomas to Hannah Whitehead 11-6-1867
Whitehead, Thomas to Hannah Whitehead 8-9-1867 (8-6?-1867)
Whitehead, Thos. to Sarah A. Whitehead 12-15-1860 (12-21-1860)
Whitehead, Thos. to Sarah Ann Whitehead 12-12-1860 (12-21-1860)
Whitehead, William C. to Nancy E. Smith 3-26-1858 (3-28-1858)
Whitehead, William to Margaret Miller 11-4-1854 (11-16-1854)
Whitehead, Wm. C. to Modena Perry 12-30-1857 (1-1-1858)
Whitemore, Thos. B. to Mary E. Robertson 7-17-18661 (7-25-1861)
Whithead, Caleb to Caroline Carrell 3-13-1871
Whithead, James H. to Julia Kales 2-2-1874 (2-8-1874)
Whithead, John to Nancy Allen 7-13-1866
Whitson, Jesse to Elizabeth McConnel 8-7-1820 (8-10-1820)
Whittemore, Robt. to Hannah Smith 8-31-1855 (9-31?-1855)
Wigon, Joseph L. to Louisa E. Smith 9-17-1866 (9-20-1866)
Wilbern, Samul to Margaret Connor 11-6-1870
Wilburn, J. P. to Margaret H. Wishler(Willis) 1-25-1859
Wilburn, J. P. to Mary (Margaret) H. Westick 1-25-1859 (1-26-1859)
Wilcox(son), James to Rebecca Wilson 9-4-1857
Wilcox, Caleb to Elizabeth Shell 10-3-1857 (10-26-1857)
Wilcox, Cobb (Caleb?) to Elizabeth Shell 10-2-1857 (10-29-1857)
Wilcox, John M. to Margret Baker 12-2-1865 (1-16-1866)
Wilcox, John W. to Margaret Barker 12-2-1865 (1-16-1866)
Wilhight, Daniel to Susanna Greer 3-29-1851 (4-1-1851)
Wilkerson, William to Mary Stafford 10-20-1867 (10-21-1867)
Willhight, Emanuel to Catharin Greer 5-5-1851 (6-1-1851)
Willialms, James M. to Elizabeth Phillips 12-30-1864 (1-8-1865)
Willialms, William A. to Joanna Bowers 12-23-1868 (12-27-1868)
William, Isaac to Delrey W. Manis 11-26-1870 (12-11-1870)
Williams, A. F. to Eliza A. Garrison 7-2-1860 (7-8-1860)
Williams, Albert P. to Susanna Cross 9-21-1850 (9-22-1850)
Williams, Alford to Leanory Gourly 1-13-1857

Williams, Alfred M. to Elizabeth C. Peters 10-18-1873 (10-19-1873)
Williams, Alfred M. to Mary E. Peters 10-18-1873 (10-19-1873)
Williams, Archibald to Sarah E. Hyder 8-14-1858 (8-16-1858)
Williams, Arther A. to Sarah J. Buckles 10-8-1865 (10-12-1865)
Williams, Christian to Elizabeth Fair 7-24-1856
Williams, Christian to Elizabeth Farr 7-24-1856
Williams, David to Fanny Love 3-5-1873 (4-13-1873)
Williams, E. D. to Silpha McCaslin 4-22-1871 (8-4-1871)
Williams, Elihu J. to Mary E. Pearce 12-30-1868 (12-31-1868)
Williams, Elijah D. to Alpha McCarthin? 4-22-1871 (8-24-1871)
Williams, Frank to Elizabeth Peoples 1-26-1875
Williams, Frank to Elizabeth Peoples 1-26-1875 (no return)
Williams, Geo. to Mariah Sharp 3-15-1866 B
Williams, George T. to Nancy S. (Nannie) Barker 10-9-1869
Williams, Harvey R. to Cathran Combs? 9-28-1877 (9-29-1877)
Williams, Isaac to Delray Taylor 11-26-1870 (12-11-1870)
Williams, J. D. to Nancy C. Elliott 9-22-1855 (9-27-1855)
Williams, James H. to Margaret M. Buckles 5-29-1866 (6-7-1866)
Williams, John to Caroline Clark 7-31-1851
Williams, Jonathan to Louisa Olliver 11-29-1855 (11-30-1855)
Williams, Joseph to Eliza Sayler 10-28-1872 (10-28-1872)
Williams, Josiah to Mary E. Eller 10-11-1875 (10-13-1875)
Williams, Montgomery T. to Margaret Payne 10-19-1850 (10-23-1850)
Williams, Nathaniel T. to Martha Daniel 1-29-1859 (2-2-1859)
Williams, Pleasant to Ann J. Headrick 11-20-1868 (11-22-1868)
Williams, Pleast. to Sally Grace 1-22-1876
Williams, Robt. B. to Martha J. McKorkle 3-3-1861 (3-28-1861)
Williams, Rufus K. to Eliza Jane Garland 1-19-1856
Williams, Rusell to Sarah C. Grindstaff 4-4-1870 (4-6-1870)
Williams, Samuel W. H. to Edna Miller 2-13-1862
Williams, Samuel to Rachal A. C. Pugh 4-10-1855 (4-?-1855)
Williams, Thomas E. to Charlotie Hodge 12-23-1874 (12-24-1874)
Williams, Thomas to Nancy J. Peters 8-17-1878
Williams, William A. to Janna Bower 12-23-? (12-27-1868)
Williams, William to Phebe Lovelace 4-?-1861 (4-14-1861)
Williams, Wm. D. to Crisa Blevins 3-9-1875
Wills, Willis to Sarah Watts 10-13-1852 (10-14-1852)
Wilson, Abraham to Nancy C. Elliott 11-14-1853
Wilson, Andrew J. to Mary A. Bowers 11-23-1856 (no return)
Wilson, Andrew J. to Nancy Ann Wilson 12-31-1857 (1-3-1858)
Wilson, B. C. to Louisa A. Pearce 10-24-1866 (10-28-1866)
Wilson, Daniel A. to Harriet E. Mullins 1-10-1854
Wilson, Daniel to Mary Demkin 8-15-1850
Wilson, David to Eliza Heatherly 12-20-1878 (12-24-1878)
Wilson, Emanuel to Ellen Slagle 9-4-1867
Wilson, Geo. W. to Mary Minton 12-24-1866
Wilson, James to Emeline Curtice 8-5-1861 (8-6-1861)
Wilson, James to Mary Carden 3-12-1856 (3-13-1856)
Wilson, James to Mary J. Blevins 10-8-1865
Wilson, John to Ellen T. A. Kinally 9-23-1847
Wilson, John to S. A. Dinzymore 7-27-1877 (?-?-1877)
Wilson, R. D. to Mary L. Fritso? 9-7-1872
Wilson, Solomon to Sarefina Cole 2-7-1874 (4-22-1874)
Wilson, Thomas H. to Sarafina Grindstaff 11-12-1864
Wilson, William to Sarah Waters 1-26-1858 (1-28-1858)
Winter, Stephen to Elizabeth Grage? 2-20-1852 (4-9-1852)
Winters, James to Eliza Jane Smith 12-31-1877
Winters, John to Catharin Crusman 10-26-1857 (10-29-1857)
Winters, John to Catharn Crosmon 10-26-1857 (10-29-1857)
Winters, John to Nancy Crusmon 10-26-1857 (10-29-1857)
Wishon, John to Celia Neatherland 1-10-1878 (12-16-1878)
Wishorn, John to Elizabeth Hicks 2-26-1879 (3-2-1879)
Woodby, Hesekiah to Elizabeth Brumit 7-14-1862 (7-15-1862)
Woodby, Jeremiah to Mary J. Chambers 9-18-1857 (9-27-1857)
Woodby, Lewis to Nancy Sloan 4-18-1855
Woodby, William to Lavicy Bennett 4-18-1856 (4-26-1856)
Woodley, James to Susanna Honeycut 3-16-1849 (3-18-1849)
Woods, Isaac to Rachel Fraser 9-28-1858 (no return)
Woods, Isaac to Rachel Frasier 9-28-1858
Woods, James to Amanda Carr 5-12-1877 (5-13-1877)
Woods, Levi to Mary A. Helton 9-3-1855 (9-6-1855)
Woods, Thomas to Mary Nediffer 12-2-1873 (12-5-1873)
Woods, Thomas to Mary Nidifer 12-2-1873 (12-5-1873)
Wrley, Joseph A. to Margaret E. Brown 3-13-1871 (3-21-1871)
Wygal, James S. to Nancy J. Fannin 12-9-1867 (11?-9-1867)

Young, Alfred to Viney Folsom 4-6-1867
Young, Henry to Deannah White 2-3-1869 (2-4-1869)
Young, John to Allace E. Patton 12-26-1860
Young, Joseph B. to Susanna J. Patton 1-2-1864 (1-2-1865)

Abner, Levicy to Isaac Nidifer 4-24-1868 (5-3-1868)
Adkins, Matilda to John Curten 2-16-1869 (2-8?-1869)
Agner, Sefrona to Healy Laws 9-5-1877
Akins, Emeline to Jonathan Poland 3-14-1874 (3-15-1874)
Akner, Cambe? to Jonathan Pollero? 3-14-1874 (3-15-1874)
Alfred, Isey to Abraham Bowers 6-22-1868
Allen, Nancy to John Whitehead 7-13-1866
Allen, Nancy to John Whitehead 7-13-1866
Ambrose, Sarah Ann to Joseph B. Loveless 6-4-1855 (6-7-1855)
Ambrous, Sarah J. to Joseph Lovless 6-4-1855 (6-5-1855)
Ambrouse, Sarah Jane to Joseph Lovless 6-7-1855
Anders, Elizabeth to Isaac N. Brown 8-21-1866
Anderson, Dicey to Valentine Garland 10-21-1871 (10-22-1871)
Anderson, Elender to Alexander Pearson 10-26-1867
Anderson, Eliza Ann to Kinchuls Carden 11-6-1861 (11-7-1861)
Anderson, Elizabeth to Daniel Campbell 4-28-1855 (4-29-1855)
Anderson, Ellen to John Taylor 4-21-1877
Anderson, Martha to Michael P. Elliott 10-6-1866 (10-18-1866)
Anderson, Mary E. to Ebanna W. McInturff 12-28-1871 (12-29-1871)
Anderson, Mary E. to Elcana W. McInturff 12-28-1871 (12-29-1871)
Anderson, Mary E. to Elcana W. McInturff 12-28-1871 (12-31-1871)
Anderson, Mary to Peter Bowen 8-6-1866
Anderson, Mary to Telir? Bowers? 8-6-1866
Anderson, Rhoda A. E. to Joseph Morrell (Murrell?) 9-14-1856 (9-24-1856)
Anderson, Sarah to Clemmons Reed 4-25-1854
Anderson, Thereby A. to Geo. W. Creed 12-31-1861
Anderson, Viney to William Garland 6-14-1873 (6-15-1873)
Andrews, Sarah to Alexander Davis 11-24-1862
Andrews, Viney to Wm. Garitain? 6-14-1873 (6-15-1873)
Andrews?, Viney to William Garlan 6-14-1873
Angel, Martha J. to William Jordon 8-31-1854
Angel, Mary to John A. Turner 11-29-1865 (11-28?-1865)
Angel, Susan M. to John G. Shell 10-12-1865 (9?-19-1865)
Angell, Ann M. to John W. Ellis 5-21-1857
Angell, Florence? to James Jackson ?-?-1875 (with spring)
Angell, Mary to John A. Turin? 11-29-1865
Angell, Susanna E. to John G. Shell 10-12-1865 (10-19-1865)
Angle, Ann M. to John W. Ellis 5-21-1857
Arawood, Elenor to James Forest 3-9-1854
Arawood, Patsy to James Trusler 4-5-1864 (4-7-1864)
Armey, Susana to John Truman 12-31-1872 (1-5-1873)
Arnell, Mary to William Arance 1-1-1876
Arnett, Matilda to William Grag 12-6-1872 (12-8-1872)
Arnold, Ann B. to Lewis Freeman 3-7-1853
Arnold, Catherin to Enoch Duncan 6-22-1850
Arnold, Docia D. to Joseph R. Cole 9-22-1864 (9-24-1864)
Arnold, Margaret to James Richardson 9-12-1866 (9-17-1866)
Arnold, Martha A. to A. B. Fincanon 3-4-1878 (3-7-1878)
Arnold, Mary to Vaught Reasor 1-9-1854 (1-28-1854)
Arnold, Rebecca to William L. Estep 2-23-1869 (2-26-1869)
Arwood, Alvina to Harison Bowman 7-16-1868
Arwood, Caraline to James Trusler 10-10-1858
Arwood, Eliza Jane to Joseph Bowman 5-1-1865
Arwood, Josephine to W. H. Jenkins 2-20-1879 (2-25-1879)
Arwood, Martha to Lewis Trusler 2-16-1867
Arwood, Mary to John N. Warren 10-27-1868 (11-1-1868)
Arwood, Mary to Joseph Trusler 9-5-1860 (9-14-1860)
Arwood, Sarah to James West 7-22-1858 (7-25-1858)
Arwood, Slavica? to Harrison Bowman 7-16-1868
Asher, Lourana to William H. Elliott 7-15-1868 (7-21-1868)
Auder, Elizabeth to Isaac N. Brown 8-21-1866
Badget, Nancy Ann to Preston W. Murphy 5-20-1852
Badgett, Sarah to D. L. Miller 4-20-1856
Bailey, Myrey R. to Grover B. Maberry 2-19-1855
Bailley, Darkus to Israel McInturff 3-6-1850 (3-7-1850)
Baker, Caroline to David Kaner (Keener) 12-21-1875 (12-23-1875)
Baker, Harrett to Edmond (Edward) Taylor 9-12-1866
Baker, Judy to Charles Grindstaff 11-20-1860 (11-24-1860)
Baker, Lovenia to James P. Noris 9-18-1857 (9-27-1857)
Baker, Margret to John M. Wilcox 12-2-1865 (1-16-1866)
Baker, Mildred to J. B. Guardner 10-21-1845 (11-20-1845)
Baker, Nancy to John Harris 5-8-1872
Baker, Sarah Ann to Mordica February 7-10-1857
Baker, Sarah to Joseph Smith 10-25-1860 (10-26-1860)
Baker, Susan to Jonathan B. Garland 2-1-1869
Ballard, Nancy to Hyram Hall 9-26-1850
Ballinger, Tewanda to William P. Badgett 12-31-1851
Bank, Fanney to Henry Hicks 4-2-1869
Banks, Catharine to Amon Troanner 2-19-1853 (2-?-1853)
Banks, Evelin to John W. Berry 10-30-1874 (11-1-1874)
Banks, Fanny to Henry Hicks 4-1-1869 (4-2-1869)
Banner, Susan to Henderson Bridget 8-4-1869
Barber, Julia to Jonah Vaught 3-23-1873 B
Barker, Lydia E. to Wm. B. C. Smith 10-12-1865 (10-17-1865)
Barker, Margaret to John W. Wilcox 12-2-1865 (1-16-1866)
Barker, Nancy S. (Nannie) to George T. Williams 10-9-1869
Barne, Rebeca to Henry Maple 4-25-1865 (4-29-1865)
Barnes, Eliza to John W. Stepp 6-18-1872 (6-26-1872)
Barnes, Lue (Luisa) to John Lilley 1-16-1876
Barnett, Martha Ann to Andrew E. Bishop 3-12-1865
Barrett, Martha E. to Andrew E. Bishop 3-12-1865
Bartee, Evaline to Daniel Elliott 6-29-1878 (6-30-1878)
Beagles, Mary C. to Elbert? H. Range 9-27-1852 (9-30-1852)
Beats?, Martha to Jas. Hatcher 12-25-1874
Beck, Elizabeth to J. M. Deloach 1-4-1879 (1-5-1879)
Beekin, Ellen to Simon League 5-28-1867 (5-29-1867)
Beener?, Jane to Alfred Benet 3-31-1864
Bell, Jane to Greenberry Burlerson (Burlison) 11-27-1868 (11-29-1868)
Bell, Sarah to Elisha Garland 2-26-1875 (3-4-1875)
Benfield, Matilda to A. H. Owen 3-9-1871
Bennett, Lavicy to William Woodby 4-18-1856 (4-26-1856)
Berry, Catharin to Isaac N. Taylor 5-28-1859 (5-29-1859)
Berry, Catharine C. to Isaac N. Taylor 5-28-1859 (4?-29-1859)
Berry, Elener to Leander Berry 8-12-1850 (8-15-1850)
Berry, Eliza to Daniel S. Bowers 12-24-1867 (12-31-1867)
Berry, Elizabeth Jane to James D. Lewis 6-9-18785 (6-10-1875)
Berry, Elizabeth to James Edens 2-11-1850 (2-12-1850)
Berry, Elizzie J. to James C. Lewis 6-9-1875 (6-10-1875)
Berry, Evelina to Rheuben Peters 11-29-1853
Berry, Lousea J. to W. C. Hunt 6-26-1855 (6-28-1855)
Berry, Mary Ann to Wilson Grindstaff 10-14-1860
Berry, Sarah E. to Henderson M. Folsom 9-29-1855 (9-30-1855)
Berry, Sarah to Samuel N. Nave 1-20-1869 (1-21-1869)
Berry, Winey to Robert Buckles 1-15-1851 (1-19-1851)
Bishop, Ann Eliza to Lenard A. Bowers 8-6-1856
Bishop, Ann Eliza to Leonard A. Bowers 8-6-1856
Bishop, Elizabeth to Alfred C. Peters 7-12-1863 (7-13-1863)
Bishop, Margaret to William Cashaday 7-13-1861 (7-15-1861)
Bishop, Margaret to William Cassada 7-13-1861 (7-15-1861)
Bishop, Martha J. to Joseph Bashor 6-21-1858 (6-24-1858)
Bishop, Martha Jane to Joseph Barker 6-21-1858 (6-24-1858)
Bishop, Mary D. to Silas M. Riche? 12-31-1867 (1-2-1868)
Bishop, Mary D. to Silas M. Rucker 12-27-1867 (1-2-1868)
Bishop, Sarafina to James M. Hickey 10-21-1850 (10-24-1850)
Bishop, Sarafinah to Robert A. Berry 9-14-1877 (9-18-1877)
Blevins, Ann to Michael Campbell 5-29-1871
Blevins, Carnelia to John Elliott 9-20-1876 (10-1-1876)
Blevins, Crisa to Wm. D. Williams 3-9-1875
Blevins, Della Cathern to Nepolion B. Creed 3-11-1876 (3-12-1876)
Blevins, Elizabeth to Peter Phipps 11-7-1865 (11-8-1865)
Blevins, Fanny to Elijah Richardson 4-10-1861 (4-11-1861)
Blevins, Julia to Robert White 8-23-1877
Blevins, Lavica to Isaac Nidiffer 4-14-1868 (5-3-1868)
Blevins, Louisa to Robert More 2-15-1853 (2-16-1853)
Blevins, Martha L. to Carac N. Ritchie 12-9-1876 (12-10-1876)
Blevins, Martha to Jas. Hatcher 12-25-1874
Blevins, Mary C. to Andrew Fletcher 6-21-1860
Blevins, Mary E. to Andrew Fletcher 6-21-1860
Blevins, Mary E. to Andrew Fletcher 6-?-1860 (6-21-1860)
Blevins, Mary J. to James Wilson 10-8-1865
Blevins, Mary Jane to Frank Hinkle 11-7-1877 (11-9-1877)
Blevins, Mary to Wm. Garland 1-22-1855 (1-27-1855)
Blevins, Mary to Wm. Miller 12-16-1855
Blevins, Matilda to Allen Hurley? 10-23-1867 (10-25-1867)
Blevins, Nancy to James Simerly 12-4-1872 (12-5-1872)
Blevins, Nancy to Landon Heatherly 2-28-1855 (2-29-1855)
Blevins, Nancy to William H. Waters 10-1-1870 (10-2-1870)
Blevins, Nancy to Wm. H. Walin 10-1-1870 (10-2-1870)

Blevins, Nany? to James Simerly 12-4-1872 (12-9-1872)
Blevins, Sarah to Daniel S. Crow 10-4-1871
Blevins, Sarah to James S. Smith 5-21-1859 (5-29-1859)
Blue, Blany to William Ensor 3-9-1875 (no return)
Bolem?, Maria to Alexander Johnson 12-21-1875 (12-22-1875)
Bolen, Marier to Alexander Johnson 12-21-1875 (12-22-1875)
Bolen, Myrey Ann to James D. Humphreys 9-28-1870 (9-29-1870)
Bolin, ---- to J. D. Humphrey 9-28-1870
Bolliln, Martha to Georg Miller 5-31-1865 (6-3-1865)
Borders?, Allice to Landon Marshall 3-1-1875
Boren, Emiline E. to J. E. Rowe 12-31-1859 (1-1-1860)
Boren, M. E. to J. E. Rowe 12-31-1859 (1-1-1860?)
Bowen, Margaret J. to John C. Carriger 9-25-1876 (9-26-1876)
Bowen, Mary L. to William A. Bowen 6-16-1858 (6-17-1858)
Bowen, Molly T. to Edward T. Heaton 5-18-1874 (5-26-1874)
Bowen, Nancy L. to Jackson Grindstaff 5-8-1866 (5-14-1866)
Bower, Janna to William A. Williams 12-23-? (12-27-1868)
Bowers, Aneliza to B. H. Peters 3-14-1866
Bowers, Elizabeth to Daniel S. Nave 3-15-1860 (3-18-1860)
Bowers, Ellen to John Hardin 10-8-1866 (10-10-1866)
Bowers, Emeline to Isaac N. Bowers 3-8-1876
Bowers, Joanna to William A. Willialms 12-23-1868 (12-27-1868)
Bowers, Margaret E. to Moses P. Roberson 12-?-1865 (12-14-1865)
Bowers, Margaret E. to Moses P. Robertson 12-?-1865 (12-14-1865)
Bowers, Mary A. to Andrew J. Wilson 11-23-1856 (no return)
Bowers, Mary E. to Alexander Lacy 1-10-1870 (1-16-1870)
Bowers, Mary E. to Alexander Long 1-10-1870 (1-16-1870)
Bowers, Mary L. to Lilbern Treadway 11-17-1850
Bowers, Mary L. to William A. Bowers 6-16-1858 (6-17-1858)
Bowers, Matilda to James Deloach 4-17-1877
Bowers, Mollie T. to Edward T. Heaton 5-18-1874 (5-24-1874)
Bowers, Nancy L. to Jackson Grindstaff 5-8-1866 (5-14-1866)
Bowers, Rebecah J. to John W. Jones 12-17-1859
Bowers, Ruthy Adaline to Isaac B. Buckles 2-28-1866 (3-2-1866)
Bowers, S. E. to Elisha Collins 10-26-1854 (10-26-1854)
Bowers, Virginia to Jackson Pearce 1-19-1878 (1-20-1878)
Bowlen, Mira to Wesley Blevins 4-8-1867 (4-11-1867)
Bowlin, Nancy to W. A. Teague 1-26-1879
Bowman, Ann to William Keane 8-1-1860 (8-2-1860)
Bowman, Elizabeth L. to Nathanel T. Haynes 7-12-1865 (7-13-1864?)
Bowman, Harriett to Francis C. Coleman 2-20-1877 (2-27-1877)
Bowman, Levina E. to Nathanl. Haynes? 7-12-1864 (7-13-1864)
Bowman, Louvina to George Bowman 11-14-1870 (11-15-1870)
Bowman, Lucinda C. to Wm. G. Anderson 7-5-1870
Bowman, Mary A. to A. B. Smith 4-23-1878 (4-22?-1878)
Bowman, Mary A. to G. W. Lynvill 9-24-1870
Bowman, Mary to Nathan Honycut 3-23-1873
Bowman, Roda E. to John Loudymilk 9-30-1858
Bowman, Rody E. to John Loudermilk 9-30-1858
Bowman, Sarahfina to Emanul McInturff 9-30-1873
Boy, Lou V. to A. B. Smallin 9-13-1873
Boyd, Ellen to Thos. A. R. Nelson 3-20-1857
Boyd, Ellenor to Thomas A. R. Nelson 3-21-1858 (3-22-1858)
Boyd, Emily to Isaac Grindstaff 8-5-1834
Boyd, Mary A. to William V. Bell 3-1-1860
Bradley, Ann to John Smith 10-25-1853
Bradley, Delia to William A. Carter 6-15-1875
Branch, Mary to John Brumit 4-18-1872 (4-19-1872)
Branch, Susan to William Brumit 8-26-1875
Branch, Susan to William Brummet 8-26-1875
Brett, Serana to William Blum 3-4-1870 (3-24-1870)
Brewer, Drusilla J. to Emery Snodgrass 2-6-1872 (7-7-1872)
Brewer, Evaline M. to James H. Neal 9-23-1852
Brewer, Martha to Abraham Rhodes 2-22-1860
Britt, Caroline to John C. Carrell 1-15-1856
Britt, Edana to Powell Philips 5-17-1862 (5-22-1862)
Britt, Eliza to Alford L. Grindstaff 8-15-1874 (8-24-1874)
Britt, Harriet E. to Nathaniel T. Peoples 1-18-1879 (1-19-1879)
Britt, Jane to David Britt 2-6-1855
Britt, Mary to John Moon 9-2-1858
Britt, Serana to William Blevins 3-4-1870 (3-24-1870)
Britt, Tiney J. to William Petty 8-24-1853
Brook, Kate E. to Geo. W. Emit 4-27-1874 (4-29-1874)
Brook, Nancy to Samuel Davis 12-13-1874 (12-16-1874)
Brooks, Catherine E. to George D. Emmit 5-27-1874 (4?-29-1874)
Brooks, Jane to Thomas E. R. Heuston? 9-15-1857
Brooks, Janie to Thomas E. R. Hunton 9-15-1857
Brooks, Margaret R. to Lawson F. Hyder 3-29-1871 (3-30-1871)
Brooks, Mary M. to Geo. P. Crouch 2-13-1860
Brooks, Nancy to Samuel H. Dover 12-15-1876 (12-16-1874?)
Brooks, Parmellia C. to Jos. Renfro 12-26-1876
Brown, Jane to Treg Thomas 11-13-1867 B
Brown, Loucille J. to Emery Snodgrass 2-6-1872 (2-7-1872)
Brown, Margaret E. to Joseph A. Wrley 3-13-1871 (3-21-1871)
Brown, Margaret P. to Joseph Werley 3-13-1871 (3-21-1871)
Bruen, Ann to Sandy Burgon 2-27-1872
Brumit, Elizabeth to Hesekiah Woodby 7-14-1862 (7-15-1862)
Brumit, Mary to A. L. Benfield 6-26-1875 (7-18-1875)
Brummett, Mary to A. L. Burfield 6-26-1875 (7-18-1875)
Brutt, Eliza to Alfred L. Grindstaff 8-15-1874
Buchanon, Elizabeth A. to Landon C. Perry 3-15-1858 (3-16-1858)
Buck, Abigail to Volentin Bower 9-30-1808 (10-1-1808)
Buck, E. J. E. to Solomon B. Snider 12-12-1869 (12-16-1869)
Buck, Mary to John Carrel 7-19-1872
Buck, Nany to Lee Bowman 12-20-1871
Buckhannon, Elizabeth A. to Landon C. Perry 3-15-1858 (3-16-1858)
Buckle, Nancy J. to J. P. Vandeventer 5-30-1870 (6-2-1870)
Bucklen, Mary Ann to James P. Ritchie 11-17-1865 (11-23-1865)
Buckles, Eliza C. to David L. Robison 8-24-1878 (8-25-1878)
Buckles, Eliza Jane to Thomas J. Patrick 9-1-1870 (9-4-1870)
Buckles, Eliza Jane to Thomas J. Patterick 9-1-1870 (9-4-1870)
Buckles, Loucinda to William Bradley 4-12-1870 (4-17-1870)
Buckles, Margaret M. to James H. Williams 5-29-1866 (6-7-1866)
Buckles, Margaret to Wilferman Reason 12-30-1873
Buckles, Mary C. to Samuel M. Berry 10-2-1878 (10-4-1878)
Buckles, Mary P. to William J. Washam 8-30-1876 (9-10-1877)
Buckles, Mary to Geo. White 9-22-1866 (9-28-1866)
Buckles, Nancy J. to Joseph P. Vandeventer 5-30-1870 (6-2-1870)
Buckles, Rachael to Christian Carriger 9-1-1859
Buckles, Sarah J. to Arther A. Williams 10-8-1865 (10-12-1865)
Buckles, Susanna to Calvin F. Coble 3-6-1852 (3-18-1852)
Bunlain, Sarah to Daniel Bowman 10-10-1871
Buntain, Mary to George Olliver 9-10-1858 (9-11-1858)
Buntern, Matilda to Pleasant Parker 3-4-1871 (3-12-1871)
Bunton, Mary A. to David Bowman 10-10-1871
Bunton, Mary to George Oliver 9-10-1858 (9-11-1859?)
Bunton, Sarah to James B. Potter 10-31-1851 (11-1-1851)
Bunton, Sarah to James B. Potter 11-7-1854 (11-11-1854)
Burchfield, Ann E. to J. S. O'Brien 10-16-1852 (10-21-1852)
Burchfield, Jane to Isaac Perkins 5-14-1860 (5-15-1860)
Burchfield, Mary E. to C. M. C. Burchfield 9-9-1871 (9-12-1871)
Burchfield, Mary to B. M. C. Burchfield 9-9-1871 (9-12-1871)
Burchfield, Sarah to Wilson McInturf 2-1-1851 (2-2-1851)
Burfield?, Mahala to A. H. Owens 3-7-1871 (3-9-1871)
Burkluts?, Rachel to Christian Carriger 9-15-1859
Burks, Emelin to John W. Berry 10-30-1874 (11-1-1874)
Burrow, Emily D. to George D. Roberts 10-29-1866 (10-30-1866)
Burrow, Emy to Geo. D. Roberts 10-29-1866 (10-30-1866)
Burrow, Louisa to Geo. W. Pharr 4-21-1870
Burrus, Louesa to George W. Farr 4-21-1870
Burton, Matildad to Pleasant Parker 3-11-1871 (3-12-1871)
Butt, Mary to John Moore 9-2-1858
Butterworth, Mary A. to George Angell 10-23-1858
Cable, Ellen to John Hollen? 12-18-1868 (12-19-1868)
Cable, Emily S. to Jacob D. Bunton 1-13-1870 (1-17-1870)
Cable, Martha C. to Granville W. Stout 10-19-1857
Cable, Mary E. to Peter H. Potter 1-9-1859 (2-10-1859)
Cable, Sarah to James Stout 8-2-1867 (8-15-1867)
Calbaugh, Mary to William Nidiffer 5-7-1877 (6-3-1877)
Calboch, Marthy A. to James C. Nidiffer 6-28-1871 (6-29-1871)
Caldwell, E. M. to Noah Coble 3-2-1874 (3-8-1874)
Caman, Mary to William Taylor 10-2-1873 (no return) B
Cameron, Elizabeth A. to Landon Carter 6-18-1866 (6-19-1866)
Cameron, Harriet to Hiram Craig 6-9-1870
Cameron, Mary N. to G. T. Magee 3-13-1850
Camm?, Elizabeth A. to Landon Carter 6-19-1866
Campbell (Bell), Sarah to Elishey Garland 2-26-1875 (3-4-1875)
Campbell, Amanda E. to Charles D. Harkland 11-26-1870 (11-7?-1870)

Campbell, Amanda E. to Charles D. Markland 11-26-1870 (11-7?-1870)
Campbell, Celia J. to William A. Lewis 12-29-1856 (1-4-1857)
Campbell, Dosha to Alexander Grindstaff 3-7-1868 (3-8-1868)
Campbell, E. E. to Lafayett Peace 5-13-1871
Campbell, Elena W. to Tarlton Dugger 7-11-1856 (7-13-1856)
Campbell, Eliza C. to Joseph Duggar 9-23-1861 (10-17-1861)
Campbell, Eliza M. to Samuel Jenkins 2-20-1873
Campbell, Elizabeth A. to H. M. Arnold 5-8-1874
Campbell, Elizabeth A. to Richard Hazlewood 12-24-1870 (12-25-1870)
Campbell, Elizabeth to George Tipton 12-27-1870 B
Campbell, Elizabeth to Harrison M. Arnold 5-8-1874
Campbell, Elizabeth to Isaac Hodge 12-23-1872
Campbell, Elizabeth to Jackson Manning 8-16-1853 (8-18-1853)
Campbell, Elizabeth to John Fry 12-15-1852 (12-20-1852)
Campbell, Elizabeth to Samuel Jenkins 2-20-1873
Campbell, Elizabeth to William Davis 4-12-1866 (4-24-1866)
Campbell, Ellen E. to Layfaette Pearce 5-13-1871
Campbell, Ellen to William Glenn 6-15-1877 (6-17-1877)
Campbell, Elvinah to Thomas D. Vanhuss 8-7-1851
Campbell, Eva to J. L. Smith 11-20-1878
Campbell, Eveline to James Taylor 3-8-1867
Campbell, Fanny I. to N. T. Campbell 11-8-1873 (11-9-1873)
Campbell, Highly (Hilley) to John Shown 3-13-1858 (3-14-1858)
Campbell, Jane to William Johnson 12-20-1856
Campbell, Jane to William Johnson 12-23-1856 (12-27-1856)
Campbell, Laura C. to J. H. Simerly 11-2-1878 (11-3-1878)
Campbell, Lavicy to Elija C. Hathaway 11-14-1853 (11-15-1863?)
Campbell, Malinda to Isaac M. Barker? 4-?-1867 (4-12-1868?)
Campbell, Malinda to Larken Blackbourn 10-6-1860
Campbell, Mary Ann to Daniel S. Allen 11-15-1865 (11-18-1865)
Campbell, Mary E. to Calvin F. Campbell 2-2-1854
Campbell, Mary J. to Henry Markland 6-27-1868
Campbell, Mary R. to William Dugless 10-12-1874
Campbell, Mary to James Glover 5-24-1876 (5-25-1876)
Campbell, Mary to James Jackson 10-11-1868
Campbell, Mary to Wm. Grindstaff 5-26-1854 (no return)
Campbell, Matilda to Isaac M. Bowers 4-12-1868
Campbell, Nancy Ann to Samuel M. Estep 10-31-1866 (11-11-1866)
Campbell, Nancy E. to D. O. Johnson 8-1-1886 (8-8-1886)
Campbell, Nancy E. to Sampson Richardson 9-24-1874 (9-29-1874)
Campbell, Nancy M. to James B. Fletcher 11-15-1871 (11-16-1871)
Campbell, Nancy to Benj. Garland 2-11-1865 (2-20-1865)
Campbell, Nancy to Daniel Hicks 11-27-1869 (11-28-1869)
Campbell, Nancy to Harrison Hendrix 3-4-1851
Campbell, Nancy to James D. Fletcher 11-15-1871 (11-16-1871)
Campbell, Nancy to Thos. James 1-25-1855 (1-27-1855)
Campbell, Nanevy to Daniel Huck? 11-27-1869 (11-28-1869)
Campbell, Rebeca to William Dugless 10-10-1874 (10-12-1874)
Campbell, Rebecca to William Dugless 10-18-1874 (10-12?-1874)
Campbell, Reda (Roda) J. to Francis M. Humphrey 11-25-1874 (11-26-1874)
Campbell, Sarah J. to Lawson L. Lewis 8-27-1858 (8-29-1858)
Campbell, Sarah to Elisha Garland no date (1850-1876)
Campbell, Sarah to Mathew Night 7-8-1865 (no return)
Campbell, Sarah to R. C. Heatherly 3-11-1875
Campbell, Saraphina to James L. Taylor 2-26-1875
Campbell, Selia Jane to William A. Lewis 12-29-1856 (12-30-1856)
Campbell, Susannah C. to George M. Duggar 2-14-1860 (3-8-1860)
Camphen?, Mary to James Jackson 10-11-1868
Camu?, Mary to Clayton Stafford 12-11-1856 (12-24-1856?)
Cannon, Elizabeth to James T. Bowers 9-18-1852 (9-19-1852)
Cannon, Jane Fen? to Godfrey Carriger 10-5-1857 (10-8-1857)
Cannon, Jane T. to Godfry Carriger 10-5-1857
Caraway, Alla (Alta) to John McFall 12-8-1858 (12-16-1858)
Caraway, Nancy A. to John McFall 12-8-1858 (12-16-1858)
Caraway, Sarah to A. S. Hollyfield 7-23-1873 (7-27-1873)
Carden, Eliza J. A. to Shaderik W. Govern 12-3-1850
Carden, Eliza to William Kees 7-10-1872 (7-11-1872)
Carden, Emeline to R. G. Crow 2-7-1864
Carden, Martha to Harvey D. Estep 10-21-1875
Carden, Mary to James Wilson 3-12-1856 (3-13-1856)
Carden, Susan E. to Joseph P. Tipton 6-22-1852 (6-24-1852)
Cardin, Eliza to William Ker 7-10-1872

Cardon, Martha M. to Harvey D. Estep 10-21-1875
Cariger, Alvena to C. C. Morrell 1-18-1862 (1-19-1862)
Cariger, Mary to Robert Jenkins 7-19-1877 (9-20-1877)
Carlton, Ellen to Henry Simerely 12-8-1860 (12-9-1860)
Carlton, Margaret S. to Drewry S. Magee 10-30-1850
Caroway, Martha to William Hester 12-25-1873
Carr, Adaline to Ezekiel Lyon 12-24-1877
Carr, Amanda to James Woods 5-12-1877 (5-13-1877)
Carr, Catharn to Landon C. Lyon 8-21-1872 (8-25-1872)
Carr, Cathrin to Landon C. Lyon 8-21-1872
Carr, Clementine to Wm. A. Vaughn 9-29-1873
Carr, Emeline to James Struls? 1-12-1854 (6-15-1854)
Carr, Hester A. to David Weaver 12-26-1877 (12-18?-1877)
Carr, Lucilla Jane to Henry Morris 6-12-1875 (6-13-1875)
Carr, Mary M. to Jas. M. Lindaman 6-25-1875
Carr, Sarah to John Cole 12-13-1860 (12-15-1860)
Carraway, Nancy Allos to John McFall 12-8-1858 (12-16-1858?)
Carrell, Caroline to Caleb Whithead 3-13-1871
Carrell, Emelin to Nat T. Buck 12-19-1868
Carrell, Etta to Nathaniel T. Buck 12-19-1868
Carrell, Hanah Ann to John Mosley 8-15-1857 (8-16-1857)
Carrell, Mary to Clayton R. Stafford 12-4-1856
Carrell, Mary to Clayton Stafford 12-11-1856 (12-24-1856)
Carrell, Nancy E. to Daniel C. Kehn? 4-3-1866 (4-29-1866)
Carrell, Rachael to Noh? D. Saylor 5-14-1877 (5-15-1877)
Carrell, Rebecca to Isaac C. Hammer 12-24-1858
Carrell, Rebecca to William Burchfield 5-2-1859
Carriage, Vicey J. to Jacob C. Pierce 2-28-1856
Carrier, Eveline to Willy Blevins 2-15-1865
Carriger, Alizina to Christian C. Morrell 1-18-1862 (1-19-1862)
Carriger, Catharin to Joseph McKinny 9-19-1865 (9-24-1865)
Carriger, Eliza Jane to James E. Hyder 11-2-1859 (11-3-1859)
Carriger, Emi J. to Jacob H. Hicks 12-15-1874 (12-16-1874)
Carriger, Emy J. to Jacob Hick 12-15-1874
Carriger, Jane to Rufus Minton 9-15-1858 (not executed?)
Carriger, Jane to Ruphus Minton 9-15-1858 (no return)
Carriger, Kenah to George Sullivan 9-16-1871 (9-18-1871)
Carriger, Lavicy to John Crow 2-18-1858
Carriger, Martha A. to J. O. L. Hyder 5-21-1857 (5-29-1857)
Carriger, Martha A. to Joseph O. L. Hyder 5-31-1857 (5-29?-1857)
Carriger, Mary Jane to Levie Buckles 5-22-1860 (5-24-1860)
Carriger, Nancy N. to William Stover 1-21-1856
Carriger, Racheal to Isaac Bowers 4-14-1868 (9-15-1869)
Carriger, Rachel J. to Isaac Bowers 9-14-1867 (9-15-1867)
Carriger, Rebecca S. to Alfred R. Bowers 10-4-1876 (10-13-1876)
Carriger, Sarah E. to Alfred J. Berry 1-29-1867 (1-31-1867)
Carriger, Susannah M. to Jacob Hicks 8-30-1858 (9-1-1858)
Carroll, Carolilne to William Bowman 9-11-1867
Carroll, Hannah Ann to John Mosley 8-15-18857 (8-16-1857)
Carroll, Nancy E. to Daniel C. Kite 4-27-1866 (4-29-1866)
Carroll, Rebecca to William Burchfield 5-2-1859 (5-?-1859)
Carson, Bettie to Joseph Logan 4-16-1872
Carter, Ann to Franklin Parker 7-12-1861
Carter, Ann to Franklin Parks 7-12-1866
Carter, Elizabeth to William Campbell 8-13-1870
Carter, Emma to John Chambers 3-6-1878 (3-7-1878)
Carter, Harrieitt to William D. Greenlee 2-27-1869 (2-28-1869)
Carter, Hester to Robert B. Bradley 8-24-1876
Carter, Littitia to Robert Stover 5-28-1870 (6-1-1870)
Carter, Lover? to Henry Johnson 3-26-1874
Carter, Margaret to William J. Carr 3-4-1874 (3-5-1874)
Carter, Mary O. to James Pearce 1-26-1852 (7-27-1852)
Carver, Julean to Eldridge Conebson? 9-17-1874 (9-20-1874)
Carver, Julian to Eldridge Cockren 9-17-1874
Carver, Margaret to N. H. Johnson 2-16-1856 (2-17-1856)
Carver, Mary to Wm. More 12-8-1854 (12-16-1854)
Carver, Nancy to Swinfield Blevins 3-28-1864 (3-31-1864)
Carver, Sarah to Henry Hicks 2-23-1878 (2-24-1878)
Carver, Sarah to Jas. M. Whitehead 2-12-1868 (2-16-1868)
Carver, Sarah to Nathaniel T. Bradley 12-24-1872
Casper, Martha to James Shell 10-3-1863 (10-4-1863)
Cass, Martha L. to Alvin P. Ritchie 12-8-1869
Cassell, Mary to Clayton Stafford 12-4-1856
Cassina, Julia A. to Anderson R. Stout 11-2-1877 (11-7-1877)
Cates, Allace to Lewis Simons 11-14-1871 (11-19-1871)

Cates, Julia to Jas. H. Whitehead 2-2-1874 (2-8-1874)
Cates, Mariah J. to David Ingram 12-3-1872
Cates, Viney to William Carver 10-21-1873 (10-27-1873)
Catton, Charlotte to Benjamin Hyder 3-19-1855
Chamber, Eliza to Young Umphrey 8-15-1855 (9-16-1855)
Chambers, Eliza to Young Humphrey 8-15-1855 (8-16-1855)
Chambers, Jane to David Forbes 8-2-1877 (11-10-1877)
Chambers, Mary J. to Jeremiah Woodby 9-18-1857 (9-27-1857)
Chambers, Matilda to David Davis 7-29-1878 (7-28?-1878)
Chambers, Sarah to Jas. Whitehead 2-2-1852 (2-4-1852)
Chambers, Susanna to John Simmerly 3-22-1850 (3-24-1850)
Chapman, Margaret to Samuel Moore 3-22-1858 (3-23-1858)
Chrisly, Eva to Robert Treadway 9-3-1872 (9-4-1872)
Church, Caroline to Simon Hodge 2-23-1858
Church, Catharin to Solomon Hodge 2-23-1858
Church, Elizabeth to John Kinley 1-10-1863 (1-11-1863)
Church, Elizabeth to John Stewaert 11-14-1861 (11-15-1861)
Church, Luisey to James W. Trivet 4-13-1878 (4-18-1878)
Claimore, Pheby E. to James F. Little 10-23-1876 (10-24-1876)
Clark, Caroline to John Williams 7-31-1851
Claymore, Lydia to Alfred Range 1-2-1873
Claymore, Sarah J. to Peter Slagle 2-9-1856 (2-10-1856)
Clemens, Martha J. to Henry B. Prestly 2-26-1868 (3-1-1868)
Clementine, Mary to Jos. Lunceford 12-30-1865 (1-7-1866)
Clemons, Marret to A. H. Whaley 6-3-1862 (6-8-1862)
Climon, Nancy C. to Michael J. Duggar 6-2-1860 (6-5-1860)
Closson, Amassa A. R. to Merit L. Hicks 4-29-1878 (4-30-1878)
Cluner, Nancy E. to Michael I. Dugger 6-2-1860 (6-5-1860)
Cobb, Emily S. to Jacob D. Buntan 1-12-1870 (1-17-1870)
Coble, Catherine to James Green 8-9-1863 (11-8-1863)
Coble, E. J. to Daniel Green 2-22-1866 (2-24-1866)
Coble, Eliza Jane to David Greene 2-22-1866 (2-24-1866)
Coble, Ellian? to John Hollen 12-18-1868 (12-19-1868)
Coble, Martha C. to Granvill W. Stout 10-19-1857
Coble, Mary E. to Peter H. Potter 1-9-1859 (2-10-1859)
Coble, Mary M. to John M. Brown 10-4-1876 (10-6-1876)
Cobler, Emey to William Hart 9-23-1868 (9-24-1868)
Coffee, Mary A. to Calvin Brewer 7-9-1878 (7-14-1878)
Coffman, Allice P. to Thomas J. Tipton 5-10-1875 (5-11-1875)
Colbaugh, Jemima J. to Geo. J. Low 12-29-1865 (12-31-1865)
Colbaugh, Martha A. to James C. Nideffer 6-28-1871 (6-29-1871)
Colbough, Elve M. to Stephen Low 6-13-1872 (6-15-1872)
Cole, Adeline to Isaac Campbell 12-22-1876 (12-24-1876)
Cole, Ann to John Lowe 6-20-1856 (6-23-1856)
Cole, Cealy Ann to Kennedy Stout 1-9-1852 (6-13-1852)
Cole, Celia A. to S. M. Taylor 10-28-1878 (10-30-1878)
Cole, Lauza to Alen Blevins 2-12-1853
Cole, Lidia to Wm. G. Howard 12-16-1854 (12-21-1854)
Cole, Louisa to S. H. Cole 3-20-1874
Cole, Mary A. to David M. Kearne 6-4-1873 (6-5-1873)
Cole, Nancy S. to Henderson Garland 12-29-1867
Cole, Saraphina to James D. Garland 10-31-1866 (10-10?-1866)
Cole, Sarefina to Solomon Wilson 2-7-1874 (4-22-1874)
Colend, Sally Cates to Roner Bukor? 6-27-1874 (no return)
Collert, Eslie M. to Noah Cable 3-2-1874 (3-8-1874)
Collier, Martha to L. T. Bowers 12-29-1874 (12-31-1874)
Collins, Cathan to Jacob F. Treadway 2-10-1866 (2-11-1866)
Collins, Eliza C. to Daniel Ellis 9-2-1876 (9-3-1876)
Collins, Elizabeth to David Perry 6-25-1867 (6-26-1867)
Collins, Emilin to William Perry 4-14-1866
Collins, Emy C. to Elbert Glover 9-27-1876
Collins, Jane to Daniel Harden 1-1-1869 (1-2-1869)
Collins, Malinda to Elijah D. Oliver 8-6-1866
Collins, Martha to L. T. Bowen 12-29-1874 (12-31-1874)
Collins, Sarah J. to James Perry 2-1-1868 (2-4-1868)
Collough, Jemima C. to George J. Low 12-29-1865 (12-31-1865)
Combs, Amanda to General Taylor 1-2-1855
Combs, Hariet J. to General Jackson Taylor 10-28-1856 (10-29-1856)
Combs, Hester to William Pugh 3-2-1868 (3-3-1868)
Combs, Nancy to G. W. Crow 5-1-1866 (5-3-1866)
Combs, Nancy to George W. Creed 5-1-1866 (5-3-1866)
Combs, Susan to Patrick H. Johnson 10-4-1860 (10-5-1860)
Combs?, Cathran to Harvey R. Williams 9-28-1877 (9-29-1877)
Connor, Margaret to Samul Wilbern 11-6-1870
Cook, Elizabeth to William Campbell 4-14-1866 (4-15-1866)

Cooper, Elizabeth to Jerdon (Jorden) Croy 2-28-1861
Cooper, Louisa E. to Henry H. Hammer 8-7-1855 (8-9-1855)
Cooper, M. J. to W. F. Calis (Cates) 7-26-1866
Cooper, Malinda S. A. to Jacob P. Taylor 7-16-1862 (7-27-1862)
Cooper, Martha E. to William J. Overholser 11-7-1865 (11-23-1865)
Cooper, Sally to A. D. Taylor 6-8-1878 (8-15-1878)
Cotton, Loucinda C. to Peter W. Emmert 8-16-1860? (8-16-1860)
Cox, Ruth E. to William Caps 4-30-1858 (5-1-1856?)
Cox, Sarah J. to James R. Little 12-3-1857
Cox, Sarah Jane to James K. Little 12-3-1857
Creed, Jane to David Richie 5-10-1862 (5-25-1862)
Creed, Phebe to James Alford 7-12-1871 (2?-3-1871)
Creed, Rebecca to James Alfred 7-12-1870
Crew, Phebe E. to Samuel Smith 11-30-1858
Cried?, Sarah C. to John F. McClure 9-17-1864 (9-18-1864)
Crockett, C. A. to J. A. Smith 12-31-1877 (1-1-1878)
Crockett, Mary E. to Geo. Alex. Anderson 7-10-1876 (7-12-1876)
Crose?, Mary J. to Thomas Sims 3-13-1867 (3-14-1867)
Crosmon, Catharn to John Winters 10-26-1857 (10-29-1857)
Cross, Susanna to Albert P. Williams 9-21-1850 (9-22-1850)
Crow, Angaline to Elijah Jenkins 5-31-1856 (6-1-1856)
Crow, Delana E. to Samuel Richardson 2-16-1875 (2-18-1875)
Crow, Delcena E. to Samuel Richardson 1-30-1869 (1-31-1869)
Crow, Elizabeth A. to Harvey Richardson 8-5-1852
Crow, Emelin to John Mathis 8-5-1869
Crow, Emily to John Mather 8-7-1869 (no return)
Crow, L. J. to Solomon Miller 1-15-1853 (1-16-1853)
Crow, Martha J. B. to Christian A. A. Pearce 12-23-1869
Crow, Martha J. B. to Christian H. Peace? 12-23-1869
Crow, Martha to Elbert C. Berry 3-24-1875 (3-25-1875)
Crow, Martha to Saml. M. Dunkin 11-8-1859 (11-9-1859)
Crow, Marthey to David T. Bowen 9-1-1860 (9-20-1860)
Crow, Marthy to Samuel H. Dunken 11-18-1859 (11-19-1859)
Crow, Mary C. to John W. Pippin 11-10-1875 (11-11-1875)
Crow, Mary J. to J. W. Pippen 11-10-1875 (11-11-1875)
Crow, Mary J. to John Lovless 1-8-1867 (1-13-1867)
Crow, Phebe E. to Samuel E. (T.?) Smith 11-30-1858
Crow, Phebe J. to Henry Pearce 5-11-1854 (5-13-1854)
Crow, Phebe to Henry J.? Nave 12-9-1865 (12-10-1865)
Crowe, Jane to Levi N. Ellis 4-12-1856
Crumbley, Nancy A. to Abraham Nave 6-18-1852 (6-20-1852)
Crumley, Evelin to A. J. Peters 7-23-1861 (8-1-1861)
Crumley, Evelin to Robert Treadway 9-3-1872 (9-4-1872)
Crumley, Eveline to A. Jackson Peters 7-23-1861 (8-1-1861)
Crumley, N. J. to Saml. A. Tipton 8-5-1853 (8-7-1853)
Crumley, Rebeca J. to A. T. Mires 12-14-1865
Crumley, Rebeca Jane to James C. R. Anderson 9-27-1865 (10-11-1865)
Crumley, Susanna P. to Henry c. Beasley 3-6-1861
Crumly, Eveline to Jackson Peters 7-23-1861 (8-1-1861)
Crumly, Rebecca J. to Alexr? Alen 12-14-1865
Crumly, Rebecca Jane to James C. R. Anderson 9-27-1865 (10-11-1865)
Crusman, Catharin to John Winters 10-26-1857 (10-29-1857)
Crusmon, Nancy to John Winters 10-26-1857 (10-29-1857)
Culbert, Elizabeth to William Taylor 12-28-1867 (12-29-1867)
Culbert, Louretta to Jacob C. Kinnick 4-7-1877 (4-8-1877)
Culbert, Mary to Hasten J. Lunis? 4-19-1860
Curtice, Eliza T. to Pleasant G. Humphrey 4-16-1861 (4-18-1861)
Curtice, Emeline to James Wilson 8-5-1861 (8-6-1861)
Curtis, Harne? H. to William D. Greenlee 1-27-1869 (2-2-1869)
Curtis, Hopper to Wm. Gibson 2-19-1851 (2-20-1851)
Custer, Eva C. to Henderson F. Perry 11-28-1878
Custer, Leelia? E. to Geo. H. Angel 1-1-1872 (1-2-1872)
Daniel, Elizabeth to Franklin Alison 9-9-1871 (9-10-1871)
Daniel, Elizabeth to Franklin Allen 9-9-1871 (9-10-1871)
Daniel, Hannah to John V. Keen 12-27-1871
Daniel, Martha to John Allison 9-9-1871 (9-10-1871)
Daniel, Martha to Nathaniel T. Williams 1-29-1859 (2-2-1859)
Daniel, Olive to Samuel Johnson 3-7-1853 (3-10-1853)
Daniel, Vira to Benjamin Ford 5-19-1866
Daniels, Emma to Thomas Crow 8-29-1878
Darnel, Mary to Solomon Turner 6-24-1860
Davenport, Catharn to Samuel W. Kite 4-9-1866 (4-10-1866)
Davenport, Martha Ann to Peter Glover 1-17-1879 (1-30-1879)

David, Elizabeth to Allen Miller 3-27-1858
David, Sarah to John Head 3-15-1873 (3-16-1873)
Davis, Elizabeth L. to Noe D. Laudermilk 2-29-1876
Davis, Margaret to Millard F. Kuhn 12-5-1872 (12-6-1872)
Davis, Margaret to Millard Kichen 12-5-1872 (12-6-1872)
Davis, Martha to George Carver 9-3-1866 (9-5-1866)
Davis, Sarah to Alexander Cook 10-4-1873 (10-5-1873)
Davis, Sarah to Andrew Cook 10-4-1873 (10-5-1873)
Davis, Sarah to Solomon Ellis 1-15-1856 (1-20-1856)
Day, Rebecca to William West 12-23-1870 (12-25-1870)
Debenport, Cathan to Samul W. Riles? 4-9-1866 (4-10-1866)
Deddley, Jane to Telanon Gragg 3-1-1873
Deel, Lucinda to Alfred Shell 1-10-1854
Deloach, Mahala to Henderson Hunter 4-25-1852 (4-26-1852) B
Deloach, Mary to John Beck 8-31-1870
Deloach, Mary to John Buck 8-31-1870
Demkin, Mary to Daniel Wilson 8-15-1850
Dinzymore, S. A. to John Wilson 7-27-1877 (?-?-1877)
Doby, Sarah to Russell Kite 5-1-1866 (5-2-1866)
Donathan, Nancy C. to Andrew Jackson 11-24-1850
Dorun?, M. A. to J. R. Ruhn 4-18-1871 (4-20-1871)
Dover, Delila A. to Thomas O. Murry 2-27-1877
Dover, Elizabeth to Alben Miller 3-27-1858
Dover, Elizabeth to Allen Miller 3-27-1858 (no return)
Dover, Julia A. to James T. Chambers 4-4-1878
Dover, Margaret A. to J. R. Ritchie 4-18-1871 (4-20-1871)
Dover, Martha to George Carver 9-5-1866
Dover, Sarah to John Head 3-15-1873 (3-16-1873)
Drake, Saraphina to Howard Murdox 9-23-1865 (9-27-1865)
Droke?, Maggie to George W. Cash 7-28-1877 (7-29-1877)
Duffield, Amanda to Rufus Taylor 12-15-1876 (12-16-1876)
Duffield, Malinda to Alfred Bly 9-22-1874
Duffield, Martha J. to Henry M. Renfro 11-25-1867 (11-26-1867)
Duggan, Hannah J. to Alexander S. Grindstaff 3-6-1868 (3-8-1868)
Duggan, Margaret to Levi N. Crew 10-2-1873 (10-9-1873)
Duggar, Ediny to J. D. Carriger 6-14-1866 (6-17-1866)
Duggar, Nancy J. to James G. Lewis 12-30-1865 (1-4-1866)
Duggar, Nancy to Charles Gaddy 11-26-1853
Duggar, Rosey J. to Elbert S. Pearc? 12-20-1852 (12-21-1852)
Duggar, Rosy Jane to Elber S. Peare 12-20-1852 (12-21-1853?)
Duggar, Sarah J. to William C. Pean (Pierce?) 7-6-1857 (8-30-1857)
Dugger, Edney to J. D. Carriger 6-14-1866 (6-17-1866)
Dugger, Ellen to William ARnold 8-3-1877 (8-4-1877)
Dugger, Margaret to Levi N. Crow 10-2-1873 (10-9-1873)
Dugger, Mary C. to Alphna Smithpeter 7-7-1857 (7-11-1857)
Dugger, Mary E. to Lawson L. Goodwind 2-23-1861 (3-8-1861)
Dugger, Mary E. to S. A. Lewceford 10-2-1875 (10-8-1875)
Dugger, Nancy J. to James G. Lewis 12-3-1865 (1-4-1865)
Dugger, Rosanna Jane to Henry Bowers 6-8-1876
Dugger, Rosy Jane to Elbert S. Pearce 12-20-1852 (12-21-1852)
Dugger, Sary Ann to F. M. Price 10-15-1857 (10-16-1857)
Duglass, Elizabeth to Andrew W. Mayton 3-27-1852 (3-28-1852)
Duglass, Jane to William P. Hyder 3-5-1873 (3-13-1873)
Duglass, Mary P. to Cosby S. P. Deals 10-28-1859 (no return)
Duglass, Rhoda A. to Theaplus Russell 11-20-1874 (11-5?-1874)
Dugless, Rhoda A. to Thepholus Rusell 10-2-1874 (11-5-1874)
Duglus, J. to Wm. P. Hyder 3-5-1873 (3-13-1873)
Duisemer?, Martha E. to John H. Cole 7-16-1875
Dun, Elizabeth to John Scott 11-15-1871 (1?-29-1871)
Dunbar, Eliza to Charles McKassay 8-31-1864 (10?-30-1864)
Duncan, Martha to James Lacy 1-24-1870 (1-23?-1870)
Duncan, Mary to Reuben McNealey ?-?-1875
Duncan, Masora to George Lyon 7-17-1875
Duncan, Nancy to Wm. Carrell 2-27-1855
Duncey, Mary J. to Robert P. Shell 9-30-1865 (10-1-1865)
Dunken, Phenith to Nathanel Brown 2-7-1853
Dunken, Sarah Ann to James Bowman 4-14-1853
Dunkin, Martha to James Long 1-23-1870
Dunn, Elizabeth to John Scott 11-15-1871 (11-16-1871)
Dunn, Margaret M. to James P. T. Carter 8-5-1851
Dunn?, Margarette M. to James P. J.? Carter 8-5-1851
Dunsmore, Mmartha E. to John H. Cole 7-16-1875
Dyar, Emily to Welcom Stephens 8-30-1856
Easir?, Martha to James Lenard 1-28-1878 (1-29-1878)
Easley, Allan to Thomas Easley 3-24-1871 (3-26-1871) B

Eden, Mary A. to Wesley Jones 10-12-1869
Edens, Elizabeth to Amber C. Jones 11-30-1871
Edens, Julia A. to Lafayette Gourley 1-20-1853
Edens, Louisanda to William M. Gourley 11-16-1851
Edens, Lousarda to William M. Gourly 11-16-1851
Edens, Lucinda Jane to William Gourley 11-16-1851
Edens, Martha C. to Eli H. Hicks 1-3-1868
Edens, Mary A. to Wesly Jones 10-12-1869
Edin, Elizabeth to Ambrous Jones 11-30-1871
Eggers, Martha C. to William Laws 6-23-1877 (6-24-1877)
Elis, Margaret to John L. Lyon 1-5-1854
Eller, Barbra to Valentine Bowers 3-3-1871 (3-23-1871)
Eller, Elizabeth to Wm. Blevins 7-29-1878 (7-28?-1878)
Eller, Mary E. to Josiah Williams 10-11-1875 (10-13-1875)
Ellers, Roda to P. C. Anderson 5-12-1873
Elliott, Catharin to Daniel Robertson 6-16-1866 (6-18-1866)
Elliott, Darthula to Lewis Pearce 12-25-1868 (12-29-1868)
Elliott, Elizabeth to G. W. Carrell 5-10-1858
Elliott, Levicy to G. W. Taylor 7-6-1868 (7-13-1868)
Elliott, Mary C. to David R. Lowe 12-26-1878
Elliott, Nancy C. to Abraham Wilson 11-14-1853
Elliott, Nancy C. to J. D. Williams 9-22-1855 (9-27-1855)
Ellis, Babary to Valentine Bower 3-3-1871 (3-23-1871)
Ellis, Louisa A. B. to Samuel B. Lyons 10-13-1855 (10-14-1855)
Ellis, Manervy to David T. Chambers 9-3-1866 (9-5-1866)
Ellis, Margarett to Joseph Kughn 7-1-1851
Ellis, Mary Ann to David Holly 11-27-1856
Ellis, Roda C. to P. C. Anderson 5-12-1873 (5-13-1873)
Ellott, Elizabeth to G. W. Carrell 5-10-1858
Emmert, Mary to Archabald Carter 1-21-1858
Emmert, Mary to Millard Edens 9-15-1877 (9-16-1877)
Emmert, Nancy J. to William A. Dyke 6-24-1857 (6-25-1857)
Emmert, Sarah Jane to Samuel Thompson 3-13-1866 (3-18-1866)
Emmert, Sarah to William Adams 12-31-1877 (1-31-1877?)
Emmit, Cathrine to William Vest 3-27-1871 (3-24?-1871)
Englishman, Sarah to David Due 1-2-1871 (1-8-1871)
Engram, Eliza to Alexander Garland 11-4-1870
Ensor, Loucreca to Landon C. Bowers 8-16-? (no return)
Ensor, Sarah E. to A. J. Ferguson 9-25-1856 (9-26-1856)
Ensor, Sarah E. to Andrew J. Furguson 9-25-1856 (9-26-1856)
Ervin, Rachel to John Ward 9-16-1871 B
Escott, Nellie to James T. Carver 6-13-1873
Estep, Ann to James W. Carden 3-6-1861 (2?-6-1861)
Estep, Caroline to C. S. Deal 3-3-1883 (3-4-1883)
Estep, Elizabeth to John Meridith 1-7-1855
Estep, Emiline to Robt. Nidiffer 5-20-1856 (5-21-1856)
Estep, Mahala to Daniel W. Lipps 12-29-1871 (12-30-1871)
Estep, Margaret to Levi Nidiffer 4-30-1877 (5-6-1877)
Estep, Matilda to John Richardson 11-22-1855 (11-23-1855)
Estep, Nancy C. to John Richardson 12-19-1868
Estep, Nancy J. to David Phair? 3-13-1868 (3-15-1868)
Estep, Rhoda Jane to Nathan Garland 3-21-1878
Estep, Roda to John M. Garland 11-5-1872
Estep, Ruth to M. B. Elliott 4-?-1878 (4-18-1878)
Estepp, Mahala to Daniel W. Lipps 12-29-1871 (12-30-1871)
Fain, Martha to Jacob L. Frasier 3-11-1876 (11-17-1876)
Fair, Amanda J. to Isaac Olliver 1-25-1875 (1-29-1875)
Fair, Clarisa to Samuel Miller 12-18-1857
Fair, Delila to Thos. H. Gourley 1-2-1851
Fair, Elizabeth to Christian Williams 7-24-1856
Fair, Elizabeth to Isaac Nave 12-26-1866 (12-27-1866)
Fair, Elizabeth to Nicholas Oliver 9-29-1862 (10-1-1862)
Fair, Hannah to Wm. Cooper 9-26-1852
Fair, Jane to Geo. W. Moody 5-7-1858
Fair, Jane to Wm. S. Thomas 11-12-1870
Fair, Julia F. to Wm. W. McKehen 1-6-1868 (1-9-1868)
Fair, Mary to James A. Nave 3-8-1873
Fair, Sarah E. to S. W. Hyder 7-1-1872 (7-2-1872)
Fair, Susan to James S. Stepp 10-24-1877
Fannin, Nancy J. to James S. Wygal 12-9-1867 (11?-9-1867)
Farr, Elizabeth to Christian Williams 7-24-1856
Farr, Elizabeth to Nicholas Oliver 9-29-1862 (10-1-1862)
Farr, Jane to William S. Thomas 11-12-1870
Farr, Sarah E. to Samuel W. Hyder 7-1-1872 (7-16-1872)
Farr, Saraphine to James W. Adams 11-14-1874 (11-15-1874)

February, Elizabeth to William G. Meridith 8-30-1856 (8-31-1856)
February, Julia A. to Isaac Hart 7-10-1852 (7-11-1852)
Ferguson, Mary Alice to Joseph C. Bowe 4-30-1878
Ferguson, Mary Ann to James Caraway 10-26-1856
Ferguson, Mary K. to Joel Carriger 12-?-1861 (no return)
Ferris, Margret to Henry Fox 4-24-1874
Fitzsimmons, Ann to Robert Carier 10-19-1867 (10-?-1867)
Fitzsimmons, Emily P. to Thomas I. Cox 12-9-1855
Fleming, Mary J. to William T. Freeman 9-24-1866 (9-25-1866)
Fletcher, Amy to John Spears 4-10-1852 (4-11-1852)
Fletcher, Cardelia to John W. Headrick 3-23-1866 (3-24-1866)
Fletcher, Elizabeth to J. H. Pharr 7-3-1866 (8-5-1866)
Fletcher, Elizabeth to Jas. M. Manning 4-17-1876 (4-20-1876)
Fletcher, Elizabeth to Reuben Peters 11-30-1867 (12-1-1867)
Fletcher, Ellen to Jackson C. Pharr 5-3-1868
Fletcher, Manerva to Stephen Lewis 6-14-1876 (6-20-1876)
Fletcher, Margaret to Robert Forbes 12-26-1873
Fletcher, Martha J. to Zachariah C. Campbell 7-29-1867 (9-4-1867)
Fletcher, Mary to David F. Elliott 1-3-1867 (1-30-1867)
Fletcher, Sarah to John Roberts 6-16-1876 (6-18-1876)
Floyd, Emalin to William Troxell 8-19-1865
Floyd, Emilin to William Fair 10-10-1866
Floyd, Emily to John S. Morrell 3-12-1866
Fluker?, Margaret to Robert Forbus 12-28-1872 (12-26?-1872)
Folsom, Eliza to Tolbert Collett 2-7-1872 (2-8-1872)
Folsom, Emilin M. to Benjamin Howard 7-28-1865
Folsom, Lemier to Solomon Crow 2-12-1878 (2-14-1878)
Folsom, Mary J. to L. C. Berry 6-3-1857
Folsom, Molly C. to N. G. T. Simerly 8-20-1876 (8-24-1876)
Folsom, Viney to Alfred Young 4-6-1867
Fondern, Margaret to John W. Steffey 6-24-1871 (6-25-1871)
Forbes, Ann to John W. Frasher 3-20-1858 (3-21-1858)
Forbes, Elizabeth to James H. Peters 3-6-1861 (3-8-1861)
Forbes, Lydia to Elija D. Hardin 1-2-1852 (1-22-1852)
Forbes, Mary Ann to Andrew W. Boyd 11-17-1864 (11-19-1865)
Forbess, Elizabeth to Eli Hardin 10-6-1866 (10-19-1866)
Forbus, Anna to John W. Frasure 3-20-1858 (3-21-1858)
Forbus, Elizabeth to James H. Peters 3-6-1861 (3-8-1861)
Forslit, Ann to Jas. Maston 9-13-1877
Forster, Margaret to Thomas A. Elis 9-6-1856 (9-7-1856)
Foster, Eliza J. to Joseph Odell 2-2-1850 (2-3-1850)
Foster, Eliza to Alfred Carr 7-29-1857 (8-1-1859)
Foster, Sarah to J. R. A. Hauger 3-29-1875 (3-30-1875)
Foster, Sealy to Cornelius Hauger 9-27-1873 (9-28-1873)
Foust, Catharine to Solomon Cole 1-6-1858 (1-7-1858)
Foust, Christena to Edmond W. Taylor 6-28-1856 (6-29-1856)
Foust, Martha to Dimmond Rockhold 10-14-1865
Foust, Mary E. to William J. Scalf 9-20-1865
Fox, Amanda to John Laner? 8-19-1872
Fox, Malinda to Pleasant Gibson 6-24-1865 (6-25-1865)
Fox, Manda to John Laws 8-20-1872
Fox, Matilda to Pleasant Gibson 6-24-1865 (6-25-1865)
Fraser, Rachel to Isaac Woods 9-28-1858 (no return)
Frasier, E. E. to Jos. L. Lewis 4-3-1878 (4-4-1878)
Frasier, Rachel to Isaac Woods 9-28-1858
Frasure, Angleine to Thomas Taylor 8-22-1856
Frasure, Mary A. to John Hollyway 1-7-1871
Frazier, Sarah to David Peters 7-2-1866 (7-8-1866)
Freese?, Joanah to Aaron Shell 10-3-1874
French, Mary to Geo. McKehn 6-14-1855
Fritso?, Mary L. to R. D. Wilson 9-7-1872
Fritts, Sarah to William Matherly 1-30-1854 (2-2-1854)
Fry, Elizabeth to Albert E. Campbell 11-6-1852 (11-9-1852)
Fry, Mary A. to William C. Campbell 10-31-1858
Fulkerson, Mary A. to David Dice? 1-2-1871 (1-8-1871)
Fulkerson, Sarah to John C. Dougherty 8-31-1866
Furgason, Elza M. to Samuel S. Duffield 11-20-1851
Furgason, Joanah H. to David A. Baker 12-22-1860 (12-23-1860)
Garland, Amy to Allen Blevins 12-1-1862 (12-6-1862)
Garland, Angaline to Levi Hodge 8-22-1865 (8-24-1865)
Garland, Eliza Jane to Rufus K. Williams 1-19-1856
Garland, Eliza to John Banks 4-17-1872 (12-18-1872)
Garland, Fany to Benjamin Vaughn 11-4-1871 (11-6-1871)
Garland, Harrett to Andrew Colie 11-15-1869 (11-17-1869)
Garland, Lilly to John R. Garland 12-30-1868

Garland, Malinda to Dillard Blevins 6-6-1861 (6-9-1861)
Garland, Martha E. to Wm. F. Richardson 6-7-1861 (6-8-1861)
Garland, Martha to Henry Estep 8-16-1866 (8-19-1866)
Garland, Mary A. to Thomas J. Jones 6-17-1874 (6-25-1874)
Garland, Mary to Robert Burchfield 12-23-1871 (12-28-1871)
Garland, Matilda to Dillard Blevins 6-6-1861 (6-9-1861)
Garland, Nancy C. to Ransom Estep 4-20-1866 (4-22-1866)
Garland, Nancy to David Garland 11-19-1859 (11-20-1859)
Garland, Nancy to David Garland 11-9-1859 (11-20-1859)
Garland, Nancy to William M. Lewis 4-15-1871 (4-16-1871)
Garland, Rebecca to Landon C. Carter 7-30-1877
Garland, Sarah J. to Charles Baker 1-19-1861 (1-20-1861)
Garland, Sarah to James Campbell 3-17-1876 (3-20-1876)
Garland, Sarahfine to Thomas Elliott 3-7-1856 (3-10-1856)
Garland, Susan J. to Francis K. Keen 5-5-1872 (5-3?-1872)
Garland, Vina to Nathaniel Payte 10-27-1871 (10-29-1871)
Garrison, Eliza A. to A. F. Williams 7-2-1860 (7-8-1860)
Garrison, Eliza to David Grindstaff 10-26-1876 (10-26-1879?)
Garrison, Harriet to John Merrit 1-4-1851 (1-5-1851)
Garrison, Jenni G. to James R. Fletcher 8-3-1869
Garrison, Louisa to Samuel Deloach 1-27-1865
Garrison, Martha Alice to William H. C. Humphrey 4-17-1878
Garrison, Mary Ann to James Merit 10-27-1854 (11-26-1854)
Garrison, Mary to William Y.? Hatcher 1-2-1879
Garrison, S. C. to J. M. Carter 8-9-1850
Gauge, Sarah to Ezekiel Burchfield 7-4-1859 (7-30-1859)
Genely?, Mary J. to Paddy O. Plurty 6-22-1874
Gentry, Louisa to Francis M. Griffith 10-2-1876 (10-4-1876)
Gentry, Sarah Jane to George O'Brien 2-27-1867
Gentry, Sarah Jane to Joseph Eliott 9-11-1868 (9-13-1868)
George, Mary S. to James P. Taylor 12-24-1865 (12-28-1865)
George, Mary S. to James P. Taylor 12-26-1865 (12-28-1865)
Gibs, Abagail A. to Jacob Bowman 1-24-1855 (1-25-1855)
Gifferson, Nancy A. to Pleasant Gibson 7-10-1866 (?-12-1866)
Gilber, C. J. to W. S. Shuffield 12-26-1874 (12-27-1874)
Gilbert, Elizabeth to John Britt 9-8-1851
Gill, Nancy to John Curtis? 5-26-1870 (5-27-1870) B
Gillen, C. J. to Willey S. Shuffield 12-26-1874 (12-27-1874)
Gillen, Martha to Johnson Potter 3-5-1874 (7-11-1874)
Gillen, Martha to Johnson Potts 3-5-1874 (7-11-1874)
Giller, Martha to Johnson Potter 3-3-1874 (7-11?-1874)
Glen, Nancy to Wm. G. Campbell 1-21-1865 (1-?-1865)
Glover, Delia C. to W. H. Campbell 12-21-1878 (12-29-1878)
Glover, Eliza J. to Owen Sams 3-24-1859
Glover, Elizabeth to John Hays 12-15-1857 (12-15-1856?)
Glover, Elizabeth to Thomas Campbell 7-20-1877 (7-22-1877)
Glover, Evaline to Thomas Morgon 12-29-1877 (12-30-1877)
Glover, Louisa to Andrew J. Meridith 7-27-1865
Glover, Nancy to John Smith 1-29-1851
Glover, Rachel to Jackson Sims 6-24-1856
Glover?, Elizabeth to Jehue Hays 12-15-1856
Goarhand?, Lettey to John R. Garland 12-20-1868 (12-30-1868)
Good, Eliza to William Jorden 1-5-1872 (1-7-1872)
Goodrum, Mary E. to Marion Lunsford 5-27-1872 (6-9-1872)
Goodwin, Caroline to John F. Lunsford 11-12-1866 (11-18-1866)
Goodwin, Catharin to William Shown 2-25-1858 (3-4-1858)
Goodwin, Eliza J. to John Shoun 5-23-1858
Goodwin, Emeline to Landon Carden 6-8-1867 (6-10-1867)
Goodwin, Emily to Landon C. Carden 6-8-1867 (6-10-1867)
Goodwin, Loucinda(Loverda?) to John F. Campbell 3-14-1870
Goodwin, Martha E. to Gideon Lewis 8-21-1860
Goodwin, Mary E. to Marion V. Lunaford? 5-27-1872 (6-9-1872)
Goodwin, N. C. to Wm. L. Lewis 11-4-1861 (11-10-1861)
Goodwin, Nancy J. to G. W. Campbell 9-14-1874
Goodwin, Nancy Jane to G. F. Campbell 9-14-1874
Gordon, Ellen to George Lincoln 11-5-1867 (11-11-1867)
Gorman, Nancy to Andy Tate 10-7-1878 (10-27-1878)
Gouge, Beddy to William Johnson 12-23-1867 (12-26-1867)
Gouge, Manervy to Johnson Miller 2-9-1869 (2-21-1869)
Gouge, Manervy to William Garland 11-12-1867 (11-24-1867)
Gouge, Martha Ann to Wilson Edwards 6-15-1867 (6-16-1867)
Gouge, Monisany? to Johnson Miller 2-9-1869 (2-21-1869)
Gouge, Rebecca J. to John Ramsour? 10-22-1870
Gouge, Sarah to Ezekiel Burchfield 7-4-1859 (7-30-1859)
Gouge, Susanna to Charles Stephens 8-11-1855 (8-12-1855)

Gourley, Elizabeth to Samuel S. Davenport 12-24-1860
Gourley, Fanney J. to W. J. Humphrey 4-13-1875
Gourley, Hariet Louisa to James Daniel 11-21-1850
Gourley, Joanna to David W. Taylor 3-17-1862 (3-23-1862)
Gourley, Louretta A. to Wm. Fainsworth 3-15-1858 (3-16-1858)
Gourley, Martha to F. M. Hyder 7-6-1866 (8-22-1866)
Gourley, Mary Ann to Jonathan H. Treadway 3-28-1878 (4-21-1878)
Gourley, Mary S. to Henry Hyder 9-26-1877 (9-30-1877)
Gourley, Mary to Geo. W. Master 6-14-1850
Gourley, Sarah (Susannah) to Henery Sims 8-1-1867 (8-4-1867)
Gourley, Saraphina to Samuel N. K. T. Lusk 5-3-1860
Gourly, Fanny J. to William J. Humphrey 4-13-1875
Gourly, Leanory to Alford Williams 1-13-1857
Gourly, Loureth to William B. Farensworth 3-15-1858 (3-16-1858)
Gourly, Susanna J. to Henry Sims 8-1-1867 (8-4-1867)
Grace, Emeline to Joseph P. Bowers 10-15-1855
Grace, Martha to John Livingston 10-1-1870
Grace, Sally to Pleast. Williams 1-22-1876
Grage?, Elizabeth to Stephen Winter 2-20-1852 (4-9-1852)
Gragg, Sarah M. to Jacob Miller 4-12-1877 (4-15-1877)
Gray, Martha to Amos Davis 3-13-1854 (3-16-1854)
Green, Emily C. to Willy S. Hatley 1-12-1866 (1-14-1866)
Green, Emily O. to Willey S. Hately 1-14-1866
Green, Josephin to Elbert Richer? 1-23-1872 (1-25-1872)
Green, Josephine to Elbert Ritchie 1-20-1872 (1-25-1872)
Green, Mary to Calvin Grage? 12-23-1877
Green, Rachel to Reby B. (Riley B.) Hately 8-13-1866 (8-18-1866)
Greenlee, Ann to George Fellers 3-2-1871
Greenvill, Nancy L. to William C. Ward 10-15-1864 (10-16-1864)
Greenwell, Mary F. to J. C. Gragg 12-14-1877 (no return)
Greer, Catharin to Emanuel Willhight 5-5-1851 (6-1-1851)
Greer, Susanna to Daniel Wilhight 3-29-1851 (4-1-1851)
Grenwell, Nancy R. to Wm. C. Ward 10-15-1864 (10-16-1864)
Grifeth, Martha to Shared Farr 1-26-1870 (1-27-1870)
Griffin, Sarah to Francis Tolly 8-1-1872
Griffith, Martha to Shared Fair 1-26-1870 (1-27-1870)
Grimsley, Carolin to Christopher F. Price 10-13-1861 (10-15-1861)
Grindstaff, Angaline to David Brooks 3-23-1871 (3-26-1871)
Grindstaff, Eliza J. to John L. Bowen 12-11-1866 (12-12-1866)
Grindstaff, Elizabeth to Oliver Hall 11-27-1855 (11-29-1855)
Grindstaff, Elizabeth to Wm. Humphrey 2-14-1877
Grindstaff, Ellen to Andrew Johnson 9-25-1876 (10-1-1876)
Grindstaff, Emily to John McKinney 3-27-1857 (3-29-1857)
Grindstaff, Eveline to William Casa 12-28-1870 (12-29-1870)
Grindstaff, Jane to Leonard Shell 10-13-1871 (10-15-1871)
Grindstaff, Louisa J. to William J. Raines 7-21-1864 (7-24-1864)
Grindstaff, Louisa to John H. Forester 12-9-1871
Grindstaff, Martha L. to Ezekiel Baker 8-10-1866 (8-26-1866)
Grindstaff, Mary E. to E. D. Myers 12-30-1876 (12-31-1876)
Grindstaff, Mary E. to John H. Harden 10-10-1870 (10-13-1870)
Grindstaff, Mary to Henry Campbell 1-2-1859 (1-8-1859)
Grindstaff, Mary to Moses Eastep 4-11-1874
Grindstaff, Mary to Saml. Livingston 8-24-1873
Grindstaff, Nancy C. to A. T. Helton 12-18-1860 (12-20-1860)
Grindstaff, Sarafina to Thomas H. Wilson 11-12-1864
Grindstaff, Sarah Ann to William Hail 6-20-1861
Grindstaff, Sarah C. to Rusell Williams 4-4-1870 (4-6-1870)
Grindstaff, Sarah to Samuel Livingston 8-24-1873
Grindstaff, Sealy to Geo. F. Peaters 1-21-1876 (1-27-1876)
Grindstaff, Susan to Zacariah Morton 2-2-1875
Grindstaff, Susana to Peter B. Elliott 1-7-1835
Grindstaff, Susanna to Zacariah Morton 2-2-1875 (2-7-1875)
Grisham, Margaret to Robert Rasmor 10-2-1868
Guge, Hariet to Elcana Glover 8-5-1871
Guinn, Nancy to George Simerly 11-30-1868
Guy, Harrett to Elcana Glenn 8-5-1871
Hacher, Nancy J. to Joseph R. Smith 1-2-1873
Hall, Dealy C. to James D. Campbell 4-13-1876 (4-14-1876)
Hamby, Amanda to R. P. Plep 11-11-1873 (11-21-1873)
Hamby, Caroline to Jeremiah Campbell 9-19-1874 (9-20-1874)
Hamby, Eliza Jane to John H. Smith 6-5-1865 (6-11-1865)
Hamitte, Mary Eliza to W. H. Cromwell 11-5-1867 (11-7-1867)
Hamley, Ema to William C. Clemens 5-5-1862 (5-8-1862)
Hamm?, Catharin to David Chambers 3-23-1869
Hammer, L. F. to A. J. Shell 5-7-1878 (5-26-1878)

Hampton, Caroline to Alexander Tener 1-1-1870 (1-16-1870)
Hampton, Catharn to Barnett Phillips 2-2-1858 (no return)
Hampton, Marah E. to L. C. Alison 9-7-1876
Hampton, Margaret to Richard Pearce 9-12-1857 (no return)
Hampton, Matilda E. to Thomas Badgett 5-26-1855 (5-27-1855)
Hampton, Matilda to James Shell 8-24-1874 (9-1-1874)
Hampton, Matilda to Thomas Badgett 12-14-1854 (no return)
Hampton, Nancy A. to Joseph Cosbia 12-29-1869 (12-30-1869)
Hamrick, Mary to Clem Gaddy 12-6-1850
Handrix, Hannah E. to William Scott 3-1-1869 (3-2-1869)
Hardin, Delila to Pleasant G. Nave 2-1-1868 (2-2-1868)
Hardin, Emiline to Samuel Campbell 5-7-1864
Hardin, Isabela to Elbert F. Cannon 5-3-1860 (5-6-1860)
Hardin, Margaret to Frederik Shown 3-2-1872
Hardin, Phebe S. to Christian C. Myer 12-1-1851? (12-15-1857)
Harkel, Eliza to Henry Bowers 2-6-1871 (2-12-1871) B
Harmen, Causby to Gorden French 9-10-1851 (8?-11-1851)
Harmon, Alis to Andrew J. Johnson 4-5-1878
Harmon, Amanda to Andrew J. Johnson 4-5-1878
Harmon, Amanda to James French 5-22-1851
Harmon, Elizabeth to Thomas French 8-2-1855
Harnett, Hannah E. to W. B. Sherass? 2-28-1872
Harris, Sarah to Frank Gibbs 11-9-1873
Hart, Elizabeth S. to Robert J. Lusk 7-25-1872
Hart, Elizabeth to Richard J. Lusk 7-25-1872
Hart, Martha J. to Isaac N. Stern (Stover?) 7-25-1869? (no return)
Hart, Mary J. to Geo. W. Dunbar 1-21-1873
Hart, Phebe C. to Calvin A. Campbell 9-1-1855 (no return)
Hart, Sarah E. to William N. Hendrix 9-13-1870 (9-16-1870)
Hartly, Rachael E. to Ninevy Patterson 7-17-1867 (8-18-1867)
Hartly, Susan to Solomon Bush 7-8-1870
Hartly?, Martha to Samuel W. Hodge 12-25-1867 (12-29-1867)
Hatcher, Ann to Isaac N. Bansy? 9-15-1872 (9-19-1872)
Hatcher, Ann to John H. Sellers 1-17-1867
Hatcher, Nancy J. to Joseph R. Smith 1-2-1873
Hathaway, Elizabeth to Lawson W. Fletcher 2-29-1844 (3-30-1844)
Hathaway, Nancy? to Geo. H. M. Smith 1-24-1877 (1-25-1877)
Hathaway, Permelia to John Taylor 3-13-1872 (no return)
Hatly, Sarah to Thomas Cooper 11-7-1877 (11-11-1877)
Hayes, Marget? E. to John W. Claymon 7-27-1863 (no return)
Hayes, Martha to Lenard Merritt 2-20-1858
Hayes, Sarah to J. R. Campbell 5-17-1871 (5-21-1871)
Haynes, Hannah to Nelson Hyder 8-27-1867 (9-3-1867)
Haynes, M. P. to W. D. Haynes 8-25-1859 (9-1-1859)
Haynes, Margaret P. to William D. Haynes 8-25-1859 (9-1-1859)
Haynes, Sarah Ann to Robert Hilton 11-25-1858 (11-30-1858)
Hays, Julia Ann to Benjamin Foust 10-8-1851 (10-9-1851)
Hays, Martha to Lenard Merritt 2-20-1858
Hays, Mary Ann to A. J. Lyon 12-8-1860 (12-9-1860)
Hays, Sarah to J. R. Campbell 5-17-1871 (5-21-1871)
Hays, Susan to John Merritt 9-3-1855 (9-6-1855)
Head, Sarah to David Berry 3-1-1875 (3-13-1875)
Headrick, Ann J. to Pleasant Williams 11-20-1868 (11-22-1868)
Headrick, Elizabeth to Jas. McCathern 9-4-1878 (9-8-1878)
Heatherly, Charlotte to William Peters 11-25-1858
Heatherly, Eliza to David Wilson 12-20-1878 (12-24-1878)
Heatherly, Eliza to Jessee J. Cole 5-4-1862
Heatherly, Elizabeth to Alfred Roberts 8-21-1867 (8-25-1867)
Heatherly, Emeline to James M. Lewis 2-19-1876 (2-28-1876)
Heatherly, Maggie E. to Thomas J. Gomer 1-23-1879 (1-26-1879)
Heatherly, Nancy to Valentine Garland 5-6-1861 (5-8-1861)
Heatherly, Pantitha to William C. Jacobs 9-21-1864
Heatherly, Rebecca to Landon Shuffield 3-9-1878
Heatherly, Sarah A. to Joseph R. Stout 11-8-1876 (11-9-1876)
Heatherly, Sarah to Jacob Taylor 6-17-1868 (6-20-1868)
Heaton, Abigail to Daniel E. Bowers 1-27-1873 (1-28-1873)
Heaton, Eliza to James N. Julian 10-16-1858 (10-21-1858)
Heaton, Eliza to Jas. N. Julian 3-8-1850 (3-10-1850)
Heaton, Hannah to Francis Miller 1-6-1868 (1-10-1868)
Heaton, Marilda to Loranze Miller 3-12-1866 (3-15-1866)
Hellin, Mahelda E. to Robert M. Headrick 1-11-1872
Heltin, Alice to J. N. Fair 5-23-1877 (5-24-1877)
Helton, Elizabeth to Jesse Mathis 5-15-1855
Helton, Loyett S. to William H. Tolsom 12-2-1865 (12-12-1865)
Helton, Mary A. to Levi Woods 9-3-1855 (9-6-1855)

Helton, Mary to Geo. W. Perry 7-10-1869 (7-11-1869)
Helton, Matilda E. to Robert M. Headerick 1-11-1872
Helton, Rosanna to Benjamin Scalf 3-22-1860
Heltone, Nancy C. to David Chambers 3-20-1869 (3-23-1869)
Hendrix, Emily B. to William G. Malloner 9-1-1875 (9-2-1875)
Hendrix, Emmy B. to William G. Mallance? 9-1-1875 (9-2-1875)
Hendrix, Hannah Jane to Alban M. Brown 5-10-1854 (5-11-1854)
Hendrix, Hannah to S. Scott 3-2-1869
Hendrix, Rutha E. to John J. McCorkle 9-18-1866 (9-20-1866)
Hendrix, Susan to William E. Morrell 10-1-1873 (10-2-1873)
Henkle, Margaret to William O. Frasier 10-2-1858 (no return)
Henley, Maryann to David Hinkle 1-26-1876
Hensley, Lavicy to Samuel Jones 5-25-1869 (5-27-1869)
Hickeny, Matilda to Jeremiah Miller 12-9-1842 (12-13-1842)
Hickey, Ann to Thomas J. Crumley 12-25-1858 (12-24?-1858)
Hickey, Emma to George W. Crumley 9-11-1860? (no return)
Hickey, Josephine to Samuel J. Scott 1-12-1871 (2-19-1871)
Hickey, Saraphin to Samuel J. Scott 1-12-1871 (2-19-1871)
Hickman, Mary to William Gibs 10-31-1860 (11-1-1860)
Hicks, Elizabeth to Andrew Murry 11-17-1873 (12-17-1873)
Hicks, Elizabeth to John Wishorn (2-26-1879 (3-2-1879)
Hicks, Elizabeth to Landon Whitehead 5-27-1858 (1-28-1859)
Hicks, Tempy to Adam Carver 2-25-1870 (3-1-1870)
Hicky, Ann to Thomas J. Crunly 12-25-1858 (12-26-1858)
Hill, Jane to John G. Townsend 4-17-1866 (4-19-1866)
Hilton, Cathern to Geo. M. Perry 3-28-1875
Hilton, Emaline to Jos. W. Parker 7-30-1855 (7-31-1855)
Hilton, Loyette S. to William H. Folsom 12-2-1865 (no return)
Hilton, Rarsanna to Benjamin Scalf 1-14-1860 (3-27-1860)
Hines?, Martha E. to Isaac Carriger 2-26-1869 (7-28-1869)
Hinkle, Margaret to William O. Frasher 10-2-1858 (10-4-1858)
Hinkle, Nancy Ann to F. J. Luner? 3-14-1863 (3-15-1863)
Hinkle, Nancy to William Gibson 11-3-1866 (11-11-1866)
Hinkle, Sally to J. N. Harden 11-29-1878 (11-30-1878)
Hinton, Clarisy to Elijah D. Hardin 2-21-1869
Hodge, Charlotie to Thomas E. Williams 12-23-1874 (12-24-1874)
Hodge, Della to James Mackland 6-9-1855
Hodge, Editha to Joseph Gentry 2-6-1863 (2-8-1863)
Hodge, Janie to N. T. Simerly 2-22-1873 (2-23-1873)
Hodge, Julia Ann to John Estip 1-13-1858
Hodge, Loucretia to Waitsel A. Hodges 1-5-1870 (1-6-1870)
Hodge, Lurana to David Stout 3-3-1851 (3-23-1851)
Hodge, Mahaley to Joseph O. Cole 6-14-1853 (6-19-1853)
Hodge, Martha E. to Albert Hugh 2-4-1869
Hodge, Mary J. to N. T. Simerly 2-22-1873 (2-23-1873)
Hodge, Nancy to David Boren 12-23-1874 (12-24-1874)
Hodge, Surrena to Samuel Miller 6-16-1869
Hodges, Ann to John Garland 1-15-1859 (1-19-1859)
Hodges, Delila to William Garland 9-24-1863 (9-29-1863)
Hodges, Julia Ann to John Estep 1-12-1858 (no return)
Hodges, Lorena to David Stout 3-30-1851 (3-23?-1851)
Hodges, Malinda to Andrew Bower 11-29-1870
Hodges, Nancy C. to David C. Boren 12-23-1874 (12-24-1874)
Holafield, Barbra to Peter D. Keton 5-18-1878 (5-19-1878)
Holden, Mary E. to Michael G. Lovett 2-14-1853 (2-15-1853)
Hollaway, Martha to Christian N. Bowers 11-15-1854 (11-17-1854)
Holly, Margaret to John S. Mothern 11-21-1877 (11-22-1877)
Holly, Nancy A. to John W. Slagle 9-2-1865 (9-3-1865)
Honeycut, Mary to Worley Brett 3-21-1866 (3-22-1866)
Honeycut, Susanna to James Woodley 3-16-1849 (3-18-1849)
Hope, Martha to James McLean 7-5-1873
Hopkins, Rebecca to William Prichard 7-26-1862 (7-27-1862)
Hopkins, Sarah A. to Jacob P. Rains 4-7-1856 (1-21-1856?)
Hopson, Margaret E. to William Simerly 5-18-1876 (7-8-1876)
Hopson, Martha to W. H. Blankenship 10-23-1872
Hopson, Rebecah to H. F. Shell 12-2-1877
Hopson, Rebecca to William Prichard 7-26-1862 (7-27-1862)
Horton, Amanda to Albert King 12-28-1865
Hose, Catharn to John B. Hampton 8-11-1860 (8-18-1860)
Hoss, Angaline to Burton Holtsclaw 1-18-1878 (1-20-1878)
Hoss, Catharin to John B. Hampton 8-11-1860 (8-18-1860)
Hoss, Marah to J. B. McLain 7-3?-1873
Houn, Cornelia J. to John W. Peoples 10-17-1877 (10-18-1877)
House, Martha E. to Isaac Carriger 2-28-1869
Housley, Angeline to Nicholas R. Lewis 10-12-1868

Houstin, Deby to John Arrowood 3-2-1879
Houston, Amanda to Albert King 12-28-1865
Howell, Cordelia to Caleb Whitehead 3-13-1871
Hughes, Caroline to Adam Erwin 7-16-1869 (7-17-1869)
Hughes, Nancy to Jacob Snider 1-7-1853 (1-13-1853)
Hughes, Phineda to Thomas Crafford 4-30-1870 (5-1-1870)
Hughes, Prulla to Samuel Hilton 11-18-1858 (11-20-1858)
Hughs, Priscilla to Samuel Hilton 11-18-1858 (11-20-1858)
Hulson, Sally to Jacob I. Drake 11-17-1871
Humphrey, Delia to Alfred Lewis 4-7-1877 (4-8-1877)
Humphrey, Julia A. to Charles E. Butterworth 11-23-1868 (11-25-1868)
Humphrey, M. E. to M. E. Hurly 5-21-1873
Humphrey, Mary Ann to Geo. Malone 1-8-1879 (1-9-1879)
Humphrey, Mary L. to T. C. Caloway 12-19-1878
Humphrey, Nancy A. to John C. Feathers 12-23-1865 (12-24-1865)
Humphrey, Okaperdelia to Landon P. Range 2-19-1866 (1-1-1867)
Hunby, Amanda to P. P. Plessee? 11-11-1873 (11-10?-1873)
Hunt, Elizabeth C. to Geo. W. Swingle 9-12-1876
Hunt, Loucretia A. E. to Andrew C. Bayless 7-20-1857 (no return)
Hunt, Loucretia A. E. to Andrew C. Broyles 7-20-1857
Hurley, Evaline to Colonel A. Estep 10-2-1869
Hurly, Mary to Valentine Garland 11-18-1863 (12-19-1863)
Hurly, May A. to David Hinkle 1-26-1876
Hutsen, Adaline to Pleasant Gibson 1-24-1852
Hutsen, Clarkey to Isaac Lacy 9-6-1851
Hutsen, Hariet to Granville Glover 3-5-1878
Hutsen, Salley to Reuben Lany 10-4-1827 (10-7-1827)
Hutsen, Sally to Jacob J. Drake 11-17-1871
Hyan?, Rebecca to John Campbell 11-9-1853 (11-10-1853)
Hyatt, Elizabeth to John A. Lynch 10-2-1857 (no return)
Hydee, Jane A. to Samuel Banner 12-7-1868 (12-16-1868)
Hyder, Amanda J. to N. E. Hyder 4-18-1871 (4-20-1871)
Hyder, Arzella J. to George W. P. McKehin 7-11-1855 (7-12-1855)
Hyder, Arzella Jane to Geo. W. P. McKehen 7-4-1855 (7-12-1855)
Hyder, Cordelia to J. T. Banner 8-8-1878
Hyder, Drusilla to John W. Livingston 12-19-1853 (12-30-1853)
Hyder, E. A. to W. M. Phillips 12-21-1872 (12-23-1877)
Hyder, Ellen to Amos Grindstaff 8-13-1872 (8-15-1872)
Hyder, Ellen to Arwine? Grindstaff 8-13-1872 (8-15-1872)
Hyder, Emeline E. to Joseph D. Price 9-5-1855 (9-6-1855)
Hyder, Emely to John Lynvill 7-8-1865 (7-9-1865)
Hyder, Emiline to William R. Hodges 3-25-1852
Hyder, Hannah C. to Robert Holley 2-20-1871 (2-22-1871)
Hyder, J. L. to Millard F. Fain 1-24-1874 (1-26-1874)
Hyder, J. L. to Millard F. Farr 1-24-1874
Hyder, Jane A. to Saml. Burrow? 12-7-1868 (12-16-1868)
Hyder, Joanah L. to D. M. Patton 6-16-1860 (6-17-1860)
Hyder, Lorena to H. H. Luvies? 2-12-1862 (2-27-1862)
Hyder, Louisa J. to M. L. Morland 10-24-1871
Hyder, Lousinda J. to Materson L. Moreland 10-24-1871 (10-26-1871)
Hyder, Magie A. to A. J. F. Hyder 6-18-1872 (6-19-1872)
Hyder, Martha A. to Preston Ensor 3-21-1870 (3-22-1870)
Hyder, Martha A. to Preston Ewan 3-21-1870 (3-?-1870)
Hyder, Martha C. to Adam Harmon 12-29-1852 (12-30-1852)
Hyder, Martha to Daniel C. Hyder 2-25-1877
Hyder, Martha to Thomas McKinney 3-21-1874 (3-22-1874)
Hyder, Mary P. to William B. W. Henry 2-19-1850
Hyder, Mary to William McInturff 4-26-1877
Hyder, Nancy M. to John S. Richards 10-23-1859 (10-25-1859)
Hyder, Nancy to William Dugless 8-27-1861 (8-29-1861)
Hyder, Rebecca to John B. Campbell 11-9-1853 (11-10-1853)
Hyder, Rebecca A. to James M. Miller (Mills?) 2-4-1875 (2-2?-1875)
Hyder, Sabina J. to Henry J. Nave 3-23-1876
Hyder, Sally L. to Jos. Hyder 1-23-1878 (3-28-1878)
Hyder, Sarah E. to Archibald Williams 8-14-1858 (8-16-1858)
Hyder, Tabitha J. to David H. Peoples 7-5-1866
Hyder, Tobitha E. to David H. Peoples 7-5-1866
Hyett, Elizabeth to John A. Lynch 10-2-1857
Ingle, Milly to Alexander Frasier 11-9-1859 (11-22-1859)
Ingram, Eliza to Alexander Garland 11-4-1870
Ingram, Helen to Rewfus Miller 8-29-1860 (8-30-1860)
Ingram, Malinda to Albert Hill 1-30-1861 (2-10-1866?)
Ingram, Sarah to William Miller 7-21-1859 (7-22-1859)
Ingrum, Matilda to Albert Hill 1-30-1866 (2-10-1866)

Inmon, Rachel E. to William L. Ensor 8-5-1853
Irick, Hannah to P. L. Walery 9-7-1869
Irick, Hannah to P. L. Water 9-7-1869
Isham?, Amanda to Isaac Oller 1-22-1875 (1-29-1875)
Jackson, Margaret to Nat T. Campbell 3-1-1867 (3-3-1867)
Jackson, Nancy A. to Archibald A. Vest 7-10-1867 (7-11-1867)
Jackson, Sarah J. to Elcana Justis 4-15-1862 (4-6?-1862)
Janes, Phebee to John Meridith 11-25-1862 (12-2-1862)
Jefferson, Nancy A. to Pleasant Gibson 7-12-1866
Jenkins, Clamida J. to J. B. Browning 7-22-1877
Jenkins, Eliza to Leonard Hart 4-19-1856 (4-24-1856)
Jenkins, Elizabeth to Thomas Hunley? 6-9-1877 (6-10-1877)
Jenkins, Harriett to Nathan Gouge 12-7-1874 (12-13-1874)
Jenkins, Jane to James Oliver 12-24-1866 (12-26-1866)
Jenkins, Margaret to John Bishop 12-23-1861 (12-25-1861)
Jenkins, Mary A. to J. F. M. Lewis 8-5-1878 (8-8-1878)
Jenkins, Mary Ann to N. M. Johnson 4-1-1855
Jenkins, Tempy Jane to Henderson Campbell 5-14-1866
Jobe, Emeline to Jeremiah B. Miller 3-23-1867 (3-24-1867)
Jobe, Emma to James A. Kelly 3-14-1878
Jobe, Harriett to James T. Ellis 3-19-1868 (3-20-1868)
Jobe, Harritt G. to Nathaniel W. Taylor 9-13-1875
Jobe, Mary Jane to E. E. Hunter 9-19-1871
Jobe, Nancy to John Smith 2-16-1865
Johnson, Amanda J. to Sion Taylor 7-9-1850
Johnson, Eliza to Willy Blevins 9-30-1861 (10-5-1861)
Johnson, Elizabeth to Alfred M. Shell 6-18-1866 (6-19-1866)
Johnson, J. M. to James L. Goodwin 2-23-1874
Johnson, Jane to George Smith 11-27-1859 (11-29-1859)
Johnson, Jane to Guy Smith 11-27-1859 (11-29-1859)
Johnson, June to Geo. Oliver 11-13-1868 (11-15-1868)
Johnson, L. A. to Hyram Bowman 3-25-1871 (3-28-1871)
Johnson, Martha E. to William Huff 5-7-1856
Johnson, Mary C. to W. T. Rucker 12-17-1867
Johnson, Matilda to John Smith 2-13-1875
Johnson, Molita to John Smith 2-9-1875 (2-13-1875)
Johnson, Nancy J. A. to James L. Goodwin 2-23-1874 (4-22-1874)
Johnson, Nancy to David Pugh 3-30-1871 (4-2-1871)
Johnson, Saraphina L. to John T. King 9-11-1866
Jolly, Martha to Jackson Bowman 7-22-1866 (7-23-1866)
Jolly, Nancy A. to Wm. J. Oliver 11-9-1874 (11-15-1874)
Jones, Allen to L. L. Rowe 6-14-1867 (6-15-1867)
Jones, Allom to Loranzo D. Rowe 6-14-1867 (6-15-1867)
Jones, Elizabeth to Charles N. Campbell 11-12-1840 (11-15-1840)
Jones, Hannah to David Marlen (Martin?) 12-31-1870 (1-1-1871) B
Jones, Mary to Geo. G. Frett 3-6-1871 (3-7-1871)
Jones, Mary to George C. Ford 3-6-1871 (3-7-1871)
Jones, Phebe to John Meredith 11-25-1862 (12-2-1862)
Jones, Susan to Jackson West 6-6-1870
Jones?, Sarah A. to James H. Ellis 6-14-?
Julion, Caroline to E. K. Bowman 1-25-1852 (1-28-1852)
Kales, Julia to James H. Whithead 2-2-1874 (2-8-1874)
Kean, Nancy Ann to James? H. Johnson 5-8-1861 (5-9-1861)
Keen, Amanda J. to Geo. W. Swamer 2-4-1856 (2-10-1856)
Keen, Martha to Carter Johnson 11-2-1861 (11-5-1861)
Keen, Mary E. to Christopher C. Bowman 6-8-1859 (6-9-1859)
Keen, Nancy Ann to Francis M. Johnson 5-8-1861 (5-9-1861)
Keene, Margaret to Wilson Baker 9-16-1875
Keener, Matilda A. R. to Nathaniel Jones 9-6-1871 (9-7-1871)
Kelley, Nancy to Jonathan Poland 8-12-1862
Kelley, Rhoda to William Carver 8-19-1873 (8-20-1873)
Kelly, Nancy to Jonathan Poland 8-12-1862
Kelly, Rhoda A. to William Carrier 8-19-1873 (8-30-1873)
Kendall, Elizabeth to R. C. White 3-21-1861 (3-24-1861)
Kener, Margaret to Wilson Baker 9-16-1875
Kenik, Matha? C. to William J. Crucher 7-11-1861 (7-23-1861)
Kenley, Mirey to Wilson Britt 12-18-1850
Kenley, Sarah to Christopher Price 12-15-1850 (12-22-1850)
Kennick, Cathern A. to Jno. L. Vanconer? 11-22-1875 (11-25-1875)
Kennick, Martha C. to William C. Crutcher 7-1-1861 (no return)
Kennick, Nancy J. to George Fulkerson 12-12-1859 (12-15-1859)
Kent, Sarahfinna to Saml. McKinney 11-1-1876 (11-2-1876)
Kettle, Sarah to Geo. Loudermilk 11-4-1867 (11-14-1867)
Kibler, Emey to William Hart 9-22-1868 (9-24-1868)
Kibler, Mary to B. F. Alexander 12-24-1861

Kidwell, Molley J. to Henry C. Austin 12-3-1874 (12-10-1874)
Kinally, Ellen T. A. to John Wilson 9-23-1847
Kincade, Margaret to Hyder Campbell 7-7-1869 (7-9-1869)
Kinley, Adaline to Geo. Price 3-7-1864
Kinnick, Martha C. to William C. Critcher 7-11-1861 (7-23-1861)
Kite, Martha C. to Murray Livingston 1-26-1874
Kite, Ruth to Ruben P. Cook 7-16-1855
Kite, Saraphina to Geo. W. Martin 10-17-1850
Kites, Martha to Mary Livingston 1-26-1874
Kitzmiller, M. J. to S. H. Millard 10-25-1873 (10-26-1873)
Klux, Polly to Alfred Snapp 4-6-1874 (4-9-1874)
Krous, Elizabeth A. to William Clark 1-9-1854 (1-12-1854)
Krouse, Mary to Henry Miller 3-3-1857 (3-5-1857)
Kughn, Cathern to Samuel Boyd 6-11-1851
Lacy, Elizabeth to John Emmert 5-4-1857 (5-5-1857)
Lacy, Emmy T. to John Roberts 8-22-1870 (8-23-1870)
Lacy, Ester P. to Thomas H. Morrell 3-2-1872 (2?-5-1872)
Lacy, Eveline G. to Isaac H. Mothern 1-11-1862 (1-12-1862)
Lacy, Hanah C. to Michael B. Hyder 9-7-1857 (9-10-1857)
Lacy, Hannah to Jefferson Moris 3-9-1851
Lacy, Hester P. to Thos. Morrell 3-1-1872
Lacy, Leah to Albert King 6-7-1856 (6-8-1856)
Lacy, Lusinda to Wesley Swiney 3-13-1861 (3-17-1861)
Lacy, Mary to Joseph H. Garland 12-5-1849
Lacy, Nancy A. E. to John F. Allen 1-7-1873 (1-?-1873)
Lacy, Nancy J. to Wm. A. Dyke 6-24-1857 (6-25-1857)
Lacy, Ruth Ann to Henry Mothern 7-17-1878 (7-18-1878)
Lacy, Sarah E. to David Curtice 7-26-1851 (7-27-1851)
Lacy, Theodosy to James C. Crow 2-21-1878 (2-24-1878)
Lains, Jamima to Henry Kee 6-29-1865 (7-2-1865)
Lane, E. A. S. to R. L. McBee 5-19-1852 (5-20-1852)
Lane, Elizabeth to James M. Martin 12-24-1851 (12-25-1851)
Lany, Elizabeth (Hannah)C. to Michael B. Hyder 9-7-1857 (9-10-1857)
Lany?, Charlottie A. to George W. Little 3-23-1866 (3-25-1866)
Law, Malinda to Jackson Green 8-26-1872
Law?, Cathan L. H. to Josiah Hodges 2-27-1871 (3-2-1871)
Lawe, Jane to David Robertson 2-25-1873 (2-26-1873)
Laws, Delilah to John W. Smith 1-5-1857 (1-8-1857)
Laws, Jemima to Henry Kee 6-29-1865 (7-2-1865)
Laws, Selia to William Ryefield 5-30-1874 (5-31-1874)
Lawson, Ellen to Isaac Taylor 8-1-1863 (8-3-1863)
Leadford, Mary to William Baker 3-2-1868 (3-5-1868)
Lee, Mary to John N. Lyon 5-30-1874 (5-31-1874)
Lelsmiller, M. S. to S. H. K. Miller 11-17-1873
Lenard, Harriett to Nathan Gouge 12-7-1874 (12-13-1874)
Lenard, Matilda to David Garvin? 2-22-1854
Lenderwood, Eliza A. to Franklin Morris 1-20-1866 (1-21-1866)
Leonard, Julia A. to Jacob B. Miller 6-7-1856 (6-10-1856)
Leonard, Rebecca to James Reed 12-3-1877
Leslie, Mary to Elija C. Hathaway 3-21-1852 (no return)
Leslie, Rebecca to John McLaughlin 6-13-1867 (6-14-1867)
Lessley, Louisa to Lawson H. Campbell 8-22-1857 (8-27-1857)
Lessly, Rebecca to John McClocklin 6-13-1867 (6-14-1867)
Lester, Martha J. to Abraham Hathaway 2-18-1855
Lewer?, Emeline to Alexander Culbert 2-5-1858 (1-3-1859)
Lewis, Casander to Vincent Carden 4-16-1874
Lewis, Catharin to James Nidifer 11-20-1855 (11-14?-1855)
Lewis, Celia Ann to William A. D. Pearce 12-29-1856 (12-30-1856)
Lewis, Cordelia to Allen Taylor 11-29-1878 (11-30-1878)
Lewis, Edney L. to William Campbell 12-18-1866 (12-23-1866)
Lewis, Eliz. J. to Cherstly Peters 2-5-1866 (2-22-1866)
Lewis, Eliza A. to James L. Smith 4-5-1871 (4-9-1871)
Lewis, Eliza L. to Chrisley Pters 2-5-1866 (2-22-1866)
Lewis, Elizabeth to Wm. E. Mothern 1-11-1854 (1-12-1854)
Lewis, Emelin to Alexander Culbert 7-5-1858 (12-6-1858)
Lewis, Jane to John V. White 7-26-1872 (8-4-1872)
Lewis, Julia to James L. White 4-27-1859
Lewis, Lovinia I. to Teter Colbough 1-3-1868 (1-8-1868)
Lewis, Manerva to Andrew River 6-2-1862 (6-3-1862)
Lewis, Manervy to Asa Foster 4-3-1858
Lewis, Margarett E. to Harrison H. Elliott 12-17-1859 (12-18-1859)
Lewis, Martha to David H. Shull 9-19-1865 (10-31-1865)
Lewis, Mary to Thomas Gloone? 1-14-1860 (1-15-1860)
Lewis, Rhody A. E. to John C. Mothison 12-8?-1866 (12-11-1866)

Lewis, Salina J. to A. B. Pearce 1-12-1852 (1-15-1852)
Lewis, Sarah to Benjamin Clemons 2-27-1862 (3-2-1862)
Lewis, Selia A. to W. A. D. Pearce 12-29-1856 (1-4-1857)
Lewis, Susan E. to Russell Weaver 4-18-1878
Lewis?, Julian S. to James L. White 4-27-1859
Lilley, Mary A. to Marron Glover 3-15-1870
Lilley, Nancy C. to George Milhorn 12-9-1868
Lindermood, Eliza Ann to Franklin Morris 1-20-1866 (1-?-1866)
Linvill, Matilda to William Britt 10-17-1850
Linville, Rosanna J. to James Hughes 11-17-1853 (11-20-1853)
Liply?, Louisa to L. H. Campbell 8-22-1857 (8-27-1857)
Lipps, Eliza C. to John Simerly 1-5-1865 (6-22-1865)
Lipps, Jane to Ira J. Kolluff? 1-16-1869 (1-17-1869)
Lipps, Jane to Philip Markland 4-3-1864 (4-10-1864)
Lipps, Mary Jane to Ira Ratliff 1-16-1869 (1-17-1869)
Lipps, Mary Jane to Landon C. Ellis 4-19-1856 (4-20-1856)
Lips, Martha W. to John A. Lowe 3-13-1861 (3-14-1861)
Little, C. A. to A. J. Feaster 10-3-1874 (10-4-1874)
Little, Cathane to Josiah Hodge 2-27-1871 (3-2-1871)
Little, Elizabeth to Jackson Scott 7-19-1866
Little, Elizabeth to William G. Humphreys 5-2-1866 (5-3-1866)
Little, Margaret to William R. Campbell 7-31-1854 (8-1-1854)
Livers, Eliza to James L. Smith 4-5-1871 (4-9-1871)
Livingston, Edy to Tobias Lewis 1-2-1856 (1-4-1856)
Lively, Ann to James Myers 4-16-1861 (4-17-1861)
Loe, Elizabeth to William Colbough 12-23-1874 (12-24-1874)
Long, Nancy to Samuel Tipton 7-25-1824 (7-27-1824)
Loudermilk, Cordelia to James E. Shell 7-11-1874 (7-12-1874)
Loudermilk, Martha J. to G. W. Hicks 11-28-1858 (12-2-1858)
Loudermilk, Nancy J. to David M. Taylor 12-29-1866 (1-10-1867)
Loudermilk, Rebecca A. to John A. Ready 9-18-1878 (9-26-1878)
Loudermilk, Susanna to Noah Saylor 1-1-1856 (1-3-1856)
Louis, Mary to Thomas Glover 1-14-1860 (1-15-1860)
Louisa?, Nancy L. to Benjamin W. Bowen 9-5-1852 (11-17-1851?)
Love, Fanny to David Williams 3-5-1873 (4-13-1873)
Love, Fanny to Landon C. Taylor 10-8-1870
Love, Julia to Lewis Harris 7-9-1866 (7-15-1866) B
Love, Lena to Timothy Greene 3-1-1876 (3-3-1876)
Lovelace, Phebe to William Williams 4-?-1861 (4-14-1861)
Loveles?, Eliza J. to Geo. W. Fair 10-5-1865 (10-7-1865)
Loveless, Amanda to Samuel Nidifer 11-15-1851 (11-16-1851)
Loveless, Ann to James Myers 4-16-1861 (4-17-1861)
Loveless, Mary to George F. Gourly 9-28-1876
Loveless, Nancy to John F. Lewis 7-15-1870
Lovless, Delitha to William Blevins 11-20-1865 (11-?-1865)
Lovless, Eliza J. to George W. Pharr 10-5-1865 (10-7-1865)
Lovless, Nancy to John F. Lewis 7-15-1870
Lovless, Tobitha to William Blevins? 11-20-1865 (11-21-1865)
Lovy, Jane to Nathanl. Edens 5-6-1861 (5-12-1861)
Low, Urry? Melvina to John S. Rusell 8-21-1865
Lowdermilk, Martha Jane to G. W. Hicks 11-28-1858 (12-2-1858)
Lowe, Fanny to Landon C. Taylor 10-8-1870
Lowe, Jane to Daniel Robertson 2-25-1873 (2-26-1873)
Lowe, Lucinda to Thomas Taylor 12-29-1877 (12-30-1877)
Lowe, Mary M. to Samuel Boyd 11-30-1857 (no return)
Lowe, Melvina to John R. Campbell 2-5-1868 (2-6-1868)
Lows, Delila to John W. Smith 1-5-1857 (1-8-1857)
Loyd?, Mary to Elbert Glover 9-15-1872
Lucas, Elizabeth to Andrew L. Renolds 11-1-1867 (11-8-1867)
Lucas, Pernina to Alphaus Howard 10-12-1850 (10-13-1850)
Lucus, Elizabeth to Andrew R. Renolds 11-1-1867 (11-8-1867)
Lunceford, Hannah R. to James W. Dugger 11-8-1875 (11-13-1875)
Luncey?, Mary J. to R. P. Shell 9-30-1865 (10-1-1865)
Luner?, Martha to David H. Shull 9-19-1865 (10-31-1865)
Lunier, Manerva to Asa H. Foster 4-3-1858
Lunsford, Mary to Andrew Whitehead 4-7-1871 (4-23-1871)
Lunsford, Nancy C. to James M. Goodwin 12-11-1866 (12-13-1866)
Lusk, Edney to Archabold Coldwell 11-5-1868
Lusk, Sarafina to K. K. Range 6-11-1860 (6-21-1860)
Lyle, Mary E. to William Baker 12-23-1871 (12-24-1871)
Lyles, Jane to Geo. W. Lyles 1-2-1867 (1-3-1867)
Lyles, Sarah L. to B. F. Daniel 2-6-1875
Lyon, Eliza to Jackson Soner? 3-20-1857 (3-21-1857)
Lyon, Margaret to William P. Davis 1-14-1871
Lyon, Mary A. M. to George Lyon 11-27-1869 (11-29-1869)

Lyon, Mary A. M. to John F. Lewis 11-27-1869 (11-29-1869) •
Lyon, Mary Jane to Joseph Walker 12-4-1877 (12-5-1877)
Lyon, Mary Jane to William S. Lacy 3-13-1855 (3-15-1855)
Lyon, Mary to Elbert Glover 9-15-1872
Lyon, Mary to Washington Cawer? 11-23-1872 (11-24-1872)
Lyon, Rebecca F. to James L. Hays 3-17-1855 (3-18-1855)
Lyon, Ruth E. to David N. Nave 10-13-1855 (10-18-1855)
Lyons, Elizabeth J. to William Mottern 11-8-1876 (11-9-1876)
Lyons, Margaret to William P. Davis 1-14-1871 (1-15-1871)
Lyons, Mary to Washington Carier? 11-23-1872 (11-24-1872)
Lyons, Selia to Alfred Peck 2-3-1866 (2-4-1866)
Maberry, Myria to James Caraway 5-10-1867 (5-11-1867)
Macy, Margaret to Kinedo Deloach 10-14-1874
Magee, Rosetta to Daniel Magee 1-3-1866 (no return)
Main, Elizabeth to Charles Moreland 7-14-1854 (7-15-1854)
Maines, Elizabeth to Thomas Cooper 5-17-1834
Manis, Delrey W. to Isaac William 11-26-1870 (12-11-1870)
Manning, Rebecca to J. M. M. Huston 3-29-1866
Mararity, Elizabeth to James L. Lewis 2-6-1873
Maring?, Rebecca to James M. M. Houston 3-29-1866
Markland, Amanda to Anderson L. Cole 2-22-1864 (2-24-1864)
Markland, Amanda to Andrew Cole 2-22-81864
Markland, Nancy A. to William Smith Archer 8-14-1861 (8-16-1861)
Markland, Nancy to Smith? Archer 8-14-1861
Markland, Sarah to Alvin Taylor 4-12-1862 (4-13-1862)
Martin, Fanny Jane to Michael Stephens 8-5-1866 (8-15-1866)
Martin, H. to Julias T. Landingham 8-11-1873 (8-12-1873)
Martin, Rebecca to John L. Murry 11-26-1851 (11-27-1851)
Martin, Sarah C. to Frederick Gibson 11-26-1875 (11-28-1875)
Maser?, Rebecca J. to Joseph Gentry 12-26-1868
Mast, Margaret A. to Thomas H. Hunt 8-19-1856
Mast, Martha J. to Henderson Smith 3-27-1866 (4-10-1866)
Mast, Sefrony E. to Newton Banner 7-1-1867
Masten, Louisa to John Hilliard 5-16-1877
Masters, Mary to Andrew Head 2-20-1872
Mastin, Julia to Henry T. Terrin 7-24-1869 (7-25-1869)
Mastin, Julia to Henry T. Turner 7-24-1869 (7-25-1869)
Matherly, Jane to Christly Simerly 9-11-1862
Matherly, Mary E. to William T. Nave 4-16-1874 (4-17-1874)
Matherly, Sarah to Thomas Gourley 1-22-1879 (1-23-1879)
Matherson, Amanda M. to David F. Nave 7-30-1873 (7-31-1873)
Mathis, Harriet to Julius Landingham 8-11-1873 (8-12-1873)
Mathis, Mary A. to Andrew Head 2-20-1872 (2-22-1872)
Mathis, Sarah to James Golehor 11-24-1868
Mathison, Amanda to David F. Nave 7-30-1873 (7-31-1873)
Mathorn, Harritt to Harrison H. Range 7-24-1865 (8-1-1865)
Mattern, Mary to B. M. Lacy 11-28-1878
Mays, Margaret to Kineda Deloach 10-14-1874
Mayton, Elizabeth to William Tapp 10-19-1850 (10-20-1850)
McAlister, Elizabeth to Joseph Lacy 3-22-1875 (3-23-1875)
McAlister, Mary Ann to William Cassida 11-24-1859
McCalister, Margarett E. to Thos. C. Frazer 4-21-1859 (no return)
McCarthin?, Alpha to Elijah D. Williams 4-22-1871 (8-24-1871)
McCaslin, Silpha to E. D. Williams 4-22-1871 (8-4-1871)
McClain, Susanna to James Lane 12-24-1853 (12-25-1854)
McConnel, Elizabeth to Jesse Whitson 8-7-1820 (8-10-1820)
McCorkle, L. M. to Joseph Hughes 5-23-1868 (5-24-1868)
McCulloch, Mary F. to A. H. Webb 5-28-1877
McDalstrale, Eliza to B. B. Cagle 10-2-1877 (10-3-1877)
McDoniel, Lousinda to Jno. C. Gourley 2-25-1852 (2-26-1852)
McFall, Nancy A. to William R. Perkins 6-21-1865 (6-29-1865)
McFally, Sarah to Harrison Hillard 1-4-1865 (1-6-1865)
McGraw, Helia to Rufus Miller 8-29-1860 (8-30-1860)
McInterff, Racheal to Christopher Norris 2-13-1855 (2-14-1855)
McIntire, Sarah B. to Philip Hendrix 6-23-1854 (6-25-1854)
McIntosh, Elizabeth to James McIntosh 8-1-1852 (8-4-1852)
McIntosh, Sarah G.? to H. C. Smith 3-8-1876 (3-9-1876)
McInturff, Ann(a) I. (J?) to T. M. Bowman 7-12-1873 (7-13-1873)
McInturff, Caroline to W. F. Norris 11-28-1867
McInturff, Lorina A. to John A. Brumet 6-12-1872 (6-14-1872)
McInturff, Lousinda to Martin Britt 9-10-1862 (9-11-1862)
McInturff, Mary to John Price 2-24-1872 (2-25-1872)
McInturff, Mary to John Price 2-24-1873 (2-25-1873)
McInturff, Rebecca M. to W. M. Bowman 5-7-1871
McInturff, Rebecca to Wm. M. Bownell 5-7-1871

McInturff, Sarah A. to John Brevert? 6-12-1872 (6-14-1872)
McIntush, Rachel to Moses Johnson 10-3-1855
McIntyre, Sarah to Daniel Bowman 2-26-1850 (3-30-1850)
McKee, Amanda to Moses Fuddle 12-5-1859 (12-9-1859)
McKeehen, Elizabeth D. to Brint P. French 8-7-1860
McKeehen, Hannah to Saml. McKehen 5-10-1860
McKeehen, Mary Jane to John A. C. Lusk 1-27-1866 (1-28-1866)
McKeehen, Nancy J. to Jonathan M. Range 6-11-1866 (6-14-1866)
McKeehen, Sarah E. to Jeremiah B. Range 10-2-1865 (10-5-1865)
McKeene, Jane to Isaac Jones 5-18-1872 (5-19-1872)
McKehen, Mary E. to Jeremiah R. Jones 10-2-1865 (10-5-1865)
McKehen, Mary J. to J. A. C. Lusk 1-27-1866 (1-28-1866)
McKehen, S. C.(E) to C. G. Snodgrass 2-26-1875 (2-28-1875)
McKehn, Caroline to John Constable 1-17-1867
McKehn?, Aletha to Johnathan Combs 5-14-1851 (5-15-1851)
McKimay, Mary Ann to Geo. W. Richards 8-16-1862 (8-17-1862)
McKiney, Delia to Jacob Martin 10-1-1877 (11-18-1877)
McKiney, Emily to Samul Street 12-16-1865
McKinney, Alice to James Crumley 2-27-1875 (2-28-1875)
McKinney, Caroline to Meredith Y. Morton 7-27-1871
McKinney, Catharn to Calvin Gouge 12-28-1870 (12-29-1870)
McKinney, Delila to Samuel Guy 11-9-1854
McKinney, Emily to Samuel Street 12-16-1865
McKinney, Judah C. to David M. Simerly 12-30-1865 (1-1-1866)
McKinney, Margaret P. to Marshall Boyd 2-21-1871 (2-23-1871)
McKinney, Mary J. to Samuel Stover 1-19-1871
McKinney, Mary to William Stephens 3-24-1859 (3-?-1859)
McKinney, S. L. to H. H. Manning 6-8-1878 (6-13-1878)
McKinney, Sarah E. to William Shipley 10-28-1871 (11-2-1871)
McKinney, Sarah to Clingman Heard 4-14-1864 (4-15-1864)
McKinny, Carolin to Meridith Y. Martin 7-27-1871
McKinny, Catharin to Calvin Gouge 12-28-1871 (12-29-1870?)
McKinny, Judah to David Simerly 12-30-1865 (1-1-1866)
McKinny, Mary Ann to G. W. Richards 8-16-1862 (8-17-1862)
McKiny, Carolin to M. Y. Martin 7-27-1871
McKiny, M. P. to Marshell Boyd 2-20-1871 (2-23-1871)
McKiny, Mary C. to Samuel Stover 1-19-1871
McKiny, Sarah E. to William Shipley 10-28-1871 (11-2-1871)
McKiny?, Sarah E. to William Shipley 3-28-1870
McKissic?, Jane to Isaac Jones 5-18-1872 (5-19-1872)
McKorkle, Martha J. to Robt. B. Williams 3-3-1861 (3-28-1861)
McKorkle, Mary to Rodney A. Webb 12-21-1857 (12-24-1857)
McKorkle, S. to Joseph Hughes 5-23-1868 (5-24-1868)
McLaughlin, M. A. to John Barnes 7-24-1874 (7-27-1874)
McLeod, Margaret to Robert R. Taylor 4-15-1873 (4-16-1873)
McLoud, Margaret A. to Robert C. Taylor 4-15-1873 (4-16-1873)
McLouglin, Martha A. to John Barnes 7-24-1874 (7-26-1874)
McNabb, Elizabeth to Wesley Johnson 7-12-1873 (7-13-1873)
McNabb, Jane to Kinchen Miller 9-7-1855 (9-9-1855)
McNabb, Lydia B. to Wm. Landreth 7-16-1870
McNabb, Lydia to William H. Rowe 11-13-1866 (maybe Dec.)
McNabb, Margaret C. to James T. Cooper 9-12-1857 (9-13-1857)
McNabb, Margarett to James T. Cooper 9-13-1857
McNabb, Martha E. to George C.(W.?) Bowman 10-20-1857 (10-22-1857)
McNabb, Mary to Thomas Buck 11-17-1866
McNabb, Sabina to Jesse Toney 1-10-1857 (1-15-1857)
McNabb, ____ to John A Shell ?-?-1871 (with spring)
McNatt, Martha E. to Geo. W. Bowman 10-20-1857 (10-22-1857)
McNeese, Rebecca to Wm. C. Roberts 2-13-1879 (2-16-1879)
McQueen, Elizabeth to Jessee Lewis 12-1-1855 (12-2-1855)
McQueen, Sarah to Isaac Cagle 7-26-1873 (7-27-1873)
Menen?, Sary J. L. to J. F. Perkins 12-13-1851 (12-14-1851)
Merdith, Louisa to David H. Mills 9-10-1870 (9-16-1870)
Meredas?, Nancy to Wesley Jones 8-24-1867 (8-20?-1867)
Meredith, Lorena to Peter Joins 11-3-1874 (11-7-184)
Merideth, Catherine to M. B. Cole 12-13-1877 (12-20-1877)
Meridith, Adaw? to Saml. Stout 7-30-1875 (8-1-1875)
Meridith, Louisa to David H. Miller 9-10-1870 (9-16-1870)
Meridith, Susanna to Andrew Whitehead 3-25-1858 (4-1-1858)
Merit, Rebeca to Jacob Hyder 10-24-1871 (10-26-1871)
Merly?, Nancy Louisa to Benjamin W. Bowers 9-5-1852 (11-17-1851?)
Merrett, Ann to Wilson McKiney 4-6-1861 (4-7-1861)
Merrett, Eliza J. to Henry Sims 9-4-1878
Merrett, Rebecca to Jacob K. Hyder 10-24-1871 (10-26-1871)

Merrit, Viney to John McKinney 7-2-1860 (7-15-1860)
Merritt, Elizabeth to William E. Montgomery 1-7-1850 (1-10-1850)
Merritt, Emeline to Nathaniel Sizemore 7-25-1878 (7-28-1878)
Merritt, Viny to W. M. Gourley 6-1-1877 (6-3-1877)
Miller, Alice O. to Saml. Bishop 12-30-1875
Miller, Ann J. to James Smith 9-17-1871 (9-19-1871)
Miller, Annie J. to E. W. Hampton 4-25-1879 (5-7-1879)
Miller, Edna to Samuel W. H. Williams 2-13-1862
Miller, Elizabeth Jane to Jacob B. Bolling 1-13-1856 (1-14-1856)
Miller, Elizabeth to Jackson Ellis 2-7-1869
Miller, Elizabeth to Jas. T. Peters 1-13-1860 (1-15-1860)
Miller, Elizabeth to William D. Geisler 8-16-1875 (8-26-1875)
Miller, Emely to William Blackburn 10-31-1867 (11-2-1867)
Miller, Eva C. to Thomas J. Brett 8-16-1878 (8-17-1878)
Miller, Eva M. to W. F. Dunney 7-19-1866
Miller, Harriet to H. E. Bell 6-17-1875 (7-11-1875)
Miller, Joanah to Aaron Shell 10-3-1874 (10-4-1874)
Miller, Julia to James I. (Jas. J.?) Boyd 5-20-1852
Miller, Lew to Thomas Buckhannon 8-13-1876
Miller, Malinda to William Smith 5-28-1854 (5-29-1854)
Miller, Manervy to William R. Fletcher 8-1-1862 (8-3-1862)
Miller, Manervy to Wm. R. Fletcher 8-1-1862 (8-3-1862)
Miller, Margaret to David Miller 12-16-1850 (12-19-1850)
Miller, Margaret to William Whitehead 11-4-1854 (11-16-1854)
Miller, Mary A. to Calvin Nediffer 7-31-1873 (8-3-1873)
Miller, Mary M. to John M. Bains 11-7-1872
Miller, Mary to Alexander Johnson 10-26-1859 (10-29-1859)
Miller, Mary to David Edens 10-22-1874
Miller, Mary to David I. Edens 10-22-1874
Miller, Nancy to John Hinkle 6-5-1850 (6-6-1850)
Miller, Nancy to John Smith 1-24-1864
Miller, Nancy to Robert Honeycut 11-26-1872
Miller, Rhoda Ann to Pryor Garland 2-14-1859 (3-7-1859)
Miller, Susan to Lawson Miller 9-28-1877
Miller, Virginia J. to David S. Bower 9-14-1874 (9-15-1874)
Miller, ____ to John McInturff 1-25-1872
Miller, ____ to John T. Campbell no date (with 1875)
Minea?, Mary R. to John K. Miller 7-20-1852 (7-22-1852)
Minton, Mary to Geo. W. Wilson 12-24-1866
Mongumery, Mary J. to Charley Simbs 11-1-1878 (11-3-1878)
Montgomery, Elizabeth to James R. Angel 9-27-1856 (10-3-1856)
Montgomery, Safrona to William Hicky 7-10-1852 (7-18-1852)
Moon, Louisa to Archabold Bradfute 10-25-1834 (10-28-1834)
Moor, Rebeca to William Beam 7-24-1866 (5?-26-1866)
Moore, Rebecca to William Bearnia? 7-24-1866 (7-26-1866)
More, Elizabeth to Henry Bishop 3-27-1855
Moreland, Mahilda to Jacob A. Miller 10-31-1867 (11-5-1867)
Moreland, Mary A. to John Hotticlaw 3-7-1860 (3-12-1860?)
Moreland, Nancy to A. J. Grindstaff 7-9-1853 (7-10-1853)
Moreland, Sarah Jane to Asa L. Bates 8-2-1853
Moreland, Susanna to James Meridith 3-23-1850 (3-25-1850)
Moresby?, Martha to Jeremiah Lyon 9-27-1873 (9-28-1873)
Morgan, Francy to Samuel Nidiffer 12-6-1875
Morgan, Frankey to Robert Nideffer 1-6-1875 (12?-6-1875)
Morgan, Jane to John Bolen 7-20-1866 (10-21-1866)
Morgan, Marah to William G. Meridith 10-12-1874 (no return)
Morgan, Mary (Nancy?) to A. H. Roberts 4-13-1874 (4-14-1874)
Morgan, Sarah to Aaron Greer 4-1-1873
Morgan, Sarah to Amos Guin 4-1-1873
Morgan, Sarah to Wm. G. Meridith 10-12-1874
Morland, Claricy to John Grindstaff 8-12-1854 (8-31-1854)
Morley, Louisa to Benjamin Bowers 11-5-1852 (11-7-1852)
Morrell, Abegal J. to Ryby Daniel 3-7-1857 (3-12-1857)
Morrell, Abigail I. to Riley Dewit? 3-7-1857 (3-12-1857)
Morrell, Louisa to Brownlow Davis 4-28-1870
Morrell, Margaret to Vol Stout 2-6-1870
Morrell, Martha to Volentin B. Stout 2-6-1870
Morrell, Mary E. to John Carter 12-30-1861 (2-10-1862)
Morrell, Mary to Wm. L. Carriger 4-10-1875 (4-11-1875)
Morrell, Mollie to Wm. L. Carriger 4-10-1875 (4-11-1875)
Morrell, Sarah to William Range 11-14-1877
Morrell, Susan to Andrew Curtis 12-29-1860 (12-22-1860)
Morris, Jane to Benja. Richards 7-22-1865
Morris, Lovena to John H. Johnson 10-23-1876
Morris, Margaret to Uriah Bauk 2-29-1828

Morrison, Amah to James M. Hill 10-15-1857
Morsley, Margaret to Moses Johnson 10-5-1850 (10-6-1850)
Morton, Fanny J. to Michael Stephen 8-15-1866
Morton, Jane to Miles Jolley 8-10-1855 (8-30-1855)
Morton, Joanna to John Warren 10-23-1866 (11-1-1866)
Morton, Nancy to Thomas Peters 10-5-1856
Morton, Rarey to John Hazlewood 5-18-1870 (6-19-1870)
Moses, Martha to Jeremiah Lyons 9-27-1873 (9-24?-1873)
Mosley, Rinda to John Vance 4-19-1850 (4-24-1850)
Moss, Lydia J. to John C. Mims? 8-16-1855
Moss, Sarah to Robert Carter 11-9-1871
Motham, Sina to Timothy Hickey 5-11-1850 (5-12-1850)
Motherly, Mary E. to Wm. P. Nave 4-16-1874
Mothern, Harriet C. to Harrison H. Range 7-24-1865 (8-1-1865)
Mothern, Matilda Ann to Guy H. Ellis 3-23-1876
Mothern, Sarah E. to William R. Morrell 2-12-1868 (2-13-1868)
Mothin?, Sinah to John H. Perrigan 4-19-1869
Mottern, Sarah to David P. O'Brien 2-19-1850 (2-21-1850)
Mullins, Harriet E. to Daniel A. Wilson 1-10-1854
Murray, Elizabeth to James L. Lewis 2-6-1873
Myers, Elizabeth to Jackson Oliver 8-23-1863 (no return)
Myers, Nancy to Joihn Q. Adams 5-12-1866 (6-27-1866)
Nance, Adelia J. to James K. Sharp 4-7-1870
Nave, Abigail J. to William D. Oliver 9-20-1871
Nave, Ann E. to Robert Jane 8-23-1871 (8-24-1871)
Nave, Anne J. to William Harden 9-14-1853 (9-15-1853)
Nave, Catherin to Abel Edwards 1-10-1874
Nave, Cheny R. to Lank Davis 11-26-1878 (11-27-1878)
Nave, E. L. to Wm. Campbell 5-27-1873 (5-31-1873)
Nave, Elizabeth to Thomas Crow 5-7-1859 (5-8-1859)
Nave, Eveline to Thomas Odell 10-14-1852
Nave, Georgie A. to Leander Hamby 4-2-1876
Nave, Jane to John Campbell 12-6-1877
Nave, Jane to John West 5-8-1870
Nave, Janie? to John Brent 5-1-1870 (5-8-1870)
Nave, Lavicy to Christian Oliver 9-14-1865 (9-24-1865)
Nave, Levicy to Alexander Stover 7-21-1877 (7-22-1877)
Nave, Martha N. to John W. Lacy 1-3-1867 (2-23-1867)
Nave, Mary C. to William A. Pearce 10-9-1860
Nave, Mary K. to Reuben Carden 1-1-1875
Nave, Mary to James J. Payne 12-5-1868 (12-10-1868)
Nave, Mary to R. Carden 1-1-1875
Nave, Nancy to Jno. L. Fletcher 11-3-1875 (11-4-1875)
Nave, Rebecca to Abraham Jenkins 12-14-1874 (12-15-1874)
Nave, Sarah M. to William H. Potter 3-1-1862 (3-9-1862)
Nave, Sarah to William Crowe 4-29-1852 (5-2-1852)
Navey?, Martha to James H. Justice 12-24-1869 (12-26-1869)
Neatherland, Celia to John Wishon 1-10-1878 (12-16-1878)
Neddon?, Margaret to A. Demsey Maples 3-12-1870 (3-24-1870)
Nedeffer, Adalin to John Blevins 4-22-1860 (4-24-1860)
Nedeffer, Eliza to Thomas Campbell 9-4-1874
Nediffer, Mary to Thomas Woods 12-3-1873 (12-5-1873)
Neely, M. E. to T. D. Griffin 3-3-1874 (3-4-1874)
Neely, Mary E. to Thomas D. Griffith 3-3-1874 (3-4-1874)
Neffer, Eliza to Thomas Campbell 4-4-1874 (9-26-1874)
Newlin, Mary to William M. Bishop 9-11-1856
Newton, Eliza to Thomas Hart 11-20-1860 (1-20-1860?)
Newton, Eveline to John Crow 10-16-1866 (10-18-1866)
Newton, Mary to William M. Bishop 9-11-1856
Newton, Racheal R. to Archabold Coldwell 10-12-1865 (10-13-1865)
Newton, Sarah Ann to Campbell Hart 1-10-1856
Nidefer, Adalin to John Blevins 11-19-1866
Nidefer, Catherine to Andy Buckler 3-9-1876 (3-10-1876)
Nideffer, Eliza to Thomas Campbell 4-4-1874 (9-26-1874)
Nideffer, Nancy to Alfred Peler? 7-18-1874
Nidifer, Eliza Jane to Michael Roberts 5-20-1865 (5-22-1865)
Nidifer, Mary to Thomas Woods 12-2-1873 (12-5-1873)
Nidiffer, Adaline to John Blevins 11-29-1866
Nidiffer, Ann E. to Levi Jenkins 2-17-1875
Nidiffer, Louisa to Alfred C. Peters 10-2-1869 (10-5-1869)
Nidiffer, Nancy to Alfred Peters 7-18-1874
Nidiffer, Permelia to John N. Collins 9-2-1878 (9-5-1878)
Nidiffer, Sarah M. to D. B. Lewis 10-21-1869 (10-24-1869)
Nidiffer, Sarah M. to Samuel B. Lewis 10-21-1869 (10-24-1869)
Nidiver, Margret to A. D. Maples 3-12-1870 (3-24-1870)

Noras, Hannah C. to Enoch Pilkington 3-25-1878 (3-27-1878)
Noris, Mary E. to John S. McInturff 11-2-1853 (11-3-1853)
Norris, Lousinda L. to Nelson McLaukin? 12-27-1873
O'Brian, Eliza E. to William J. Folsom 12-8-1865 (12-10-1865)
O'Brian, Elizabeth to Geo. W. Lenard 12-26-1865 (12-28-1865)
O'Brian, Ellen V. to G. H. Scott 7-12-1875 (8-5-1875)
O'Brian, Hanna A. to Andrew C. Fondrin 9-22-1865 (9-24-1865)
O'Brian, Jane to John Remine 1-11-1863
O'Brian, Margaret J. to James E. Hyder 3-4-1858 (2?-4-1858)
O'Brian, Martha to George Miller 5-31-1865 (6-3-1865)
O'Brian, Mary A. to Joseph C. Renfro 5-1-1856
O'Brian, Mary to J. I. Garland 10-13-1874 (10-14-1874)
O'Brian, Sarah J. to Wm. A. McInturff 4-13-1874 (4-16-1874)
O'Brien, Elizabeth to George Hickey 7-4-1852 (7-25-1852)
O'Brien, Ellen V. to Geo. H. Scott 7-12-1875 (8-5-1875)
O'Brien, Martha S. to Ezekiel Burchfield 1-23-1853 (1-?-1853)
O'Brian, Darthula to James W. Cochren 10-27-1865 (10-29-1865)
Oak, Emaline to William H. Simerly 2-15-1873 (2-16-1873)
Oaks, Nancy to Wm. M. Richardson 3-29-1877 (4-1-1877)
Obrien, Elizabeth to John Lunis? 12-23-1871 (12-25-1871)
Odell, Eliza J. to James M. Smith 7-12-1855 (7-15-1855)
Odell, Eveline to William Rutledge 12-31-1875 (1-1-1860)
Oliver, Amanda to Camern Pearce 9-21-1875 (9-23-1875)
Oliver, Amanda to Joseph Saylor 3-7-1862 (4-15-1862)
Oliver, Elizabeth to Isaac Estep 9-17-1856 (9-18-1856)
Oliver, Elizabeth to John Lewis 12-23-1871 (12-25-1871)
Oliver, Evellin to Gideon Lewis 12-4-1866 (12-9-1866)
Oliver, Frelove to H. P. Richardson 11-26-1871 (11-28-1871)
Oliver, Levisa to B. H. Peters 3-2-1861 (3-3-1861)
Oliver, Nancey C. to Chrisley Oliver 12-23-1871 (12-25-1857?)
Oliver, Nancy to Reuben Peters 9-1-1865 (9-2-1865)
Oliver, Sarah J. to Ansel C. Carden 6-18-1867
Oliver, Sarah J. to Ephrom C. Gentry 12-27-1860 (1-5-1861)
Oliver, Susan to H. P. Richardson 11-26-1871 (11-28-1871)
Oliver, Susan to John Deloach 1-20-1857
Oliver, Susan to John Gentry 10-26-1871
Oliver, Susan to John Simerly 5-2-1871
Oliver, Susann to Christian B. Bowen 1-8-1875 (1-?-1875)
Oliver, Susanna to C. B. Bowers 1-8-1875 (1-9-1875)
Oliver, Susanna to John Deloach 1-20-1857 (2-20-1857)
Oliver, Winny L. to Christley Oliver 12-23-1871 (12-25-1871)
Ollee?, Margaret to Lewis Harris 1-4-1875 (no return)
Olliver, Louisa to Jonathan Williams 11-29-1855 (11-30-1855)
Olliver, Sarah J. to Ephraim Genetry 12-27-1860 (1-5-1861)
Osborn, Sarah Jane to Thomas Douglas 11-13-1877 (12-18-1877)
Overbee, Eury to Lawson Overbee? 1-13-1871?
Overholser, Martha to Landon McKeehan 12-20-1855
Overholser, Mary J. to James F. Matison 10-8-1868 (10-11-1868)
Overhulser, Emelin to Elijah Grindstaff 9-16-18871
Overhulser, Hanah A. to James L. Moreland 2-13-1875 (4-5-1875)
Overhulser, Martha J. to William West 10-1-1866 (10-2-1866)
Overhulser, Martha to Elisha Briant 8-6-1858 (8-9-1858)
Overhulser, Rachel A. to Hampton West 9-5-1866 (9-9-1866)
Overhulser, Rhoda A. to N. T. Y. Tolson? 11-18-1869 (11-20-1870)
Owens, Synthey to George McKeehen 6-23-1865 (6-25-1865)
Pagin (Pugh), Jane to Morgan Treadway 2-19-1867
Pain, Ludora E. L. to Jackson Brooks 5-22-18783 (4?-23-1873)
Paregoy, Sanora F. to M. M. Martin 3-17-1873 (3-19-1873)
Parker, Delia C. to James M. Peoples 11-29-1870
Parker, Eliza to Nathaniel Ingrum 10-14-1875
Parker, Julia C. to James H. Peoples 11-19-1870
Patton, Allace E. to John Young 12-26-1860
Patton, Mary A. to Moses A. Miller 8-19-1858
Patton, Sarah A. to William J. Silvers 9-7-1859 (9-8-1859)
Patton, Susanna J. to Joseph B. Young 1-2-1864 (1-2-1865)
Paulett, Amanda V. to W. C. Hunt 4-10-1860
Payne, Edney to David T. Miller 12-25-1867 (12-26-1867)
Payne, Edney to Edmond Silvers 5-25-1859
Payne, Elizabeth to William Boyd 2-24-1869 (2-25-1869)
Payne, Emiline to Edmond Silvers 5-25-1859
Payne, Evelin to Martin Smalling 1-30-1878
Payne, Margaret to Montgomery T. Williams 10-19-1850 (10-23-1850)
Peak, A. to Samuel Carr 4-9-1870
Pean (Pruis?), Mary A. to John H. Campbell 11-25-1857
Pean, Anzella to Frederick F. Crumly 11-30-1865 (1-11-1866)

Pean, Carolin to R. F. Hazelwood 7-22-187? (with 1871)
Pearce, Carie to Furdinand Gentry 8-5-1877
Pearce, Easther to Isaac White 5-12-1866 (5-13-1866)
Pearce, Emilin E. to David J. Linus? 2-4-1848 (2-24-1848)
Pearce, Every to Lawson Overby 1-13-1871
Pearce, Eviline to Philip Markland 3-7-1878
Pearce, Julia to Jno. Estep 9-17-1886 (9-18-1886)
Pearce, L. J. to Thomas S. Ryon 12-26-1854 (12-28-1854)
Pearce, Laura to Wm. O. Phillip 10-8-1875 (10-14-1875)
Pearce, Lerunsa? to Smith McKee 12-9-1871 (12-10-1871)
Pearce, Loritia to John Taylor 11-13-1872 (11-15-1872)
Pearce, Louisa A. to B. C. Wilson 10-24-1866 (10-28-1866)
Pearce, Martha A. L. to John A. Glenn 1-29-1873 (1-30-1873)
Pearce, Mary C. C. to William J. Berry 2-15-1877
Pearce, Mary E. to Elihu J. Williams 12-30-1868 (12-31-1868)
Pearce, Sarah C. to Thomas A. Dugger 5-7-1859 (5-15-1859)
Peaters, Phoeba to Ruphus G. Minton 10-16-1858 (10-17-1858)
Peek, Ann to Elcana May 4-27-1874
Peep, Ann to Elcana Hays 4-27-1874
Peeps, Sarah to Andrew May 2-19-1867
Peirce, Eliza I. to J. B. Douthet 7-19-1861 (7-21-1861)
Pendeana?, Milli to Jon Taylor 11-1-1875
Peoples, Elizabeth C. to William Bushong 10-6-1862 (10-7-1862)
Peoples, Elizabeth to Frank Williams 1-26-1875
Peoples, Elizabeth to Frank Williams 1-26-1875 (no return)
Peoples, Martha to John W. Bowman 11-17-1869
Peoples, Mary to Jas. M. Taylor 11-3-1859
Perdue, Matilda to William Akers 12-21-1874
Perigory, S. E. to S. P. Bollen 6-19-1873
Perkins, Laura to A. C. White 12-14-1877 (12-20-1877)
Perrigory, Sanora to M. M. Martin 3-17-1873 (3-19-1873)
Perringer, Margaret A. to James W. Hughes 12-8-1856 (12-11-1856)
Perry, Adala to James C. Birnham? 1-18-1871
Perry, Edilin to John Stout 4-6-1866
Perry, Eliza to Owen Sams 8-19-1872
Perry, Elizabeth to Thomas Gourley 1-25-1858 (1-28-1858)
Perry, Elizabeth to William Glover 6-15-1859
Perry, Elzina to Owen Sams 8-19-1872 (8-25-1872)
Perry, Florance A. to Thomas A. Goodwin 9-24-1871
Perry, Florance M. to Thomas A. Goodman 9-24-1871
Perry, Jenney to David S. Helton 4-13-1869
Perry, Leriza to W. D. Pricharad 11-28-1877
Perry, Luster to A. J. Fletcher 9-9-1869
Perry, Martha to Alexander Richardson 12-16-1856
Perry, Modena to Wm. C. Whitehead 12-30-1857 (1-1-1858)
Perry, Nancy to James H. Hoss 1-30-1866 (1-31-1866)
Perry, Sarah to Nathan Almony 2-10-1865
Perry, Viney to Joseph Kughn 8-23-1854 (8-24-1854)
Perry?, Malinda to William Akin 12-21-1874
Persinger, Margaret Ann to James W. Hughes 12-8-1856 (12-11-1856)
Peters, Amanda C. to Eli C. Taylor 12-19-1865
Peters, Eliza C. to William Jenkins 12-22-1875
Peters, Eliza J. to Wm. R. Morrell 1-16-1851
Peters, Elizabeth C. to Alfred M. Williams 10-18-1873 (10-19-1873)
Peters, Elizabeth to Eli Hardin 10-6-1866 (10-14-1866)
Peters, Elizabeth to Wm. E. Nidiffer 3-14-1872
Peters, Emelin to Levi Taylor 7-10-1875 (7-11-1875)
Peters, Eveline to Alvlin P. Haardin 7?-25-1857 (7?-28-1867)
Peters, Mary Ann to Isaac O. Morrell 4-2-1856 (4-26-1856)
Peters, Mary E. to Alfred M. Williams 10-18-1873 (10-19-1873)
Peters, Nancy J. to Thomas Williams 8-17-1878
Peters, Phebe to Benj. H. Peters 5-26-1858
Peters, Phebe to Rufus G. Minton 10-16-1858 (10-17-1858)
Peters, R. E. to James C. Lewis 1-22-1878 (1-23-1878)
Pharr, Hannah to William A. Feathers 3-2-1877 (5-10-1877)
Pharr, Jane to George W. Moody 5-7-1858
Pharr, Margaret to Christian Oliver 11-20-1858 (11-21-1858)
Pharr, Rosana to John Gibson 1-1-1866
Pharr, Sarah A. to Hardin Smith 10-1-1859 (10-6-1859)
Phenix, Susan to B. F. Felty 12-6-1856 (12-8-1856)
Philips, Hanna to James K. P. McNabb 8-21-1861 (8-22-1861)
Phillips, Elizabeth to James M. Willialms 12-30-1864 (1-8-1865)
Phillips, Julia to Joshua M. Patton 6-1-1859 (6-2-1859)
Phillips, Mary Jane to Thomas Y. Patton 10-17-1861 (10-24-1861)
Phillips, Nancy to Francis Hodge 8-15-1875 (8-17-1875)

Phinick, Susan to B. F. Fellig 12-6-1856 (12-7-1856)
Phipps, Monas to Taylor Phipps 12-13-186
Phuen?, Sarah to James Nance 3-8-18783
Pickerieng, Elizabeth to William H. Price 10-18-1859
Pierce, Carline to Alen T. Carriger 9-21-1852 (9-22-1852)
Pierce, Eliza to M. S. Bowers 11-27-1860
Pierce, Elizabeth to Nelson Lipps 8-21-1886 (8-23-1846?)
Pierce, Leodacia R. C. to Jackson Brooks 4-22-1873 (4-23-1873)
Pierce, Lovina V. to Saml. M. S. Myers 2-26-1876 (2-3?-1876)
Pierce, Martha R. to H. N. Crow 1-11-1855
Pierce, Mary A. to John H. Campbell 11-25-1857
Pierce, Mary J. to William H. Dugger 12-12-1868 (12-16-1866)
Pierce, Mary to John T. Bowers 4-19-1856 (4-20-1856)
Pierce, Nancy to Nelson J. Markland 2--19-1851 (3-16-1851)
Pierce, Nancy to Thos. P. Elliott 4-11-1868 (4-13-1868)
Pierce, Sarah J. to David P. Blevins 8-7-1853 (8-8-1853)
Pierce, Sarah to John Archer 10-14-1860
Pleasant, Mary J. to Daniel R. Forbes 12-29-1862 (1-6-1863)
Pleasant, Nancy C. to James M. Richardson 8-5-1875 (8-8-1875)
Pollums, Frances to Philander S. Egbert 9-27-1869 (10-11-1869)
Poor, Josephine to Eli Hardin 4-2-1859 (4-3-1859)
Porch, Hannah to David Saylor 11-8-1865 (11-10-1865)
Potter, Caroline to Elija D. Harden 10-9-1858
Potter, Delila to William Treadway 3-3-1867 (3-30-1867)
Potter, Hanah to John Jones 11-12-1877 (11-19-1877)
Potter, Jane to Gasper Dugger 10-20-1877 (10-21-1877)
Potter, M. L. to M. L. Holly 9-26-1875
Potter, Marah Ann to T. N. McGinis 8-25-1874 (8-24?-1874)
Potter, Martha to James Perkins 11-8-1872 (11-9-1872)
Potter, Mary A. to John W. Morgan 9-14-1873
Potter, Mary to Samuel Montgomery 2-17-1859
Potter, Sarah Ellen to Jas. L. Clawson 7-28-1854 (7-30-1854)
Potter, Susanna to Wm. G. Bowen 9-5-1866
Potter, Tempy to George W. Miller 2-16-1849 (2-18-1849)
Potter, Tempy to Malden Kite 9-28-1859 (10-13-1859)
Powell, Malinda to L. D. Liphford 12-7-1864 (12-20-1864)
Powell, Rachel L. to William L. Powell 3-18-1866 (3-19-1866)
Powers, Martha A. L. to John A. Glover 1-29-1873 (1-30-1873)
Poyner?, Ednay to David T. Miller 12-25-1867
Preen?, Sarah to Alexander Carrell 9-20-1860
Price, Evelina to Wm. Toney 1-25-1855
Price, Nancy C. to Samuel Bowman 1-13-1872 (1-14-1872)
Price?, Susanna C. to Thomas A. Duggar 5-9?-1859 (5-15-1859)
Prichard, Malinda to William B. Simerly 7-14-1862 (7-16-1862)
Prichard, Mary to Robert Jones 3-8-1855 (no return)
Prichard, Matilda to William B. Simmerly 7-14-1862 (7-16-1862)
Prigory, S. E. to S. P. Bolton 6-18-1873 (6-19-1873)
Prock, Hannah to David Sayler 11-8-1865 (11-10-1865)
Profett, Malinda to David L. Goan 6-12-1859
Pruett, Mary to Calvin Milem 7-6-1876 (7-10-1876)
Puden, Mandy to Eli C. Taylor 12-19-1865
Pugh, Chany to Charles Campbell 1-1-1867
Pugh, Manery J. to James P. Price 1-9-1861 (1-10-1861)
Pugh, Mary M. to John H. Treadway 9-23-1868
Pugh, Rachal A. C. to Samuel Williams 4-10-1855 (4-?-1855)
Pugh, Sarah E. to William H. Treadway 6-20-1866 (6-24-1866)
Radin, Eliza to Allen Hamby 2-8-1871 (2-9-1871)
Rainbolt, Elizabeth C. to William A. Lipford 8-14-1866 (8-16-1866)
Rains, Louisa to Sampson Robertson ?-?-1875 (with spring)
Raly, Charlotte Ann to George W. Little 3-23-1866 (3-25-1866)
Range, Barsha A. to Alvin P. Shell 1-24-1862 (1-30-1862)
Range, Barshaby to Elcana D. Range 8-3-1866 (8-5-1866)
Range, Deborah to Abraham Fulkerson 11-10-1856 (11-13-1856)
Range, Delial E. to Joseph Boren 8-17-1857 (8-20-1857)
Range, Ditha? to W. A. Taylor 12-20-1875
Range, Eliza to Abraham Fulkerson 11-17-1858 (11-18-1858)
Range, Lydia A.? to Jacob Lenard 11-15-1871 (11-16-1871)
Range, Mary Ann to John Little 8-11-1854 (8-13-1854)
Range, Mary Eliza to William H. Mothern 2-20-1867 (2-28-1867)
Range, Mary F. to James T. Kelly 4-20-1867 (5-19-1867)
Range, Mary Jane to Jacob Range 9-10-1866 (9-13-1866)
Range, Nanie E. to W. H. M. Smith 3-10-1877 (3-22-1877)
Range, Susanna to John Hyder 8-29-1865 (9-7-1865)
Raper?, Margaret to Joseph P. Ellis? 10-7-1865 (10-10-1865)
Rasor, Eliza to James Cole 3-8-1875

Rasor, Elizabeth to Robert Pearce 4-8-1875 (4-9-1875)
Rasor, Martha A. to S. E. Hampton 12-26-1878
Readie, Eliza to Allen Hamby 2-8-1871 (2-9-1871)
Reason, Eliza to James Cole 3-18-1875
Reckey, Elizabeth to Lewis D. Taylor 3-2-1872 (3-3-1872)
Reece, Hanah A. to Willis Hochs 10-1-1872 (10-3-1872)
Reese, Esther to Isaac White 5-12-1866 (5-13-1866) B
Reeser, Hannah A. to Willis Hicks 10-1-1872 (10-3-1872)
Reno, Sarah Jane to William A. Gibson 1-18-1851 (1-19-1851)
Rewir?, Rebecca to George Blevins 2-27-1862 (3-2-1862)
Richards, Susana to Mattison Bridgman 10-25-1868
Richardson, Carolin to George W. Livingston 12-28-1872 (12-29-1872)
Richardson, Eliza to Isaac Perry 3-6-1875 ((3-7-1875)
Richardson, Eliza to John W. Morgan 3-18-1874 (5-22-1874)
Richardson, Hannah to Geo. W. Arnold 8-13-1876
Richardson, Mary to James Blevins 6-27-1866 (7-1-1866)
Richardson, Mary to Nathaniel T. Smith 11-13-1867 (11-16-1867)
Richardson, Phebe to William Morton 12-30-1856 (12-31-1856)
Richardson, Sarah to Wright Harly 10-23-1876
Richey, Mancy to Isaac C. Laws 9-10-1858
Richie, Elizabeth to Lewis D. Taylor 3-2-1872 (3-3-1872)
Richie, Mary Ann to John Simerlin 12-27-1857 (12-17?-1857)
Richie, Mary J. to Daniel Hardin 1-4-1862
Ritchie, Margaret to Joseph P. Ellis 10-7-1861 (10-10-1861)
Roberson, Margaret to John Howell 10-19-1869
Robert, Carolin to Amos Guinn 9-9-1873
Robert, Lidda M. to D. N. Morliver? 10-8-1871
Roberts, Caroline to James Morgan 9-9-1873 (9-12-1873)
Roberts, Elmira E. to Robert A. Smith 7-22-1873 (9-22-1873)
Roberts, Emeline to David Crawford 9-17-1864 (9-20-1864)
Roberts, Fereby to Andrew J. Harden 8-15-1868 (8-16-1868)
Roberts, Leticia E. to Calvin Custer 7-4-1861
Roberts, Lidda M. to D. N. Morton 10-8-1871
Roberts, Lillia to George H. Angell 1-1-1872 (1-2-1872)
Roberts, Loucinda to Noah Whisenhunt 5-5-1873 (5-6-1873)
Roberts, Mahala to William Grindstaff 10-30-1869 (10-31-1869)
Roberts, Nancy Ann to John M. Hodge 8-2-1877 (8-5-1877)
Roberts, Phebe to Patrick H. Webb 5-12-1858 (5-13-1858)
Roberts, Rebecca to Powell Arnold 9-20-1855
Robertson, ——— to Thomas Nideffer 1-23-1875
Robertson, Charlotte to Richard Glover 12-12-1863 (no return)
Robertson, Delley C. to William Huckler 8-8-1874 (8-9-1874)
Robertson, Dilley C. to William Hinkle 8-8-1874 (8-9-1874)
Robertson, Docia I. to Isaac Estep 7-31-1873 (8-1-1873)
Robertson, Elizabeth to David Owens 8-25-1861 (8-26-1861)
Robertson, Elizabeth to John C. Lacy 3-19-1868
Robertson, Elzena to John Garland 6-22-1875 (6-25-1875)
Robertson, Mahala to Tandy Lee 2-2-1875
Robertson, Mary E. to Thos. B. Whitemore 7-17-18661 (7-25-1861)
Robertson, Mary J. to Samuel Glover 1-3-1850 (no return)
Robertson, Mary Jane to Samuel Glover 1-3-1850
Robertson, Mary to Thomas Nidiffer 1-23-1874 (1-24-1875?)
Robertson, Rachel to John Watson 11-29-1850 (12-1-1850)
Robertson, Sarah to Samuel Taylor 12-18-1871 (12-19-1871)
Robertson, Vina to Lervicy Glover 1-12-1850
Robinson, Emeline to Alexander H. Owens 5-2-1857 (5-3-1857)
Robison, Margret to John Hamet 10-19-1869
Rockhold, Mahala to William Gourley 8-15-1866
Roddie, Martha A. to Henry T. Berry 8-9-1854 (8-10-1854)
Roe, Melviny C. to Paxton Linby 1-1-1857
Rose, Elva L. to William Campbell 5-27-1873 (5-31-1873)
Rourk?, Mary J. to James M. Krouse 10-17-1870 (10-18-1870)
Row, Ann J. to Isaac D. English 10-19-1858 (4-7-1858)
Rowe, Julia A. to John W. McInturff 12-29-1868 (1-3-1869)
Rowe, Mary M. to Samuell Boyd 11-30-1857
Rowe, Melvina C. to Paxton Leslie 1-1-1857 (1-2-1857)
Rowen, Mary J. to James E. Krouse 10-17-1870 (10-18-1870)
Royston, Margaret to Andrew Perry 2-17-1871 (2-18-1871)
Ruber, Jamima to Isaac L. Laws 9-10-1858 (2-18-1871)
Ruber, Mary Ann to David F. Bowen 7-8-1857
Rulen, Mary A. to John Simerliln 12-27-1857
Runge?, Delila E. to Joseph Boren 8-17-1857 (8-20-1857)
Rusell, Emma R. to W. Kethporal 3-24-1875 (4-1-1875)
Rusell, Sarah to Abraham Mores 10-17-1868 (10-18-1868)
Rusk, Edney to Archabald Caldwell 11-5-1868

Russell, Elizabeth to Henry Lyon 10-17-1868 (10-18-1868)
Russell, Sarah to Abraham Moser 10-17-1868 (10-18-1868)
Ryon, Sarah to Benjamin F. Folsom 7-24-1856
Sagle, Cynthia E. C. to Henry Slage 8-26-1845
Salls, Emily to Thomas Jenkins 4-27-1870
Sams, Martha to G. W. Perry 6-28-1873
Sanders, Martha J. to John S. Walker 10-19-1868
Sayler, Eliza to Joseph Williams 10-28-1872 (10-28-1872)
Sayler, Martha to Alen L. Barnes 3-7-1854
Sayler, Mary to N. G. McFarland 5-25-1870 (5-26-1870)
Sayler?, Mary E. to John N. Lyon 5-30-1874 (5-31-1874)
Saylor, Elizabeth to James Barnes 11-6-1861 (11-9-1861
Scalf, Rebecca to James Hinkle 9-2-1856 (no return)
Scalp, Mary E. to G. W. Emmert 2-3-1879
Scott, Martha to Daniel Rowe 12-21-1865 B
Scott, Sudia to Wm. McKinney 9-22-1886
Segan, Margaret A. to Lankester Davis 7-22-1871
Seller, Mary A. to Albert Lacy 4-16-1873
Seller, Sarahfina J. to John Ellis 10-18-1869 (10-21-1869)
Seller, Saraphine E. to John Ellers 10-21-1869
Sellers, Margaret A. to Wm. W. Garland 10-14-1871 (10-15-1871)
Sewerly, Sarah to John Blevins 8-25-1877 (no return)
Sharp, Jane to James M. Simmons 9-26-1866 (9-27-1866)
Sharp, Mariah to Geo. Williams 3-15-1866 B
Shea, Sarah to Alfred J. Campbell 3-25-1851 (3-27-1851)
Shell, Abby to Aaron Shell 12-24-1853 (12-25-1853)
Shell, E. C. to D. T. W. Clark 12-16-1870
Shell, Elizabeth to Caleb Wilcox 10-3-1857 (10-26-1857)
Shell, Elizabeth to Cobb (Caleb?) Wilcox 10-2-1857 (10-29-1857)
Shell, Ellen to Larken Caraway 1-5-1878
Shell, Emaline Catharine to D. T. W. Clark 12-16-1870
Shell, Harriett to Geo. Mothern 4-30-1877 (5-6-1877)
Shell, Hester Ann to John Prichard 4-4-1866 (4-5-1866)
Shell, Lousana to Peter Potter 10-10-1870 (10-23-1870)
Shell, Luona to Jacob Miller 6-10-1876 (6-?-1876)
Shell, Malinda to Hillsberry? Richardson 12-24-1844 (1-8-1845)
Shell, Margaret to James Hinkle 8-18-18871 (8-20-1871)
Shell, Martha A. to Andrew M. Humphrey 4-30-1877 (5-6-1872?)
Shell, Martha to Adam? Baker 3-19-1868
Shell, Martha to William Baker 3-18-1868 (3-19-1868)
Shell, Mary E. to James W. Gates? 12-21-1869
Shell, Matilda to John S. Snodgrass 8-21-1871
Shell, Sarah to Archibald Curtis 5-25-1850 (5-27-1850)
Shell, Sarah to G. W. Miller 9-24-1870
Shell, Susan E. to William Duncy 9-3-1865 (10-1-1865)
Shell, Susanna E. to William Demsey 9-30-1865 (10-1-1865)
Shoemaker, Caroline to Geo. W. Gourley 5-18-1872
Shoemaker, Hannah to Andrew Taylor 11-30-1865
Shufferd, Clary to William Cole 8-10-1874 (8-13-1874)
Shuffield, Amanda to R. B. Reeser 2-16-1875
Shuffield, C. J. to David H. Grindstaff 12-4-1872 (12-25-1872)
Shuffield, Clarecy to William Cole 8-10-1874 (8-13-1874)
Shuffield, M. J. to Richard White 5-25-1877 (5-27-1877)
Shuffield, Martha A. to William S. Green 8-22-1871 (8-24-1872)
Shuffield, Mary A. to Alfred Shuffield 7-14-1870 (7-15-1870)
Shuffield, Mary L. to Alfred Shuffield 7-4-1870 (7-16-1870)
Shuffield, Mary to James White 11-26-1862 (12-8-1862)
Shuffield, Melvena to Silas Perdue 7-12-1871 (7-14-1871)
Shuffield, Nancy to W. A. Perkins 8-28-1851 (8-31-1851)
Shuffield, Selia J. to D. K. Grindstaff 12-4-1872 (12-5-1872)
Shuffield, Selia to Ambrose Jones 4-19-1862 (4-20-1862)
Simerly, Carlin to John Hyder 9-1-1859
Simerly, Cashin (Cathan) to Nicholas Carriger 1-1-1873
Simerly, Catharin to James Lee 6-5-1865 (6-8-1865)
Simerly, Catharine to William Chambers 10-12-1868 (12-29-1868)
Simerly, Catharn to James Leu? 6-5-1865 (6-8-1866?)
Simerly, Catharn to John L. Hyder 9-12-1859
Simerly, Elizabeth to Sanford Miller 9-18-1854 (no return)
Simerly, Hannah to Reuben Gouge 1-29-1870 (1-30-1870)
Simerly, Hannah to Samuel Howard 8-12-1867 (8-13-1867)
Simerly, Jane E. to A. S. Badgley 9-29-1865 (9-30-1865)
Simerly, Mary Ann to Markus G.(D?) Cochran 7-8-1867 (7-14-1867)
Simerly, Mary J. to David Gouge 1-23-1873
Simerly, Mary Jane E. to A. S. Badley 9-29-1869 (9-30-1869)
Simerly, Mary to William Johnson 3-22-1851 (3-27-1851)

Simerly, Mary to William S. Carrell 9-13-1866
Simerly, Perlina J. to William M. McKeehen 5-31-1862 (6-1-1862)
Simerly, Sarah J. to David N. Gourley 11-9-1854
Simerly, Sarah to Reuben Mosley 10-2-1853 (10-4-1853)
Simerly, Selia to William McKinney 2-8-1868 (2-9-1868)
Simerly, Susanna to Benjamin D. Cable 12-3-1855 (12-9-1855)
Simerly, Susannah to David N. Gourly 11-9-1854
Simerly, ____ to Elcana D. Heaton ?-?-1871 (with spring)
Simery?, Mary C. to John P. Walker 10-23-1867 (10-31-1867)
Simmerly, Nancy to Alexander Campbell 3-9-1855 (3-11-1855)
Simmerly, Sarah to Reuben Mosley 10-3-1853 (10-4-1853)
Simmons, Margaret to Henry Fox 4-24-1874
Simons, Elizabeth to Thomas Rowe 9-12-1871 (9-14-1871)
Simons, Elizabeth to William Hicks 2-19-1867
Sims, Jane to Alexander Matherly 6-24-1857 (6-29-1857)
Sims, Jane to Alexander Matherly 6-28-1857 (6-29-1857)
Sims, Julia to John L. Henry 2-4-1877
Sims, Mary to Allen Hamby 11-12-1877 (11-24-1877)
Sims, Rachel to Jackson Sims 6-24-1856
Singletary, Elizabeth C. to George Rain (Ryan) 4-30-1856 (5-4-1856)
Singletary, Elizabeth J. to B. M. G. O'Brien 9-16-1869
Slagle, Ellen to Emanuel Wilson 9-4-1867
Slagle, Emilie to John H. Mollen 1-13-1873 (1-14-1873)
Slagle, Emilin to John H. Mottern 1-13-1873 (1-14-1873)
Slagle, Martha to George O. Step 12-2-1873
Slagle, Mary to Jonas M. Keen 1-24-1875 (1-25-1875)
Slagle, Mollie E. to Geo. O. Stepp 12-12-1873 (12-18-1873)
Slagle, Virginia A. to Isaac N. Crow 8-31-1878 (9-1-1878)
Slimp, Eliza to David Grindstaff 8-9-1856? (8-10-1856)
Slimp, Louisa to David Grindstaff 8-9-1856 (8-10-1856)
Sloan, Nancy to Lewis Woodby 4-18-1855
Smallen, Catharin E. to Geo. Mothorn 8-24-1850 (no return)
Smalling, Clemy J. (Clericy?) to H. B. Houston 10-14-1875 (10-17-1875)
Smalling, Jane to William Gourley 7-27-1878 (7-28-1878)
Smalling, Nancy A. to Wm. H. Dickson 9-10-1874
Smith, Ann to Albert M. Johnson 3-6-1866 (3-15-1866)
Smith, Carrie to Andrew Richardson 3-11-1875
Smith, Catharin to Jefferson Morris 2-9-1866 (2-10-1865?)
Smith, Charlotte to Joseph McFarland? 6-19-1868
Smith, Charlotte to Joseph P. Richardson 6-18-1868 (6-19-1868)
Smith, Delitha to A. M. Loveless 3-16-1860 (3-18-1860)
Smith, Eliza Jane to James Winters 12-31-1877
Smith, Eliza to Wilson Hill 1-6-1858 (1-8-1858)
Smith, Elizabeth J. to David Taylor 3-1-1851 (4-3-1851)
Smith, Elizabeth to David Duggar 3-31-1863 (4-1-1865)
Smith, Elizabeth to William Colbough 8-1-1850
Smith, Emelin to James Akers 2-21-1869 (2-25-1869)
Smith, Emelin to John Lovless 2-13-1869
Smith, Emeline to James Akers 2-24-1869 (2-25-1869)
Smith, Evaline to Jno. Manis 7-22-1878 (8-2-1878)
Smith, Eve Newsom to John Crow 10-16-1866 (10-18-1866)
Smith, Eveline to John Loveless 2-13-1869 (2-14-1869)
Smith, Eveline to Joseph P. Lyon 7-27-1859
Smith, Hannah to Robt. Whittemore 8-31-1855 (9-31?-1855)
Smith, Jane R. to John H. Bowman 1-1-1851
Smith, Jane to Pleasant Hazelwood 10-14-1871 (10-16-1871)
Smith, L. J. to Abner Slagle 1-8-1857
Smith, Lorena T. to Samuel Angell 11-20-1865
Smith, Lorina T. to Findley M. Smith 12-7-1847 (11?-18-1847)
Smith, Lorrina to Samuel Angel 11-13-1865 (11-?-1865)
Smith, Louisa C. to Joseph L. Waggoner 9-17-1866 (9-20-1866)
Smith, Louisa E. to Joseph L. Wigon 9-17-1866 (9-20-1866)
Smith, Louisa Eliza to Wilson Hill 1-6-1858 (1-8-1858)
Smith, Lucinda Ann to Abner Slagle 1-8-1857 (1-15-1857)
Smith, Lydia to Martin Bentley 2-10-1874 (2-11-1874)
Smith, Malicia C. to David W. White 9-21-1866 (9-23-1866)
Smith, Malinda to Samuel H. Meridith 2-17-1868
Smith, Malinda to Samuel H. Meridith 7-17-1868
Smith, Malissa J. to Edmon Gilbert 5-10-1877 (5-20-1877)
Smith, Margaret C. to James F. Floyd 3-12-1864 (3-17-1864)
Smith, Martha to Jeremiah Lacy 10-23-1855 (10-28-1855)
Smith, Mary A. to Nathanel T. Smith 11-12-1866 (11-22-1866)
Smith, Mary A. to Thos. C. White 8-9-1862 (8-14-1862)
Smith, Mary Ann to Elcana Richardson 11-9-1853 (11-11-1853)
Smith, Mary Ann to Turner? Chambers 10-1-1853 (10-18-1853)
Smith, Mary E. to John W. Hathaway 6-28-1872
Smith, Mary to John B. Treadway 11-22-1877 (11-24-1877)
Smith, Mary to John Campbell 6-15-1867
Smith, Mary to John H. Carver 2-17-1870 (3-17-1870)
Smith, Mary to Wm. H. Curren? 2-17-1870
Smith, Mattie E. to T. Y. Snodgrass 3-6-1872
Smith, Mollie C. to Thomas Y. Snodgrass 3-6-1872
Smith, Nancy E. to William C. Whitehead 3-26-1858 (3-28-1858)
Smith, Sarah A. E. to Carter Campbell 3-23-1867 (3-24-1867)
Smith, Sarah A. to Alpheus? Smith 11-9-1875
Smith, Sarah E. to David H. M. Smith 2-16-1878 (2-24-1878)
Smith, Sarah F. to James Davis 1-2-1871
Smith, Sarah to A. R. Toncray 12-30-1872
Smith, Sarahfina to Jeremiah Blevins 8-2-1851 (8-3-1851)
Smith, Selia C. to Jeremiah Lyon 8-20-1856
Smith, Selia C. to Jeremiah Lyons 8-2-1856 (no return)
Smith, Selia to Hamilton Hurley 8-25-1877 (8-26-1877)
Smith, Susan E. to John W. Bowen 5-5-1868
Smith, Susana to Andrew Johnson 2-23-1873
Smith, Susaner to Andrew H. Johnson 2-22-1873 (2-23-1873)
Smith, Susanna to Edmond Phillips 2-2-1866 (no return)
Smith, Susanna to Grugham? Ash 12-10-1853 (12-11-1853)
Snider, Elizabeth J. to William D. Jenkins 3-11-1853 (3-15-1853)
Snider, Emeline to Jacob S. Hampton 2-12-1853
Snider, Mary Ann to Johnson Heaton 8-11-1855 (8-13-1855)
Snider, Nancy A.(E?) to John Whitehead 12-4-1857 (10?-4-1857)
Snodgrass, Mary F.(S?) to F.(Q?) H. H. Lusk 1-30-1872 (2-1-1872)
Southerland, Mary to Thomas Collett 5-30-1874 (3?-31-1874)
Spears, Sarah to Jas. Troxwell 12-25-1876 (12-27-1876)
Spring, Mary D. to Samuel Lacy 3-25-1871
Stafford, Margaret to Robert L. Rowe 1-15-1857
Stafford, Mary to William Wilkerson 10-20-1867 (10-21-1867)
Stalcup, Sarah Surena to Joseph Campbell 12-24-1865
Standley, Nancy to Ezekiel L. Garland 10-1-1853 (10-2-1853)
Stephens, Biddy to Samuel McKinney 11-3-1860 (11-4-1860)
Stephens, Dicy? to Houston Gourley 12-26-1850
Stephens, Eviline to Jonathan Street 11-8-1875 (11-11-1875)
Stephens, Jane to William Baker 12-3-1857 (1-3-1858)
Stephens, Jane to William Baker 12-3-1857 (1-30-1858)
Stephens, Mary J. to Elijah Smith 10-4-1864 (10-15-1864)
Stepp, Molley C. to M. N. Taylor 8-3-1873 (9-2-1873)
Stepp, Molley C. to Mailer N. Taylor 8-30-1873 (9-2-1873)
Stern, Juie? to Cornelus Seal? 6-12-1870
Steve, Mary E. to John B. Smith 5-12-1875 (5-13-1875)
Stevens, Seally to Jacob Cunstabl 8-17-1867 (8-18-1867)
Stewart, Charlott to William Vaughn 8-21-1875 (8-26-1875)
Stone, Tempey to Willy W. Jones 4-19-1866
Stoner, Delila to Mat Jordon 11-5-1865
Stoner, Martha to Peter E. Hart 8-20-1867 (8-22-1867)
Stoner, Rody to William D. Bowers 5-16-1857 (5-17-1857)
Stout, Cordelia to Benjamin Baird 12-19-1877 (12-20-1877)
Stout, Elizabeth to John Stephens 10-12-1865
Stout, Mabla? to Michael Grindstaff 7-26-1862 (7-27-1862)
Stout, Martha to William H. Caraway 11-1-1865 (11-3-1865)
Stout, Mary to Alexander Morton 6-22-1875 (7-4-1875)
Stout, Rhoda E. to James L. White 11-27-1864 (12-7-1864)
Stout, Rossella? to James Morgan 9-24-1873 (9-26-1873)
Stout, Rosseller to James Morgan 9-24-1873 (10-26-1873)
Stout, Sarah J. to James A. Owens 1-6-1852 (1-22-1852)
Stout, Sarah Jane to Isaac Grogen 11-9-1865 (11-13-1865)
Stover, Antonette to Elija D.(C?) Hardin 2-11-1857
Stover, Eliza M. to Thomas Maloney 10-14-1875
Stover, Eliza to James Hinkle 11-22-1862 (11-23-1862)
Stover, Elizabeth to John Hays 12-15-1857
Stover, Eveline to David A. S. Head 8-9-1866
Stover, Eveline to David B. Jenkins 10-13-1869 (10-14-1869)
Stover, Jane to Cornelius Seal 6-11-1870 (6-12-1870)
Stover, Margaret A.(S?) to James A. Dugger 1-16-1866 (1-25-1866)
Stover, Martha to Peter E. Hart 8-20-1867 (8-22-1867)
Stover, Mary E. to John B. Smith 5-12-1875 (5-13-1875)
Stover, Mary J. to William M. Camern 2-22-1876
Stover, Rachel to Jackson Sims 6-2-1856
Stover, Rebeca to Nathaniel J. Pierce 12-24-1857
Stover, Rebecca to Nathanl. J. Pean 12-24-1857

Stover, Roda to Wm. G. Bowers 5-16-1857 (5-17-1857)
Stover, Sarah to W. S. Tipton 11-15-1870
Street, Elizabeth to John Stephens 10-10-1865 (10-12-1865)
Street, Mary to Eli Fry 12-14-1856 (12-15-1856)
Sumers, Elizabeth to Thomas Rine 9-12-1871 (9-14-1871)
Surland?, Mary A. to Nathan Farr 6-17-1874
Swan, Rachel to William Carver 10-9-1874 (10-11-1874?)
Swaner, Sarah to Risen Carver 1-28-1866 (4-28-1866)
Swanger, Margaret to Worley Linville 1-24-1857 (1-25-1857)
Swerin, Raheal to William Caron? 10-9-1874
Swiney (Swinney), Mary C. to John P. Walker 10-23-1867 (10-31-1867)
Syler, Mary E. to Wm. Baker 12-23-1871 (12-24-1871)
Talley, Jane to George Oliver 11-13-1868 (11-15-1868)
Tally, Martha to Jackson Bowman 7-22-1866 (7-23-1866)
Tapp, Lydia E. to Samuel B. McNabb 1-11-1858 (1-17-1858)
Tate, Alice to Samuel Ray 2-23-1872
Taylor, Adalade to Martin Crow 2-19-1873 (2-?-1873) B
Taylor, Amanda to George Hinkle 3-19-1876
Taylor, Cleursy? to William Carrell 1-22-1878
Taylor, Deleny to Geo. Humphrey 8-3-1878 (8-4-1878)
Taylor, Delia to William Harris 12-24-1875 (12-29-1875)
Taylor, Delray to Isaac Williams 11-26-1870 (12-11-1870)
Taylor, Dicy to Abram Bly 4-21-1875
Taylor, E. E. to Osborn D. Buck 12-4-1865 (12-7-1865)
Taylor, Edna D. to John I. Edins 1-1-1852
Taylor, Eliza to Alexander Love 4-28-1873 (no return)
Taylor, Elizabeth A. to G. W. Nediffer 9-9-1872
Taylor, Evaline to James M. Anderson 10-15-1872 (10-17-1872)
Taylor, Evelin C. to N. T. Gourley 8-13-1859 (8-14-1859)
Taylor, Evelin to William Lacy 11-26-1860 (11-27-1860)
Taylor, Eveline E. to Osburn D. Buck 12-4-1865 (12-7-1865)
Taylor, Frances to James H. Foster 4-14-1871
Taylor, Jane E. to Samuel P. Shell 6-12-1867 (6-13-1867)
Taylor, Lousa to John Taylor 3-29-1873 (3-30-1873)
Taylor, Lylie to William Harris no date (with 1875)
Taylor, Malinda to Mathew E.(F?) Parker 9-9-1856
Taylor, Margaret to Aury P. T. Ensor 11-30-1873 (12-4-1873)
Taylor, Margaret to Avery C. P. Ensor 11-30-1873 (12-4-1873)
Taylor, Margaret to George Hart 9-2-1875
Taylor, Martha to John Estep 7-6-1877 (7-10-1877)
Taylor, Mary C. to Jesse Pepper 12-9-1867
Taylor, Mary E. to E. D. Jobe 2-8-1877
Taylor, Mary E. to G. A. Hamm 11-12-1868
Taylor, Mary E. to J. H. Pippin 12-9-1867 (12-?-1867)
Taylor, Mary E. to Thadeous(Theopholus) Loudermilk 3-10-1872
Taylor, Mary J. to A. N. Kitzmiller 1-30-1855
Taylor, Mary to Harmon Myers 5-4-1875 (5-9-1875)
Taylor, Mary to William Aram 4-24-1869 (4-25-1869)
Taylor, Mary to Wm. H. Hendrix 1-23-1853 (1-24-1853)
Taylor, Nancy A. to Jonathan Taylor 12-25-1869
Taylor, Rhoda E. to John D. Reeves 4-17-1876 (4-18-1876)
Taylor, Sabra E. to John E. Price 3-25-1870 (3-27-1870)
Taylor, Sabra to John Pearce 3-25-1870 (3-27-1870)
Taylor, Sarah I. to David M. Bowman 8-15-1876 (8-17-1876)
Taylor, Sarah J. to Noah D. Taylor 1-1-1856
Taylor, Sarah T. to Wm. R. Perry 8-18-1868
Taylor, Sarah to Lawson Campbell 10-1-1870 (10-2-1870)
Taylor, Saraphina Jane to Samuel Miller 3-20-1858 (3-21-1858)
Taylor, Tobitha to Benjamin G. Hyder 2-21-1852 (2-22-1852)
Taylor, ____ to James Reges? 8-21-1874
Taylor?, Mary to Harrison Myers 5-4-1875 (5-9-1875)
Thomas, Nancy E. to Joseph Perkins 10-8-1860 (10-14-1860)
Thompson(Jenkins), Barbery to M. Y. Morton 12-12-1861 (12-21-1861)
Thompson, Hannah to Cane Shell 4-18-1859 (4-19-1859)
Thompson, Hannah to William G. Dempsey 3-24-1854
Thompson, Sally to William Edmundson 2-8-1877
Tipton, Cornelia E. to Alfred M. C. Taylor 7-22-1856 (7-24-1856)
Tipton, Eve V. to John C. Smith 12-22-1868
Tipton, Fanny C. to John K.(R?) Miller 1-22-1866 (1-23-1866)
Tipton, Harriet J. N. to George A. Haun 1-8-1856
Tipton, Hester Ann to Caleb M. Emmit(Emmert) 5-27-1873
Tipton, Julia A. to Wm. A. Aldrige 10-30-1861 (10-31-1861)
Tipton, M. E. to Jas. M. Cameron 2-6-1855

Tipton, Margarett to Isaac S. Bowers 8-20-1861
Tipton, Martha Adalade to C. M. D. Gourley 9-8-1856
Tipton, Martha J. to John M.(W?) Jones 7-16-1867
Tipton, Martha Jane to J. J. R. Boyd 10-2-1847 (10-7-1847)
Tipton, Nancy Jane to John Ingram 12-23-1854
Tipton, Rachael to James Brown 11-4-1867 (11-6-1867)
Toney(Tomy), Mahala to C. C. McInturff 1-9-1851 (1-30-1851)
Topp, Lydia E. to Saml. B. McNabb 1-11-1858 (1-17-1858)
Toppins, Catharine to Elkanah Shell 10-4-1854
Townsend, Ellen E. to Samuel Hill 11-23-1865
Townson, Marah to James D. Townson 4-13-1878
Treadway, Catherine E. to Isaac M. Heaton 3-28-1877 (3-29-1877)
Treadway, Cathern to Isaac M. Heaton 7-31-1875
Treadway, Jane to D. N. Carriger 5-23-1876 (5-25-1876)
Treadway, Rebecca to William McKinney 10-30-1852 (11-2-1852)
Treasure, Angeline to Thomas Taylor 8-22-1856 (8-23-1856)
Trexwell?, Catharine to Thomas Gibson 8-9-1860? (8-10-1860)
Tripp, Jane A. to James Johnson 8-27-1872 (8-28-1872)
Tronell, Martha to John Olive 7-14-1873
Troutman, Saraphina to Nathan Barnet 12-22-1857 (12-23-1857)
Troutmon, Sophrona to Nathan Bennett 12-23-1857
Truman, Mary A. to John Holloway 1-7-1871 (1-10-1871)
Trusler, Lydia to Ezekiel Hamit 6-21-1866 (6-22-1866)
Tucker, Caroline to Jasper Briant 2-18-1879 (2-20-1879)
Tume, Margaret to Jacob Dane 9-4-1865 (9-6-1865)
Turner, Ann E. to Samuel H. Fair (Farr) 12-23-1869 (1-2-1870)
Turner, Harriet to David M. McIntosh 12-26-1853 (1-1-1854)
Turner, Priscilla to Thos. M. Slimp 9-30-1865 (10-2-1865)
Twigs, Alis E. to Thomas S. Prichard 4-5-1877 (4-8-1877)
Vance, ____ to James L. Lewis 6-17-1875
Vandeventer, Bettie to James Barnett 11-13-1878 (11-14-1878)
Vandeventer, Elizabeth to Stephen Jones 12-31-1850 (1-9-1851)
Vanhouse, A. B. D. to Abraham Nave 11-8-1861 (11-9-1861)
Vanhulser, Rhoda A. to Nathanel F.? Y. Tilson 11-18-1869 (11-20-1869)
Vanhuss, Mimi to Isaac Morrell 2-23-1877
Vanhuss, Roda E. to Samuel W. Farry? 6-26-1867
Venable, Matilda to John H. Rainbolt 9-3-1848
Verick?, Mary E. to John F. Buntain 4-20-1874
Vernon, Betty E. to Geo. F. L. Smith 6-10-1869
Voncanon, Martilia to Jas. Wagoner 9-5-1877 (9-10-1877)
Wadkin, Malinda to William Carter 2-16-1869 (2-18-1869)
Waggoner, Amanda C. to Christopher C. Branch 2-6-1877
Wagner, Nancy J. to William Cash 9-19-1851 (9-20-1851)
Wagoner, Catharine to David Wagoner 6-12-1879
Walker, Adelin to Fielding McIntush 8-21-1861 (8-22-1861)
Walker, Edalin to Fielding McIntosh 8-21-1861 (8-23-1861)
Walker, Emile to George Ramsom 7-26-1873 (7-27-1873)
Walker, Sarah to Thomas Usry, jr. 6-6-1856
Wallace, Martha to Jonathan Head 8-26-1873 (8-29-1873)
Waller, Susan to Henry Spergin 11-19-1878 (11-24-1878)
Walling?, Nancy A. to John W. Slagler 9-2-1865
Walters, Martha to Jonathan Head 8-26-1873 (8-29-1873)
Ward, Ann to Corneleas Seals 3-13-1868 (3-14-1868)
Ward, Sarah to Samuel Grimes 5-4-1878 (5-5-1878)
Waters, Sarah to William Wilson 1-26-1858 (1-28-1858)
Watson, Elizabeth to Isaac McNabb 10-9-1856 (10-16-1856)
Watson, Lousanda to Adam Whisenhunt 12-30-1852
Watson, Phenith to Thomas Roberson 6-11-1855 (6-16-1855)
Watts, Sarah to Willis Wills 10-13-1852 (10-14-1852)
Welch, Sarah R. to Thos. Dillard 5-12-1865
Welcus?, Rachel N. to Carlos W. Lewis 9-23-1867 (9-24-1867)
Wellan, Clary to William Chanler 1-27-1875 B
West, Nancy to John Hollowman 1-2-1867 (1-3-1867)
Westick, Mary (Margaret) H. to J. P. Wilburn 1-25-1859 (1-26-1859)
Whalen, Elizabeth to John Burk 2-1-1865 (2-1-1866?)
Whitacer, Martha to James U. Hardin 2-24-1874
Whitacre, Caroline to James C. Harden 2-24-1874 (2-25-1874)
White, Beloadory? to Jacob Taylor 10-3-1878 (10-4-1878)
White, Belvedora to Richard L. White 1-3-1867
White, Caroline to Wm. K. Miller 2-4-1869 (3-11-1869)
White, Deannah to Henry Young 2-3-1869 (2-4-1869)
White, Eliza E. to Bethervill Farr 5-2-1870 (5-3-1870)
White, Eliza E. to Rethual Pharr 5-2-1870 (5-5-1870)
White, Elizabeth to Thomas Hamby (Harnby) 8-9-1856 (8-10-1856)

White, Elizabeth to W. L. McQueen 5-11-1870 (5-15-1870)
White, Elizabeth to William Deloach 11-12-1869
White, Gillen (Gillie) M. to Robert Pool 9-3-1874 (9-6-1874)
White, Josephine to William Arrance? 1-22-1878 (1-25-1878)
White, Julia A. to Benjamin B. Ferguson 12-29-1868 (12-30-1868)
White, Mary C. to George L. C. Pierce 11-6-1869 (11-7-1869)
White, Mary C. to Robert L. Smith 4-8-1866 (4-19-1866)
White, Mary E. to Lafayett D. East 12-2-1865
White, Mary to Alfred Pearce 8-2-1873 (8-3-1873)
White, Mary to John F. Hately 5-5-1866 (5-13-1866)
White, Rachel to Munroe Gragg 12-4-1868 (12-7-1868)
White, Susanna to George W. Livingston 12-29-1868 (12-19?-1868)
White, Susannah to George W. Livingston 12-29-1868 (1-30-1869)
Whitehead, Biddy to Ezekiel Hill 5-8-1857
Whitehead, Eliza Jane to James Miller 11-7-1865 (1-25-1866)
Whitehead, Hannah to Thomas Whitehead 11-6-1867
Whitehead, Hannah to Thomas Whitehead 8-9-1867 (8-6?-1867)
Whitehead, Hiley (Hilly) to David Blevins 8-12-1870 (8-14-1870)
Whitehead, Hilley to Thomas Grindstaff 7-8-1865 (7-12-1865)
Whitehead, Malinda to Richard Cable 3-5-1875
Whitehead, Margaret to David A. Whitehead 11-19-1869
Whitehead, Martha A. to Wilborn Hicks 1-25-1878
Whitehead, Martha J. to James O'Lenard 12-29-1858 (1-12-1859)
Whitehead, Martha Jane to James O. Lenard 12-29-1858 (1-12-1859)
Whitehead, Martha to David A. Kates 12-29-1877 (12-30-1877)
Whitehead, Martha to H. D. Guinn 11-3-1874 (11-5-1874)
Whitehead, Mary to Abner Vance 4-17-1853 (4-24-1853)
Whitehead, Mary to John Chambers 10-15-1856 (10-16-1856)
Whitehead, Miley to Thomas Gantt 7-8-1865 (7-12-1865)
Whitehead, Modena to Strawberry Thomas 10-19-1865 (12-26-1865)
Whitehead, Rachel to Joseph W. Green 3-15-1866
Whitehead, Rebecca to Daniel Tolly 4-28-1864 (5-7-1864)
Whitehead, Rhoda to Waits Odaner 10-3-1878 (10-8-1878)
Whitehead, Sarah A. to Thos. Whitehead 12-15-1860 (12-21-1860)
Whitehead, Sarah Ann to Thos. Whitehead 12-12-1860 (12-21-1860)
Whitehead, Susanah to Isaac Hopson 2-23-1871 (2-26-1871)
Whitehead, Susanah to Isaac Hopson 2-23-1871 (7-26-1871)
Whitehead, Yanaby to Lowis P. Bill 7-21-1847 (7-23-1847)
Whithead, Caroline to James H. Miller 2-5-1869
Whitson, Emeline to Landon Brett 4-4-1871 (4-6-1871)
Whittemore, Mary to Thomas Bowman 10-2-1867 (10-7-1867)
Wilcox, Malinda to James Miller 1-16-1855 (1-17-1855)
Wilcox, Martha C. to F. V. Banner 12-11-1878 (12-15-1878)
Wilcox, Martha E. to David (Daniel) Crow 4-2-1873
Wilcox, Rachel Allenella to Corlos W. Lewis 9-23-1867 (9-24-1867)
Willcox, Mary Ann to John H. Vance 8-2-1859 (8-10-1859)
Williams, Allace T. to John M. Simerly 10-6-1870
Williams, Ann Eliza to William Carrell 10-8-1857
Williams, Arsilla Jane to Willy W.(O?) Boren 12-4-1859 (12-6-1859)
Williams, Deborah to William R. Miller 8-27-1866 (9-2-1866)
Williams, Deborah to William R. Miller 8-29-1866 (9-12-1866)
Williams, Eliza A. to J. W. F. Dugger 9-30-1876 (10-1-1876)
Williams, Eliza E. to William Buck 3-5-1866 (3-8-1866)
Williams, Eliza J. to George Toppens 9-20-1864
Williams, Eliza to Henry Jones 10-1-1853 (10-2-1853)
Williams, Eliza to Saml. Jenkins 10-28-1875
Williams, Elizabeth to Abraham Floyd 5-29-1851 (5-25?-1851)
Williams, Elizabeth to Elijah G. Lovless 12-19-1870 (12-22-1870)
Williams, Eveline to Watson Collins 8-6-1844
Williams, Frances T. to Caswell C. Taylor 11-21-1867
Williams, Hester Ann to Peter W. Emmert 2-3-1866 (2-4-1866)
Williams, Jane to James Deloach 3-8-1869
Williams, Julia C. to Jorden C. Hardin 11-24-1861 (12-4-1861)
Williams, Julia to Michal E. Hyder 11-21-1877 (11-22-1877)
Williams, Julia to Wm. T. Range 8-30-1865 (8-31-1865)
Williams, Lou to James Houston 12-25-1875 (12-30-1875)
Williams, Loucretia M. to A. C. Hampton 12-22-1870
Williams, Loucretia M. to A. C. Humphrey 12-22-1870
Williams, Louisa P. to Thos. Clark 7-21-1860 (7-22-1860)
Williams, Louisa to Milton Penland 12-23-1877 (12-27-1878?)
Williams, Lue to James Houston 12-25-1875 (12-30-1875)
Williams, M. E. to David H. Hyder 2-21-1872 (2-22-1872)
Williams, M. T. to N. H. Hyder 6-6-1870 (6-9-1870)
Williams, Margaret L. to Charles P. Toncray 3-9-1859
Williams, Margaret M. to Isaac H. Brown 11-30-1855 (12-2-1855)

Williams, Margaret to Thomas H. Berry 3-9-1875 (3-11-1875)
Williams, Margart to Thomas H. Berry 3-9-1875 (4-11-1875)
Williams, Martha to Thompson Cole 4-15-1875
Williams, Mary A. to Elbert A. Barns 12-19-1872 (12-24-1872) *
Williams, Mary A. to Elbert A. Barns 12-?-1871
Williams, Mary Amanda to Adam Gourley 8-14-1856
Williams, Mary E. to David H. Hyder 1-21-1872 (1-22-1872)
Williams, Mary E. to David H. Hyder 2-21-1872
Williams, Mary E. to John W. Camern 12-31-1857
Williams, Mary to Kenedy Peoples 6-6-1859 (6-12-1859)
Williams, Mary to Nelson Duffield 4-25-1878 (4-26-1878)
Williams, N. A. to James L. Hail 10-21-1875
Williams, Nancy J. to James L. Hart 12-21-1875
Williams, Nancy J. to Wallace D. Coble 11-20-1868
Williams, Nancy to John Kelly 11-3-1847
Williams, Racheal A. C. to W. T. L. Scott 4-8-1869
Williams, Racheal A. to William H. Scott 4-8-1869
Williams, Racheal C. to William A. Cooper 5-7-1873 (5-8-1873)
Williams, Racheal to Wm. H. Cooper 5-7-1873 (5-8-1873)
Williams, Rachel to Milton Penland 7-25-1867
Williams, Rhoda Ann to P. A. J. Crocket 9-27-1852 (9-30-1852)
Williams, Rhoda J. to Henry H. Hyder 12-19-1866 (1-9-1869)
Williams, Rhoda Jane to Geo. T. Anderson 2-17-1855 (2-20-1855)
Williams, Rhoda to James I.(J?) R. Boyd 2-7-1860 (2-28-1860)
Williams, Rhoda to Robert Bunch 7-6-1867 (7-7-1867)
Williams, Rody to Easterly Blevins 3-29-1855
Williams, Salley F. to Wm. A. Beriens? 5-18-1875
Williams, Sally F. to William A. Bowers 5-18-1875
Williams, Sarafina to David Floyd 7-5-1852
Williams, Sarah C. to William J. Tinen 10-15-1868
Williams, Sarah C. to William J. Toncray 10-15-1868
Williams, Sarah J. to Wm. H. Taylor 4-4-1860 (4-5-1860)
Williams, Sarah to Thomas Hampton 12-30-1876 (12-31-1876)
Williams, Sarah to William Hilton 1-?-1875
Williams, Selia to Thomas J. Buckles 4-14-1869 (4-22-1869)
Williamson?, Rhoda to Montgomery C. Cooper 1-24-1879
Willson, Charlotty to Henry Lineback 10-2-1872 (10-4-1872)
Wilson, Allan to William Carray 9-9-168 (9-12-1868) B
Wilson, Eliza J. to Doc Hodge 5-2-1875
Wilson, Eliza J. to Luny B. Taylor 8-30-1878 (9-4-1878)
Wilson, Eliza to Kenedy Garland 11-4-1871 (11-8-1871)
Wilson, Elizabeth to Geo. G. February 11-2-1856
Wilson, Elizabeth to Kenedy Garland 11-4-1871 (11-8-1871)
Wilson, Jane to Findly Shell 5-9-1852
Wilson, Lillie to Henry Jensbuck? 10-2-1872
Wilson, Lorana to John F. Puket? 12-17-1868
Wilson, Martha L. to Nelson Markland 8-2-1853 (8-7-1853)
Wilson, Mary Ann to E. D. Lovelass 11-19-1876
Wilson, Mary to John M. Garland 5-5-1875
Wilson, Matilda to Henry Richardson 7-6-1878
Wilson, Nancy Ann to Andrew J. Wilson 12-31-1857 (1-3-1858)
Wilson, Nancy Ann to Andrew Jentry 6-9-1867
Wilson, Nancy Ann to Willey B. Lyles 9-22-1862 (9-24-1862)
Wilson, Nancy Ann to Willy B. Lyle 4-15-1862 (9-24-1862)
Wilson, Pricilla to Wellington Hodge 10-10-1865 (10-15-1865)
Wilson, Rebecca to James Wilcox(son) 9-4-1857
Wilson, Susanna to George Buck 3-29-1863 (3-30-1863)
Winters, Jane to Andrew Franklin 3-4-1859 (3-13-1859)
Winters, Lyda A. to Ranson M. Hays 3-19-1878 (3-28-1878)
Wishler(Willis), Margaret H. to J. P. Wilburn 1-25-1859
Woodby, Martha to Sith? Sneyd 10-15-1853
Woods, Catharin E. to John W. Edwards 12-24-1858
Woods, Louisa to Jas. Richards 9-30-1863
Worley, Amanda to Mompy Magee 12-24-1869
Wright, Sarah (Susah?) to Henderson J. Shell 5-18-1871 (5-21-1871)
Wyatt, Emma E. to Joseph W. Price 8-22-1873 (8-24-1873)
Wyatt, Loucretia to Wartsel A. Hodges 1-5-1870 (1-6-1870)
Yarboro, Nancy to John Cook 11-16-1870 (11-17-1870)
Yarbrough, Nancy to Andrew J. Ward 12-13-1851 (1-11-1852)
Yates, Allice to Samuel J. Berry 2-23-1872
Yates, Bethana to Charles N. Campbell 12-30-1869
Yearber, Nancy to John Cook 11-16-1870 (11-17-1870)
Younce, Hannah to Matison Stout 7-25-1868 (7-26-1868)
Young, Elizabeth to Samuel Thomas 12-28-1866
Young, Rebecca J. to Westly Johnson 10-1-1870

Zapp, Jane A. to James Johnson 8-27-1872
_____, Marga to Harrison M. Elliott 12-17-1859
_____, Susanna to Jackson West 6-6-1870
_____, _____ to John Tinnen? 12-31-1872
_____, _____ to Samuel Jones 3-25-1869

www.ingramcontent.com/pod-product-compliance
Lightning Source LLC
LaVergne TN
LVHW081401060426
835510LV00016B/1926